Contents

Contents

Appendices   209

Remedying Damp

Ralph F. Burkinshaw

Chartered Building Surveyor BSc, FRICS, MA, CSRT, PGCHE
Independent Dampness Consultant

with contributions from

Dr Chris George,
Stuart Athol

and

Nigel Hewitt

Acknowledgments

Crown copyright material is reproduced with the permission of the Controller of HMSO and the Queen's Printer for Scotland

Permission to reproduce extracts from BS 5250: 1989, *Code of practice for control of condensation in buildings* and BS 8102: 1990, *Code of practice for protection of structures against water from the ground*, is granted by BSI. British Standards can be obtained in PDF or hard copy formats from the BSI online shop: www.bsigroup.com/Shop or by contacting BSI Customer Services for hardcopies only: Tel: +44 (0)20 8996 9001, Email: cservices@bsigroup.com.

Extracts from BRE publications are reproduced with permission (www.ihsbrepress.com).

Extracts from National Flood School training materials are reproduced with permission from the National Flood School.

Published by the Royal Institution of Chartered Surveyors (RICS)
Surveyor Court
Westwood Business Park
Coventry CV4 8JE
UK

www.ricsbooks.com

ISBN 978 1 84219 305 1

Typeset in Great Britain by Columns Design Ltd, Reading, Berks
Printed in Great Britain by Page Bros, Milecross Lane, Norwich

Text printed on Core Silk 100gsm
Cover board Core Silk 300gsm

List of tables

Personal acknowledgments

Mrs Ashby; Tessa and Dave; Catherine Edwards; Anne Joliffe; Dora Heaton; Dr Tony Wainwright; Peter Mawer; Nigel Hewitt; Mr W. J. Hargreaves; Kate and Simon; Sue Astle; Mrs Dawn Rogers; Jamie Nash; Mr and Mrs Murphy; Andrew Dallen; Chris Netherton; Sen and Jun; Nigel Hewitt; Patrick Gallagher; Chris Burbridge; Ashley Wood; John Lowday; Peter Thompson; Morten Resslev; Dr Malcolm Richardson; Phil Hewitt; Philip Leach; Dr Chris George; David Lockyer; Ian Poole; Sean Fallon; Stuart Athol; David Lambert; Warren Muschialli; Costa; Martin Barnard; Elizabeth Burkinshaw; Marguerite Clark; Nina Stovold; Mark Brickell; Graham Coleman; Peter Reay; Bill Hargreaves; Philip Wingfield; Robert Deary, Robin Sibley; Mustafa Koray Kazim; John Kelly; Andy Habbershaw; Jagjit Singh; John Housden; Howard Morley; Jon Donaldson; Christopher Newton; Mr W. A. Burkinshaw; David Smith.

Many thanks to all others who have helped, and most particularly close family: Elizabeth Burkinshaw and Marguerite Clark for encouragement over many years, and thanks to my wife Susan, and wonderful sons Douglas and Edmund for their love, support and patience during the preparation work for this book.

All photographs, unless otherwise stated, are by the author.

The following line drawings, sketches and diagrams are by the author:

1 Introduction

BACKGROUND AND CONTEXT

I believe that my earlier work, *Diagnosing Damp*[1] took understanding of damp diagnosis to a new level. We showed how inspection of damp problems begins with visual examination, but could move on to make use of all manner of techniques and equipment. It was not within the scope of that text to explore remedial options once a diagnosis had been made. *Remedying Damp* seeks to take this important next step. I have no knowledge of any other publication dedicated to this subject range.

In the guidance note *Building Surveys of Residential Property*[2], surveyors are firmly advised to arrange further investigation of structure or services from persons 'free of any financial self-interest'. Unfortunately, obtaining independent advice on dampness problems – either for their diagnosis or remediation – is likely to be difficult over the next few years. Unless more chartered surveyors, engineers and architects learn how to measure and interpret dampness in buildings, the contractors out there in the industry will remain the main source of further advice.

'Further investigation' may or may not always require use of additional diagnostic equipment or more invasive surveying. Sometimes a re-evaluation of evidence and symptoms presented will be all that is needed, by a more experienced surveyor able to make a stronger professional judgment.

Surveying of dampness problems can no longer be labelled a *specialist* activity, when so many building problems are caused by moisture imbalance. We are talking *basic defects analysis*: the home ground of house surveyors.

THE REMEDY PROCESS

A successful remedy should in my opinion satisfy the following key criteria:

- meet client aims and objectives;
- achieve occupier/user needs; and
- achieve building needs.

There is also a wider national and, increasingly, global perspective. The resources used to remedy defects need to be allocated efficiently in economic terms. Methods and materials used need more and more commonly to be appraised for their global impact – when, for example, alternative remedy strategies could be more or less carbon efficient, or could incorporate materials from more renewable sources. Some construction techniques are reversible (i.e. they may be removed in the future without causing undue damage to the original building fabric), or perhaps the materials and components themselves could be recycled at the end of their useful life.

The remedy process is shown in Figure 1. The key elements of the remedy process are summarised as follows:

The seven-stage remedy process

Diagnosis:

1 Careful assessment of the building problem, cause and effects of the dampness.

Remedy:

2 Identification of the various short- and long-term strategies to cure or manage the dampness.
3 Short-listing of suitable remedy options.
4 Selection of the most appropriate remedy (e.g. by feasibility report).
5 Detailed remedy design.
6 Remedy implementation.
7 Monitoring and evaluation.

Any errors of judgment at the earlier stages of the process will tend to have a greater impact on the likelihood of successful remediation.

Education, training and research can feed into the process at all stages and are very much an underpinning driving force.

If any of the seven remedy stages are ignored, the final remedy as implemented is unlikely to meet client, user and building requirements – certainly over the longer term and very likely over the shorter term too.

A remedy may also fail if insufficient funds are made available to produce a quality job. A client, or the one who pays, must be fully informed of the risks of an inferior job specification.

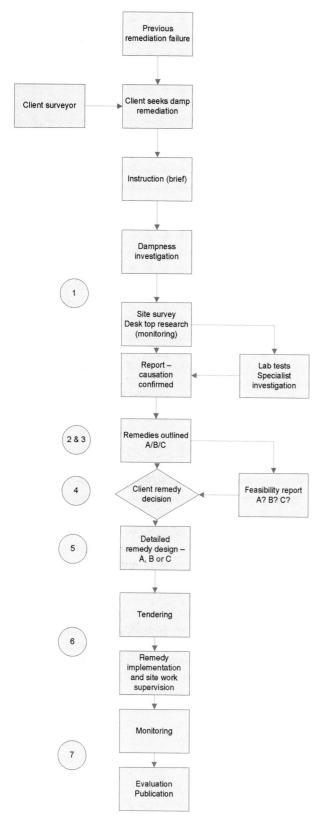

Figure 1: The remedy process.

Key features of the remedy process

- A coordinator is central to the evaluation of the remedial options available. A dampness investigator – if *independent* – can most effectively co-ordinate the remedy process. Stage 1 may include a diverse collation of information to feed into diagnosis and remedy design – including of course the dampness investigation on site, as well as desk top research and a dialogue between all parties with knowledge of the subject damp problem. It is sometimes necessary to commission specialist testing and site investigation – for example, thermal image survey work or electronic leak detection.

- The remedial options may be researched by the co-ordinator, with input from contractors, the client, the client's surveyor and any other knowledgeable party.

- Several alternative remedial options are tendered for.

- The client is presented with feasibility reporting either before or after tendering. One of the key requirements of any remedy will be 'value for money'; this can be more closely assessed once contractors' tenders have been received.

- Feasibility reporting explains to the client how alternative remediation strategies meet key requirements, and assesses their strengths and weaknesses.

- In most cases the client will make the final decision on remedy selection: hopefully a decision informed by research compiled by the remedy coordinator.

- The remedy process may *produce research output* that can be fed back into the system by publication. And the whole process needs to be supported by research input from the industry.

- Feedback on the remedy process may be fed into the industry by formal publication of the project design and implementation, or informally via internet discussion forums or peer group interaction.

- The coordinator has professional protection (from being sued or loss of reputation) from an option appraisal that flags up the *strengths and the weaknesses* of remedies available – in meeting the key client (and sometimes wider) aims. And also the fact that no remedy will be perfect.

- The coordinator of the remedy process could take part in later stages such as supervision of works on site or monitoring, and could be a professional outside the usual cohort of architects, engineers, surveyors, etc. This role requires *project management skills.*

- A contractor should not usually be the remedy coordinator, but can have an important role in offering technical input at early stages of remedy evaluation, and at later stages in the fine detailing of the remedy selected. It is the coordinator's role to maintain an independent perspective at the early stages of remedy design and selection.

We must *always* have it at the forefront of our minds that with the general public being fed a diet of quick-fix building improvement TV programmes, there is an expectation that building work can be executed at tremendous speed. While it is true is that the more skilled craftsperson, well equipped with the right tools and using the best trade methods, can be expected to produce a better quality of work, and usually faster than the less able, speed must not be the driver. Quality of work, achieved over a reasonable timeframe, should always be the number one aim – especially when dealing with such problematic issues as dampness.

There is a growing trend amongst home owners to view the home more as an 'investment', managing it accordingly. So when improvements are planned, considerations of profit can dictate the choice of remedial options. Fast change seems to be the emphasis in TV projects. But without a longer-term perspective on maintaining and improving our homes, time, materials and indeed energy can be wasted on the more short-term solutions. So instead of using highly durable lead sheet for a flat roof covering, complementing what would otherwise be a quality building extension, we find the cheaper felt roof alternative being used – destined to last perhaps only 15–30 years. Hardly a sustainable and environmentally responsible option! Best to find a long-term solution and get it right first time.

The remedy process may be driven by available funds and our professional motivation as individuals, but it is underpinned by the knowledge base of research, learning and experience within the industry, and more immediately by the level of education and training of all those involved, from surveyors, designers and administrators, to those at the workface 'on the tools'.

Craft training seems to many to have suffered over recent years, as more extended traditional training in the building crafts seems to have been replaced by quick-fix shorter courses in specific craft skills. Attempts are even afoot to convert pinstriped office workers into working plumbers in weeks or months, rather than by the year-on-year apprenticed route from plumber's mate to fully fledged plumber. The subtle WHY of the trade operation being taught will be overbalanced by the more simplistic HOW. This cannot be good for the construction industry, and heralds potential problems at stage 6 of the seven-stage remedy process!

There have been other weak links in the remedy chain over the years. One could look first to how remedies are selected and designed. Too often there has been a reliance on contractors to select appropriate remediation. Contractors will have intimate knowledge only of the particular systems and materials they use, and which they may naturally attempt to adopt, whether or not this is in the best interests of client, occupier/user or building – or indeed the wider world. So if you were to request a further investigation of a damp basement by a company that mainly installs drained cavity waterproofing systems, the diagnosis might well be that there is lateral damp penetration requiring comprehensive waterproofing to achieve the grade of use required, and that the waterproofing should be by a drained cavity waterproofing system! In the same way, if you were to request a ventilation company to check out a mould-ridden flat, and that company manufactures and installs heat recovery ventilation units as their flagship product, do not be surprised to be presented with a quotation for installing heat recovery ventilation units from that specialist.

A specialist company, in surveying a property with a damp problem, will usually seek evidence which supports the installation of the system they wish to install. This is where an independent voice such as a surveyor should much more often be there, to offer more impartial advice on options to the client. (See *Free from the water board* below.)

Free from the water board

In a recent case, a damp-proofing contractor was called in to assess a lower ground floor flat's dank and wet store room which was situated under the steps to the upper flat. A comprehensive belt and braces multi-coat render system was priced for – nearly £4,000-worth of tanking work. This would certainly hold back the dampness – no question. But before this remedial work was put in hand, I advised the surveyor, a former student of mine, to contact the water board, who could check the water main for leakage (the main is nearly always sited under the front step zone of this kind of older Victorian property). I visited the property with the student a few days later. It was occupied by an elderly lady, who had been able to use the front steps space for storage over many years without recourse to specialist waterproofing. I noticed some new black tarmacadam on the pavement near the outside service valve access flap. The student informed me that the water board had just repaired a leaking water main. The pooling water causing all the fuss had nearly dried up. So the water board gave not only a free survey – but also a free remedy!

As a general rule of thumb, if you have not identified at least three ways to remedy a damp problem, or indeed to carry out any construction repair or improvement, then you have jumped the gun. The three remedy options would preferably be completely different approaches, but may sometimes simply be three ways of installing pretty much the same remedy. These three remedy options need to be evaluated carefully, and the client informed of their relative strengths, weaknesses and indeed risks. The client, briefed on the options, is usually then able to make an informed decision. If you offer the client just one way of doing anything, you might be failing as a professional advisor.

The author, in preparing this book, has sought to offer examples of alternative strategies for damp remedy by direct illustrated examples, and to offer technical advice on the various remedies available today. As house surveyors, even if we do not possess detailed knowledge of methods A, B or C, we should at least understand the implications of the alternative remedy options and help drive the remedy process towards the best option. Often the very first task will be to verify whether there *is* a damp problem, and to find out whether a standard building repair is all that is needed, rather than damp-proofing or water proofing.

THE KNOWLEDGE BASE WITHIN THE INDUSTRY

In the author's opinion, there has been a dearth of technical writing on building defects over the years, particularly on damp-related defects. The truth is that many very knowledgeable construction professionals hug their experience closely to their chests. This can be to maintain a market lead or an advantage in expertise, or more often because surveyors, architects and engineers have not the time, resources or funding to enable preparation of published works.

Beginning at the very base of a building – we really have not yet come to fully understand why wall bases become too damp! Some can measure the amount of moisture in the wall, but few can really be sure where it has come from.

We have not yet devised the best methods to remedy the dampness – if indeed it is deemed significant, and some damp-proofing methods seem to be of unreliable performance, e.g. chemical dpc injection. There has not been the independent research of real buildings to verify effectiveness of the various retrofit damp coursing methods. We have tended to mask dampness and guarantee the masking for a specified period, which has prevented us from really learning more about it. Why is there not yet a thick manual with large-scale architectural details of alternative wall base detailing we might draw from? Buildings may be 'different', but many are similarly built and detailed, lending themselves to common ground rules.

CHANGES IN THE INDUSTRY

We begin our design of remedy for a damp problem by considering how to incorporate combinations of the three ways to control or manage moisture in building elements, i.e. by drainage, evaporation or barriers.

In older more traditional buildings, we may manage moisture more by 'breathing' – where a porous fabric takes in and releases moisture to maintain a suitable equilibrium. In an older building that appears to be successfully managing low-level dampness pretty much just by efficient breathing of the wall base, you would nearly always find that any dampness soaking into the base of walls faces a 'high jump test', with a good vertical distance between wetting wall base and vulnerable timber or decorative interior. Height means more opportunity for evaporation in terms of breathing surface area, and a hard climb too against gravity. Just think of castle building – so often on a hill top, so invading marauders could be repelled!

We are becoming more and more knowledgeable concerning breathing walls that incorporate lime mortar or lime pointing. Many surveyors and architects who manage the conservation of listed property are already familiar with the materials and methods, and it is becoming increasingly likely that older buildings will be repaired in the future using lime-based products. We have seen many failures of masonry, pointed in dense cement-rich mortars, which themselves crack, and where spalling of brick faces is exacerbated or walls where damp has been trapped by use of dense unforgiving cementitious renders – a common cause of dampness spreading and indeed rising.

The hand skills needed to apply and use lime materials can be easily learned by modern plasterers and bricklayers, as the more traditional bricklaying and pointing methods require a less perfect and exacting skill. However, the selection of suitable mortars and the tools to apply them may require the modern tradesperson to at least attend short courses for familiarisation with the older materials and methods. We need to cherish those who have these skills and can pass them on. The more traditional materials need to be locally available, at mainstream builders' merchants, and the knowledge to use them tacked onto or running in tandem with existing trade courses.

Mould may or may not be the next asbestos. The truth will finally out. Those with a commercial interest to sell products connected with the identification of mould or the cleaning of mould would tend to emphasis the health risks. As we learn more about mould and related health issues, we will know more about how to assess the risk of mould to the building user and the building itself. In the future, the medical profession as well as mycologists, chemists and biologists may be involved much more in our surveys in a team surveying approach, when dampness is affecting, or might affect human health. The condition of a building and the health of its occupants are traditionally viewed separately. The health of an individual is normally assessed away from the very place (work or home) that may be the prime cause of the ill health.

The main debate on mould now seems to be whether we should be alert to *specific* risk species (following on from the US experience of *stachybotrus chartarum* in a ground-breaking legal case, *Melinda Ballard v Farmers Insurance Group*), or whether the sheer *amount* and/or *location* of mould present may be more important. We really need to think more holistically here. We need to be aware of moulds that are a known health risk, assess their proliferation in the subject building and the associated air contamination, in relation to the presence of *susceptible individuals* who may come into contact with them.

Damp and mouldy buildings are a proving ground for all manner of ventilation solutions to control condensation and the associated mould colonisation. There really is a battle out there amongst manufacturers of ventilation systems. Some of the alternative systems that control indoor humidity, create enough air changes and improve air quality are touched on in this book. It is difficult for us non-scientists to know how we can evaluate the best ventilation option for each building. Until there is sufficient independent research to draw from, surveyors are at risk of being blinded by the claims of systems manufacturers and installers.

In timber treatment there have been huge changes over recent years. Many dangerous chemicals have now been withdrawn. A new climate seems to be developing, where chemicals may take back-stage. We are becoming less afraid of dry rot! True, it can spread and cause enormous damage, but we can learn to control it by withdrawing its life support system – principally the water it needs to live. By getting to grips more with measuring moisture in materials and monitoring changes in moisture condition using the sophisticated logging equipment now available (see Chapter 8) we will be able to repair buildings and monitor moisture in the building fabric, and know whether or not we have reduced the dampness sufficiently to make it impossible for rots to continue to survive. Through the work of Dr Singh, who has discovered much about how such organisms grow and spread, we can be more confident of killing them off without recourse to chemical treatments. The way forward is to come to an understanding of how the building as a whole deals with moisture in *sinks and reservoirs* – rather than blitzing a particular designated dry-rotted zone with chemicals to provide a limited zoned guarantee against recolonisation. As a general principle, when one roof slate has failed, others on the roof may soon fail too! So a damp problem in one part of the building could happen elsewhere when similar design and construction deficiencies are present.

As surveyors learn more about beetle and other infestations, the blanket treatment of roofs or floors with chemicals will become a thing of the past. Experienced remedial treatment surveyors are able to verify whether or not an insect infestation is live or historic. We need to learn from the specialist surveyor, so that we as house surveyors can carry out a more telling investigation, rather than pass on basic investigations to the remedial treatment industry. That industry's key role should be to assist in the design and implementation of appropriate remedial treatment, rather than basic diagnosis.

As the climate changes, the threat of floods and storms is likely to intensify. More buildings will find themselves at risk from rising sea or river levels, or surcharges from urban sewers, unable to cope with flash flood situations. We need as house surveyors to read the signs. Many buildings show symptoms of past flooding. Many buildings are not built of materials resilient to flood. After flooding, many occupiers suffer frustrating problems that drag on and on, and are unable to get help in locating the source of water leakage. Alternatively, a professional drying contractor may need assistance in making sense of the existing building, which may be home to all manner of pre-existing damp problems that

complicate the drying-out phase. As it stands, policy holders are very much at the mercy of the drying contractor and building contractors called in to make good flood damage – some of whom, it has to be said, create work by over-zealous stripping out. Surveyors need to *be there*. We have experience in reading older property, but more of us need to be able to measure and interpret moisture in the building elements and components we are already familiar with. Armed with these skills, we could be an invaluable team member in the restoration of buildings after flood.

Advice from the BRE on drying buildings can sometimes lag a little behind today's sharp edge in the industry – possibly through lack of resources to keep digests up to date. The BRE offers little advice on drying buildings, and appears out of kilter with the damage management industry. For example, BRE Good Repair Guide 11 *Repairing Flood Damage* Part 4[3] advises that the drying-out of masonry may take months, 'even using dehumidifiers'. This advice is at odds with the leading manufacturers of drying equipment and known industry experts in this field. Modern drying strategies can often dry out masonry in days, sometimes weeks, but rarely months. But drying *can* take many months, if carried out unprofessionally using unsuitable equipment and techniques, and if the drying contractor misinterprets the building construction.

The job of being a chartered building surveyor, engineer or architect extends in scope year by year. Degree courses are stretched to cope with an ever-expanding knowledge base. Generally it is the core building surveying agenda that has always been squeezed out – and less defects analysis, the bread and butter of surveying. With so little time available for learning the finer points of property inspection, there seems now to be a strong case for a dedicated diploma or degree programme covering how we should conduct property inspections, the site survey, and the underpinning research we can draw on regarding all manner of defects in buildings. Hands-on survey work has to be at the heart of such a study, perhaps with mock-up construction elements and building examples in a covered workshop setting, as well as real buildings that students can crawl in, under and over – with experienced surveyors there to help and advise.

The current home inspection initiative is very interesting to observe. There is much positive work we can admire. The standard homebuyer inspection format has been to all intents and purposes taken apart and rebuilt from scratch to a different format. The need for dedicated training in house inspection has been acknowledged by all those involved in the home inspector training programmes. The author has attended some home inspector training modules and found the practical survey training extremely useful.

I applaud any initiative to train surveyors 'on the job'. When I attended my first brickwork training programme, we had what were called 'shop talks' in which practical bricklaying was mixed with short seminars grouped round a blackboard. It really was an ideal teaching and learning environment – *learning by doing*. A hands-on approach helps surveyors to become more familiar with materials and trade operations – and therefore better equipped to design and specify construction details.

CPD conferences abound. They can be expensive to attend but while many are extremely useful, the plain truth is that often they are not challenging enough for delegates and do not usually have any built-in check that anybody has actually learned anything. Top-up courses with an end test, although perhaps not as relaxing as a typical seminar event, would at least verify that delegates had listened and learned. Skills need to be updated, and in the same way as scouts can earn badges for acquired skills, why not adopt this approach for surveyors?

Much (often excellent) training is now available from manufacturers, although such events may inevitably slant eventually towards particular products. As good as the seminars often are, however, the key question concerning whether or not the subject remedy is *even necessary* may never be asked, and alternative generic remedial options are usually only touched on. The author has attended many manufacturer-led seminars – always technically up to date and extremely valuable – but requiring you to read between the lines to make objective judgments on the value of the particular remedy option for particular buildings and circumstances.

There is an additional and quite serious problem here. The objectivity and indeed the honesty of some surveyors can really be put to the test. Some manufacturers of patent damp remedies offer surveyors commission for sales. So if a surveyor recommends a particular product, there can be a fee-earning opportunity – and this could obviously sway selection of remedy towards profit-earning opportunities. So be on your guard here. House surveyors must stand at a little distance from particular manufacturers' products, so advise generic systems in the first instance.

GETTING THE MOST OUT OF *REMEDYING DAMP*

This book covers key dampness problems, chapter by chapter. The general issues are discussed in the chapter main text. Case studies then follow, illustrating remedy options in relevant situations. The author's line drawings are all based on as-found construction detailing for the diverse selection of buildings encountered, as well as scale drawings of new remedy ideas. Some of the case studies also feature hands-on construction work carried out by the author to trial various remedial approaches. The appendices provide useful further detailed information, along with some detailed tables and charts.

I hope you will find the book both practical and informative.

Ralph Burkinshaw can be contacted by email at: rf.burkinshaw2@ukonline.co.uk or via his website: www. damp-diagnosis.co.uk, or by telephone: 0207 737 4868, or mobile: 07949 959 170.

2 Flood remediation

A GROWING CAUSE FOR NATIONAL CONCERN

Every year seems to bring disastrous flooding some-where in the country, at some point. The consensus of opinion on climate change and global warming is that the UK is likely to experience heavier rainfall more often in the future, and that flooding will be more frequent and widespread as a result.

The Environment Agency's website (www.environment-agency.gov.uk) informs us that two million properties are situated in flood risk areas in England and Wales. In addition to this, according to the Association of British Insurers, some 6,000 houses are flooded by sewage every year. Each clean-up costs between £50,000 and £100,000. Additionally, there is some question as to the ability of the sewage system to cope with more regular flash flooding.

HOW TO REDUCE FLOOD RISK

It's probably almost too obvious to mention, but the best way to avoid flood damage is to avoid building in flood risk areas!

The excellent DTLR publication *Preparing for Floods*[4] (DTLR, 2002) sets out in great detail all manner of permanent and temporary measures to reduce the risk of flood.

Measures may be divided into two categories:

- external/site measures; and
- internal measures.

GENERAL ADVICE

External and site measures

External landscaping and/or barriers

Free-standing flood barriers can be used to protect an individual house or a group of houses. Barriers must be carefully thought out and of a suitable height in relation to the anticipated height of floodwater. There have been cases where the erection of temporary flood barriers has protected the homes they were designed for, but floodwater has diverted to other nearby homes to devastating effect. There is a useful Environment Agency guide: *Temporary and Demountable Defences*[5].

Floodskirts

Floodskirts are a permanent installation which can be activated to provide a temporary dam around a building. Where a high water level is anticipated or develops, temporary barriers will not be capable of withstanding the pressures induced by the sheer weight and pressure of the water. Barriers such as floodskirts are permanent protection measures that are expensive to install. A floodskirt would be more suitable for a detached house, subject to repeated danger of flooding (see figure 2).

Physical barriers erected around a property will of course not be able to stop water seeping up into the home from below ground, unless the barriers are taken down to foundation level. Pumps and sumps are often installed, with back-up battery-operated systems.

Even if physical barriers are unable to effectively keep out water, they may reduce the ingress for long enough for occupiers to move possessions to a safer place – e.g. an upstairs room. Reducing the sheer volume of water entry can also reduce the amount of silt build-up – and the associated build-up of contaminants.

Temporary covers – removable plastic covers fixed over openings, air bricks, etc.

Plastic, metal or wooden flood boards – commonly fixed across doorways, low-level windows and other

Figure 2: A floodskirt in use. Photo © courtesy of Floodskirt: www.floodskirt.com

openings – are said to be more effective than sandbags. Frames may be fitted to house sliding boards. Such an arrangement is most effective if a good seal can be achieved between the framing and the substrate, and between the movable boards themselves and the framing, Bear in mind that any security measure is only as good as the weakest link.

If water is dammed around a house the external house walls in effect become 'retaining walls' – a role for which they were probably not designed. But high water on either side of a wall would tend to cancel out the loading.

Any covers need to be removed after the flood has receded, to encourage ventilation of the house and help it dry out. Ventilation must be restored to rooms housing gas appliances. Leaving ventilation openings sealed up could promote secondary damage, such as the development of mould in the home after the flood.

Following flooding, it is not uncommon to see condensation streaming down house windows because the drying contractor has failed to achieve a low enough internal relative humidity during drying out.

Installation of anti-backflow devices

Anti-backflow devices, such as non-return valves and bungs, prevent the backflow of sewage. Manhole covers may be secured.

In the same way that the use of strong house locks can reduce home insurance costs against forced entry burglary, the use of recommended flood defence products can help reduce insurance premiums too.

Filling cracks and gaps in external walling

Good advice on how to protect a building from flood water is contained in an Environment Agency booklet: *Flood Products – Using Flood Protection Products – A guide for home owners*[6] (see www.highpeak.gov.uk/environment/flood/EAbooklet_flood_product_guide.pdf). CIRIA have also produced eight advice sheets (www.ciria.org/flooding/advice_sheets.html) giving practical guidance on how the various elements of a house can be protected[7].

Most of the above measures require a householder to be at home in time to install them, requiring good advance flood warning. If an occupier is away from home, e.g. on holiday or business, a flood could cause much greater damage as the house will be left to fend for itself.

Application of waterproof coatings to external wall faces may help keep out flood water but will also reduce the speed at which any flood water dries out. If coatings are considered worthwhile, then walls should be coated to sufficient height in relation to expected flood water height, and cracks, holes, etc. prepared and filled before application, including making good around pipe entry positions, etc.

Internal measures

Removal of vulnerable items

Valuables may be transported to higher floor levels for safety. This is the reason why a single-storey building is so vulnerable to flood damage – there may be no safe place to store precious or valuable items. What often causes the greatest distress to an occupier suffering from flood damage is the loss of irreplaceable personal items e.g. wedding photographs, rather than the more expensive goods.

Lighter-weight furniture

Selecting lighter-weight furniture for easier transportation away from the flood risk rooms, perhaps to an upper floor, may be an option. See Case Study 2 of this chapter.

Raising building services

It is common practice for critical building services, such as electrical installations, to be raised high enough to be safe from the flood water level. See Case Study 2 of this chapter.

You may find raised sockets in homes subject to flooding, but consider too running the ring main within the first floor, with vertical drops down to sockets. Also consider raising the height of meter boxes or consumer units, and switch gear.

Flood resistant materials

Water-resistant boarding may be used for kitchen cupboards, rather than vulnerable chipboard.

Plasters that are more resistant to flood may be used. Gypsum plasters, and most particularly 'Carlite Bonding' plasters, deteriorate when subjected to persistent water soaking. Suitable replacement plasters could incorporate cement or lime. Tiles fixed to a cementitious render backing plaster could often be a suitable wall finish.

Plasterboard suffers seriously from wetting and could be replaced with a more resilient finish. It can help if plasterboard linings are set as far as possible above the floor.

Cupboards and furniture

Cupboards and furniture can be raised higher off the floor using spacers, or in the case of kitchen cupboards, plastic adjustable legs. Kitchen units can be replaced with more flood resistant materials, such as durable water-resistant plywood or PVCU.

Floor coverings

Removable rugs can be used rather than fitted carpets with underlay. (See Case Study 2 of this chapter.)

Changing to rugs could be the best option if fitted carpets have been contaminated by sewage. Specialist cleaning is likely to be expensive and success unpredictable. Even if a carpet can be cleaned technically, reusing a previously contaminated floor covering may be totally unacceptable to the occupier.

If there is a risk of a repeat flood, floor coverings should be selected that allow easy access to the subfloor, e.g. to lift floorboards to help drying out, etc.

Wall finishes

More sacrificial wall paint finishes can be used, rather than more easily damaged patterned wallpapers. Permeable wall paints, such as water or lime-based paints, rather than oil-based product, should be considered.

Drainage

Weep holes and drains can be provided to allow water in cavities to escape following a flood. Cheap metal wall ties can suffer corrosion following flooding, particularly if subject to sea water ingress, so in some cases you should consider their replacement with stainless steel ties.

Insulation

Quilted insulations, whether between dry-lining and a masonry substrate, between brick and block walls of a cavity, or within timber stud inner walls, may need to be replaced with a more flood resistant insulation.

Any insulant in a cavity wall will make it more difficult to dry out the wall.

Some insulating materials can become heavy when water-logged, and slump unseen within a cavity.

It is very important that timber stud walls are not relined until it is certain that timbers have dried through their thickness. Relining over timber that is still significantly damp is a recipe for disaster.

Timber floors

Traditional timber floors should dry out reliably, but the ends of joists where they are built into masonry should be checked. Joist ends will be particularly difficult to dry out, and may be subject in any case to pre-flood damp damage. Consider re-supporting joist ends on metal joist hangers.

Although a traditional timber floor can be dried out with success, it may be necessary to clear the sub-floor void (i.e. crawl space) of debris, rubble, etc., as this can act as a reservoir for damp. You may also wish to create a drained sub-floor void – by installing screeds laid to falls, discharging by gravity to drains or provided with sumps and pumps.

Chipboard floors

Any chipboard floor coverings will probably have swelled beyond redemption from exposure to flood water, and should be replaced with more resistant materials, such as water-resistant plywood or standard builder's softwood – pre-treated if desired.

Floor finishes

Ground-bearing concrete floors can soak up a considerable volume of water, especially if water has been standing on it for some time. So be extremely careful to check that the concrete and screed toppings have dried out sufficiently to accept floor finishes that might themselves be moisture sensitive. (See Chapter 8.) Old concrete slabs without a damp-proof membrane will probably never completely dry out.

Timber windows

Timber windows may warp from wetting by floodwater, and double-glazed units may suffer water entry, meaning replacement is inevitable. Survey windows carefully after flood to assess their integrity.

Wall plasters

If wall plasters are removed, it may be most practical to replace skirting boards completely. Firstly skirtings may suffer some damage from their removal, and secondly the original mitres and end cuts will not reassemble together neatly on new plasters. Smaller-sized skirtings would often be cheaper to replace than restore. However, original mouldings that are difficult to replicate, or large section period skirting boards, should be salvaged where possible.

PROFESSIONAL WATER DAMAGE MITIGATION

Drying out buildings is becoming more professional and more scientific.

Like so many activities in the construction industry drying out has become a *specialised* activity, undertaken within a complex framework of codes and specifications to:

- meet health and safety needs;
- produce a user-friendly and accountable service for customers; and
- ensure that 'cowboys' in the industry find it increasingly hard to operate.

In the early days, drying buildings was more often left to general building contractors, or perhaps carpet cleaners, plumbers and sometimes electricians. All well-intentioned, no doubt – but so often lacking the necessary technical know-how.

Even today, damage management contractors are often called out when a general builder's attempt at drying after a simple pipe leak flood has gone horribly wrong. Secondary mould and rot can proliferate, increasing the flood damage bill. It is common to find that redecoration has been carried out too soon, before fabric has been properly dried, resulting in decorations and finishings unnecessarily damaged by underlying dampness that has resurfaced.

Where insurance companies are involved in claims, it would be more usual for loss adjusters to recommend

---

Lest we forget: the two drying phases

a) Drying of flood water.
b) Drying of newly applied wet finishes prior to re-decoration.

Decorations will fail if either a) or b) have not been successfully concluded, or if a pre-existing damp problem defeats either of the two!

---

flood remediation by a reputable specialist drying contractor.

The BDMA (British Damage Management Association) aims to promote high standards amongst members involved in restoration of buildings damaged by fire or flood – not forgetting that buildings damaged by fire frequently will have been deluged by water from the fire brigade hoses. After a fire, the building will often need to be temporarily re-roofed, to keep water out until restoration has been completed.

Professional water damage mitigation code of practice

Reputable flood remediation contractors will take on board advice within the publicly available specification PAS 64: *Professional water damage mitigation and initial restoration of domestic dwellings*, a code of practice developed in collaboration with the British Standards Institution (BSI)[8].

The code is not 'law' in the same way as an Act of Parliament, but should be regularly built into drying contracts. It is an important yardstick by which the performance of drying contractors can be judged.

The public is becoming increasingly knowledgeable in all things concerning property.

Many television programmes have focussed on the plight of flood victims and how their homes were restored. The consumer lobby will therefore help to ensure that advice contained in codes such as PAS 64 is taken heed of.

The code is well worth referring to should you wish to know in detail how flood damage restoration is executed and managed. For example, once a building has suffered flood, the restoration may be divided into two core activities:

- drying; and
- cleaning.

'Drying' includes physical drying of elements, components and materials, as well as decontamination. From the moment drying contractors arrive on site, considerable care must be exercised to prevent contamination and the development of moulds. A contractor must identify health and safety risk and advise or implement the necessary mitigation action.

Drying contractors are geared up and ready to respond to a flood at very short notice. You cannot work in this kind of industry and be a 9–5 person.

Floods are not 9–5! They can be sudden, unexpected and cause severe damage relatively quickly. A drying contractor can be expected to respond to a call within two hours. It may well be that others, such as emergency plumbers, electricians or the fire service are on site earlier.

Contractors may need to manage a surge of call-outs when widespread flooding has occurred, and will manage the response to meet the needs of the most badly affected properties or most vulnerable victims first. Be on your guard – there may be a shortage of drying equipment so some properties may not be properly dried.

The relevant insurance company will be contacted very soon after the event, and the loss adjuster would be one of the first 'suited professionals' to visit the affected property. In more minor flood incidents, claim management may be delegated to a reputable contractor and a loss adjuster may not be involved on site.

Drying out buildings – outline of PAS 64 procedures for damage management contractors

Stage 1 – Initial survey

- Assess health and safety issues – action as required.
- Draw up the drying goals and a moisture map.
- Decide on appropriate drying method/equipment.
- Removal of standing water/soaked material.
- Application of anti-microbial agents.
- Removal of vulnerable effects for storage/restoration.

Stage 2 – Site work

- Install equipment.
- Monitoring of air condition.
- Monitoring drying of building fabric.

Stage 3

- Completion of drying phase.
- Issue a report confirming drying achieved.

Confirmation of drying

It would be extremely risky for a contractor to issue a 'certificate of dryness', when many buildings can never be 'dry', no matter how long or effective the drying process. This is for two principal reasons:

- The building could be subject to dampness or wetness from a building fault other than the flood event. A fault, such as a pipe leak, could happen at any time – before, during or after the flood event.
- Some buildings will never actually be 'dry'. For example, older buildings seem to cope for years and years with levels of moisture that could seriously damage modern buildings. Sometimes

the dampness is just 'tolerated', and owners and occupiers use sacrificial or breathing finishes and decorations.

There is a huge opportunity for chartered surveyors to become more closely and regularly involved in drying contracts – to advise where there might be problems drying a house and to help check that the building fabric has dried out to an acceptable moisture level. Advice may be needed on the specification of restoration works. Surveyors can also help track down the source of a leak or extraneous moisture ingress when the contractor has not been able to do so. Drying contractors, whilst having a good practical knowledge of house construction, will not usually have studied construction, surveying or architecture to higher levels of certification.

Water is classified under four categories by PAS 64 – commonly described as:

Category 1 – Clean water
Category 2 – Grey water
Categories 3 and 4 – Black water.

Classification of flood water in the damage management industry[9]

Category 1 – clean water

Source of water not a risk to humans, just damages materials, e.g. water directly out of a mains water tap. Such water remains category 1 for a short time only. Once this water makes contact with floors, building materials, etc. it will become contaminated – moving to category 2 or 3.

Category 2 – grey water

An insanitary source, e.g. washing machine, dishwasher, urinal. It carries micro-organisms or nutrients for micro-organisms. Contains a degree of contamination and could cause sickness or discomfort to humans.

Category 3 or 4 – black water

Contains sewage. Humans are at risk from bacteria. Potentially harmful micro-organisms present, such as E. coli, Salmonella or Listeria. Water may look clear and uncontaminated, but is not. In the right conditions, microbes can double in number every 15–20 minutes (source: www.microban.com).

Key site tasks for a drying contractor

- Pump out standing water to lower parts.
- Remove water from flooring e.g. carpets.
- Release water from cavities and voids – e.g. by use of bradawl to bore small hole(s) to ceiling plasterboarding.
- Open up wall cavities, remove finishings as necessary, use specialist drying techniques.

- Remove building finishes and insulants to walls and floors, to aid drying.
- Apply anti-microbial agents to prevent contamination.
- Wet carpets may be removed – either to be disposed of or to be professionally cleaned.
- Or: float carpets to help drying.
- Furniture, carpets to be saved and/or cleaned and other personal effects are often removed and stored.

HOW TO DRY OUT BUILDINGS – KEY METHODOLOGIES

To encourage evaporation of water from the building fabric, it is common to find that impervious wall finishes have been at least partly removed, or plastic floor finishes taken up. Bathroom or kitchen wall tiling may be removed. Some unsalvageable finishes will have been discarded, e.g. carpets deemed too badly soiled to be cleaned, gypsum plasters damaged by water, plasterboard linings and soggy insulation material.

Drying contractors will use anti-microbial products to limit the development or spread of harmful contaminants. As well as controlling, stopping and preventing harmful contamination, and drying the building, cleaning will be required. Contractors should find out if occupants are sensitive to particular contaminants, e.g. moulds or the materials used to treat them.

Following a flood, a building will contain unwanted water as follows:

- Standing water in lower parts of the building, e.g. below ground spaces, such as basements and cellars. Deep standing water is traditionally pumped out by the fire brigade.
- Standing water on floors can be removed by a range of suction equipment.
- Collected water in cavities or other voids – of constructional elements, materials, components or finishes.

Some cavity walls may need to be drained of collected water. Drain holes and openings can be cut in the inner masonry skin.

Specialist drying techniques can be employed to dry out cavity construction, be it external cavity walling or internal partition work. See Figure 10.

- Water absorbed by porous materials.

For wet porous materials to dry out, evaporation (the transferral of liquid water into a gaseous state) must take place. Evaporation requires available energy, a water supply and the ability of the atmosphere to receive it[10].

In nature, the main source of energy for evaporation is the sun.

Water will evaporate more rapidly from porous materials with a high *permeance factor*. Materials that give up their moisture more reluctantly to evaporation have a lower permeance factor, e.g. 225mm-thick brickwork at 0.38, compared to 25mm-thick pine timber at 5.3.

Water will evaporate more quickly when the air is at a higher temperature, there is air movement, and the air is at a suitable relative humidity.

A drying contractor aims to maintain suitable drying conditions in a building so that efficient evaporation of moisture can continue until such time as 'drying goals' have been achieved. A balance will need to be drawn between the need to dry out quickly, and the potential damage this could cause, e.g. warping of timber doors or frames.

Evaporation is faster:

- for materials with a high permeance factor;
- when materials holding water are warmer;
- when materials are wetter;
- if air is less humid;
- if air temperature is higher;
- if vapour pressure is lower;
- if there is more air movement.

A leading manufacturer of drying equipment has produced a useful graph (see www.corroventa.com/dryingtechnology/theoreticalbackground), which divides the drying process into three phases:

- liquid water;
- drying of the surface; and
- drying of the material.

The graph shows the third phase to be the more drawn out.

The drying chamber

Drying contractors have found from experience that good drying conditions exist if an indoor temperature of 21°C and relative humidity (RH) of 40% is maintained. When air in the flooded house, or perhaps in part of the house, is brought to these temperature and humidity levels, a 'drying chamber' has been achieved.

Moisture in the damper, solid, porous building fabric will move (according to the laws of physics), to the drier air. From there, it can be processed by dehumidification plant and fed to collecting vessels or piped away via the property's drainage system.

Drying chamber conditions are not too difficult to achieve in the UK, with proper dehumidification plant.

Mould is the number one enemy of drying contractors. When humidity within a building is high, mould develops on surfaces that are at or below dew point. Mould colonies can develop within 48 hours, so prompt reduction of relative humidity in a flood-damaged house is of paramount importance. Maintaining drying chamber air conditions should reduce the risk of secondary mould.

Contractors should fully understand the relationship between air temperature, its relative humidity and dew point temperature. Such an understanding should enable contractors to produce and maintain safe, mould-free conditions, in which air is kept too warm and dry for condensation to form on surfaces.

If we consider our drying chamber air condition (i.e. 21°C and RH 40%) – we can plot the air at position **A** in figure 3 and the vapour pressure can be read off to the right, at approximately 1kPa. Such air would contain 6 grams of water per kg. If we describe air in terms of the actual amount of moisture in it, we are referring to 'specific humidity'. Crucially, condensation will not take place from this air unless it contacts a surface whose temperature is around 7°C or less. We know that mould colonies are not likely to form if air is maintained below RH 65%. If, however, we failed to maintain such a relative humidity during the drying process, with the air in the flooded house allowed to increase in relative humidity to 80%, this would mean that now at position **B** in figure 3 any surface at a temperature of 17.5°C or less would produce condensation. In such an unsatisfactory air state, not only is condensation inevitable on surfaces at or below 17.5°C, but the relative humidity condition of 80% is likely to encourage formation of mould colonies.

Drying contractors need to continually be vigilant, so that correct temperature and humidity conditions are maintained to encourage efficient drying and reduce the likelihood of mould development.

The combination of 21°C and RH 40% is not *the only* effective drying chamber condition, but is the combination of air and humidity condition commonly aimed for by drying contractors.

Closed drying

In closed drying, a good drying environment is created artificially inside a property, using dehumidification to maintain low relative humidity by continually removing moisture from the air. We may raise internal temperature utilising the house heating system, and we create essential air currents to help evaporation using air movers.

Efficient drying depends on contractors understanding psychrometrics. The psychrometric chart is the key reference for all those drying buildings, as it helps us understand key relationships between the air's temperature, relative humidity, dew point and vapour pressure.

The type and amount of equipment needed to create the drying chamber conditions can be calculated scientifically, and the exact positioning of air movers will be decided from site experience.

'Closed drying must be used when the outside conditions are above RH 55% or below 16°C. It should always be used when the structure is sealed, indoor

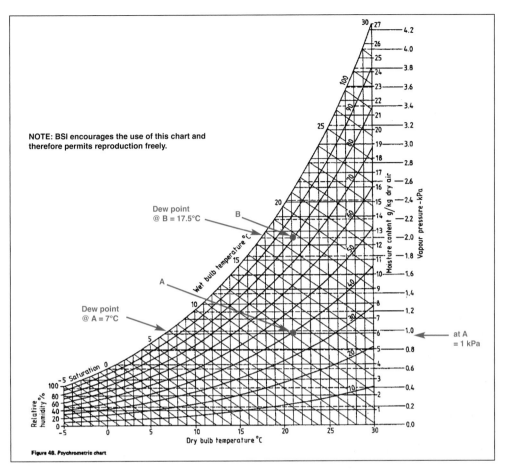

Figure 3: Psychrometric chart (figure 46 from BS 5250: 1989). Permission to reproduce extracts from BS 5250: 1989, Code of practice for control of condensation in buildings, is granted by BSI. British Standards can be obtained in PDF or hard copy formats from the BSI online shop: www.bsigroup.com/Shop or by contacting BSI Customer Services for hardcopies only: Tel: +44 (0)20 8996 9001, Email: cservices@bsigroup.com. Annotations in red are author's additions. A to B = vertical shift = change in RH of 40 to 80%.

humidity is sustained above RH 55% and where there are wet structural components or contents that require drying'[9].

Open drying

Most of us would instinctively open windows to help a wet room or building dry out, and we would naturally consider this most productive for drying in the summer rather than the winter. But we could be wrong. Warm air is not necessarily dry air – as a glance at a psychrometric chart proves. In summer, outside air could be at 25°C and RH 70% – meaning there is a high vapour pressure of 2.2kPa, with inside conditions of 20°C and RH 50% – 1.2kPa – meaning that the drying process may not be helped by opening windows.

Conversely, in winter you could find internal conditions of 25°C and RH 80% (i.e. vapour pressure just under 2.6kPa), with outside air much drier at 10°C and RH 50% (i.e. vapour pressure 0.6kPa). In this condition, the outside air is 'hungry' for moisture, and opening windows would help to dry out a building. By using the psychrometric chart we are able to understand the true difference between the relative dryness of internal

and external air. Opening windows would also create additional air movement to help evaporation.

Because relative levels of dryness of internal and external air can change even during the course of a day, in open drying we would need to continually monitor the difference in vapour pressure between inside and outside air to use the vapour pressure differential to best advantage. Typically, air conditions can change late in the afternoon, when the outside air temperature drops, increasing relative humidity and therefore raising outside vapour pressure, and open drying may cease to be effective – so we would close the windows.

Top-down drying

In this drying procedure, carpets and underlay remain in situ while drying continues above – usually in the first instance by use of powerful suction wands and pads. Flood rollers may also be used for larger areas. It is important to remember that if floor coverings remain in situ, any water or contaminant damage caused to the floor substrate, or any cavity or crawlspace below could remain undetected. Also, in many flood scenarios it is not economical to try and salvage underlays or the cheaper and more easily replaceable carpets.

Convectant drying technology

It *is* possible to use outside air to dry a wet building, by just opening windows when the vapour pressure outside is lower than inside. However, you would see slow progress in drying, as the difference in vapour pressure would not be great.

But outside air can be manipulated. It can be heated up and directed into a building.

In convectant drying, the equipment is typically trailer-mounted. One manufacturer's set-up uses banks of propane gas burners to heat outside air which is then directed into the wet house. The fresh air is conditioned to less than RH 2%, and huge volumes of this conditioned air are routed into the building through very large diameter hoses. This air is as hungry for moisture as desert sand! The dry hot air takes up moisture from within the wet building and is then pumped out.

This method is being very vigorously sold in the UK by a US company. Of course, we are told only of the great advantages, and only time will alert us to any problems with this method, if there are any.

Time, of course, is money. Time saved means the building can be brought back into use faster. Rents can be earned again, and less costs are incurred in temporary housing or other facilities during the drying and restoration process.

It is claimed that 2,000 pints per day can be removed using a trailer-mounted system – see figure 4, and independent testing backs up the claims, with times of drying reduced by 90% in comparison with traditional methods such as refrigerant or desiccant dehumidifiers. The very high temperatures and low humidity environment produced in a building during drying with this

system would mean secondary damage from mould should not occur.

As it stands at present, this new technology is more suitable for the larger or more seriously water-damaged buildings. The trailers need to be parked, and congested urban streets could present logistical difficulties.

Concerns have been raised concerning damage that could be caused from rapid drying, such as warping, excessive shrinkage, etc. One account of drying using this method stated that 'within 24 hours the [items] were *bone dry*'. This does flag up one key issue – technicians using a fast-dry method need to make sure that materials are not **over-dried**. Most building materials are happiest when they are *slightly damp*!

It is likely that, in time, smaller, more portable units will become available, so this highly efficient drying method can be used in much more modest situations.

It is also possible to make use of industrial machines to clean carpets – housed in dedicated vehicles, and able to efficiently clean large areas of carpet using powerful equipment. Again, the vehicle would need to be parked in close proximity to the subject building.

Cautionary note

When it is stated that buildings have dried out in days, the structure may not have been checked for dryness at great depth. Most moisture meter probes are used at depth to say 50mm, and a thick wall could potentially *still be wet* at greater depth.

Where a particular building element still holds unwanted water at depth, if finishes allow future evaporation this lingering moisture may eventually find a way out. However, there could be problems if the moisture is sealed in by non-breathing finishes.

Figure 4: Trailer-mounted driers drying out a medium-rise residential block that suffered widespread internal flooding from a mains burst. Note the huge tubes directing hot air into the building to promote efficient drying. Surprisingly, this trailer-mounted drying machine runs off a standard house power socket! Photo © courtesy Action Dry.

How the tower block was dried

Figure 5: A Stevenage tower block being dried using trailer-mounted drying technology. After electricity failure on the 15th floor, portable gas bottle heaters were used as a temporary measure. But a fire ensued from use of the gas bottle heaters, and tragically the fire brigade suffered two fatalities in attending the blaze. And as so often happens, flood follows fire. Photo © courtesy Action Dry.

The water damage (it is believed from fire-fighting) was extensive, with all the floors below the 15th suffering damage enough to prompt decanting of tenants – 90 apartments were water damaged.

A trailer-mounted drying operation began. Hot air at 120°C with a relative humidity of 2% was pumped into the building via huge 355mm diameter tubing. This is very thirsty air. Some tubes you may see are channelling wet air out of the building. There were unforeseen problems. What was expected to be a 20-day drying programme soon extended, as fresh leaks occurred during the drying. The source was soon discovered – plastic mains pipes had been damaged by the original fire, and sporadic leaks in many flats caused further havoc. Additional drying conundrums surfaced: damp patches near ceiling level refused to dry and were finally found to be due to a hollow floor construction that the drying contractor was not informed of – the hollow construction had trapped litres and litres of water – needing a dedicated approach to achieve successful drying. Drying in the end took 56 days – still a pretty quick result (small homes often take much longer to dry out using standard dehumidification equipment).

As well as huge pipes pushing in and pulling out air, air moving equipment can be set up in the building. Monitoring is undertaken to help drying specialists gauge the building's response to the drying methods, and to help the specialists detect the occurrence of any additional water escape during the drying process – as happened above. Dozens of humidity and temperature sensors are used with data logging, as well as the manual taking of measurements. Weather is also recorded – sometimes such painstaking monitoring can also identify linkage of high rainfall to a water ingress.

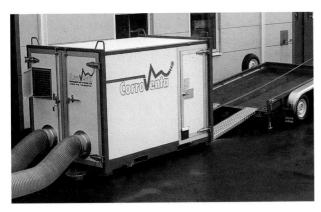

Figure 6: Desiccant trailer-mounted dehumidifiers may also be used to fast-track the drying of water-damaged property. Warm, dry air is powered into the wet building to achieve outstandingly fast drying times. The equipment pictured is more commonly used on the Continent. Photo © courtesy Corroventa, www.corroventa.com

Occupiers in situ

Closed drying regimes can be thwarted by occupiers – and I have great sympathy for anybody enduring weeks and weeks of noisy dehumidifiers and windy air movers!

Houses can become very noisy and hot, and suffer air movement blowing personal papers off desks.

In the aftermath of a flood, many occupiers will prefer to stay put rather than seek alternative temporary accommodation during the drying phase. They may reduce the effectiveness of the drying regime in any of the following ways:

- switching off dehumidifiers;
- opening doors and windows in a closed drying regime;
- moving equipment;
- turning off heating;
- de-compartmentalising drying by opening internal doors or disrupting a 'tented' area, etc.

All this is understandable, especially if the drying is taking longer than expected and there seems to be no end to the process (although contractors can keep track of whether dehumidifiers have been switched off, as modern units incorporate time clocks).

It has to be said, though, that an occupier can also help the drying process enormously by keeping track of building conditions, e.g. air temperature and relative humidity – so the drying contractor can consider any equipment adjustments or other fine-tuning to maintain efficient drying conditions. Contractors commonly leave humidity and temperature sensors on site so that occupiers can monitor conditions – perhaps to open or close windows as conditions dictate. Seeing that humidity is being maintained at a low level can also give comfort to anxious occupiers and clients.

Some occupiers take on an extremely proactive role in the drying and can soon become quite expert in keeping track of internal conditions, including monitoring internal and external vapour pressure using a psychrometric chart.

EQUIPMENT USED TO DRY BUILDINGS

Equipment is used to *heat*, *dehumidify* and *move* air.

Dehumidifiers

These can almost be classified according to colour. Blue and red ones are usually commercial – white ones are for consumers.

Dehumidifiers used by contractors are extremely robust and considerably more efficient than their consumer cousins.

Refrigerant dehumidifiers are the type most commonly used, with three main elements: condenser coil, evaporator coil and a compressor.

Such a dehumidifier reduces the temperature of moist air down to dew point, where moisture condenses on the evaporator coils. Water drips onto a tray, into a large plastic drum or is discharged via a pump into a tube fed into the house plumbing. This process creates heat – which in turn reduces relative humidity and specific humidity.

See Appendix C for dehumidifier notes.

One of the downsides of refrigerant dehumidifiers is that refrigerant coils can periodically frost up at lower temperatures, and the dehumidifier is then out of action during a defrosting cycle. More sophisticated refrigerant dehumidifiers incorporate a 'hot gas bypass', which speeds up the defrost phase to make the dehumidifier more efficient. Refrigerant dehumidifiers work much less efficiently below 20°C, and are more energy efficient in high humidity situations. Technically, a refrigerant dehumidifier can dry air down to 1°C, but would then be extremely inefficient, as much of its working time would be spent in the defrost cycle.

Consideration needs to be given to how much heat is generated by dehumidifiers and air movers running constantly. It is important to keep aiming for the ideal drying chamber condition of RH 40% and 21°C. As air temperature rises above 21°C, extremely un comfortable living conditions can develop for occupiers in situ. Humidity must not rise above RH 60%, and drying contractors would probably accept internal air temperature as high as 25°C. Higher humidity conditions would potentially create a risk scenario in which secondary mould could develop on

Figure 7: A modern refrigerant dehumidifier, manufactured for the professional market.
Photo courtesy Dri-Eaz Products Ltd, www.dri-eaz.eu.com

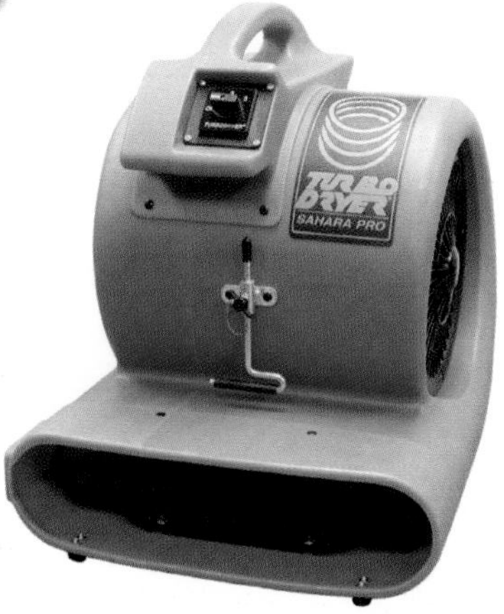

Figure 7a: This modern air mover provides high velocity airflow – essential to drying. It directs airflow across wet surfaces to force moisture into the air where dehumidification plant can then remove it. Photo courtesy Dri-Eaz Products Ltd, www.dri-eaz.eu.com

colder surfaces subject to condensation, or dampen materials (e.g. absorbent fabrics) so they become mouldy. And not forgetting that as well as the main room spaces, there will be unseen voids that could be colder, damper and more of a mould risk.

Contractors would normally place humidity and air temperature sensors in each room of the property being dried, which would give the occupier the opportunity to keep a check on any change in internal conditions. The occupier could then turn down the central heating to lower air temperature, or if faced with rising humidity – a potentially major problem – could immediately contact the drying contractor so that the drying regime could be adjusted.

A dehumidifier may give considerable comfort to a householder in situ. Water is very often collected in a large drum and it is then easy to see that the dehumidifier is doing its job. If, however, water is directed straight into the house plumbing system via a flexible tube from the dehumidifier (typically fed into a washing machine standpipe) it is not obvious how much water has been collected. In flood remediation we are dealing with often quite traumatic scenarios, and anything that can help convince the householder or occupier that drying is taking place is extremely helpful.

Refrigerant dehumidifiers work best in warm air and high humidities.

Low-grain refrigerant dehumidifiers

We have here opportunity to take advantage of the very latest technology.

A more sophisticated refrigerant dehumidifier, incorporating an extra sealed circuit filled with freon gas, is fitted to the hot gas bypass to improve efficiency of dehumidification. Such a dehumidifier is able to reduce water vapour down to around 5.7 grams/kg of air, and uses less electricity. When drying a larger property, one efficient low-grain dehumidifier could do the same drying work as three or four standard refrigerant dehumidifiers.

Desiccant dehumidifiers

These machines are more expensive than the more commonly used refrigerant dehumidifiers, but more efficient. In an absorption process, moisture is attracted to the particulate surfaces of a silica gel wheel. Silica gel is an *adsorbent* – a veritable magnet for moisture. An adsorbent does not change chemically as it absorbs moisture. These dehumidifiers are more thirsty for electricity, which would normally be paid for as part of the house insurance claim. The great advantage of desiccant dehumidifiers is that they work down to temperatures even below freezing, far colder conditions than a refrigerant dehumidifier could operate in. They are also able to produce a much lower relative humidity in a drying chamber. Such a dehumidifier can reduce humidity down to RH 10% and can work very efficiently below 10°C. Achieving a lower drying chamber RH can considerably help drying of structural materials.

Desiccant dehumidifiers can be a great boon when there is no power supply on site to activate the house heating system. In the winter floods that devastated many homes in Carlisle, desiccant dehumidifiers were used to great effect, as conditions in the houses were too cold to enable standard refrigerant dehumidifiers to work efficiently. As there is no defrost cycle there is no 'down time' for this type of dehumidifier. The silica gel wheel is continuously reactivated by an air stream that literally 'cooks' the moisture out of the desiccant rotor.

Desiccant dehumidifiers are useful for drying hard to dry materials, i.e. with low permeance factors, such

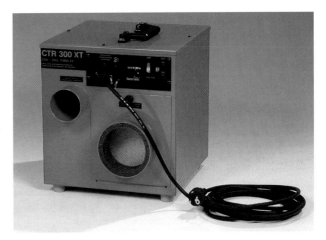

Figure 8: A desiccant dehumidifier. Photo courtesy Corroventa.

as hardwood floors, concrete and plaster. Desiccant dehumidifiers are also often comparatively lighter to transport than their refrigerant cousins.

Beware mounting hire charges! One of the common issues lies in the way contractors earn fees from drying. The longer dehumidifiers and air movers are in situ in a property, the greater will be the hire charges and fees earned by contractors – this is a big issue in the industry. Drying can be strung out unnecessarily over long periods , while fees gradually mount for the contractors. Loss adjusters acting for insurance companies are not necessarily experts in drying technology, and may not always appreciate whether drying is being carried out in the most efficient manner.

Refrigerants are particularly useful at the early stages of drying after flood, when air may be warm and humid. But at later stages of drying, when you need to pull moisture out of wet and denser structural materials, desiccant dehumidifiers come into their own, and put in place a more targeted drying strategy.

When conditions suit a refrigerant dehumidifier, e.g. when air is warm and humid, the desiccant would also be *technically* efficient in removing moisture from the air, but possibly not so *energy* efficient as the refrigerant.

Dehumidifiers can be used with a range of accessories suited to the drying strategy. Some desiccants, for example, have a variety of inlets and outlets of differing sizes that may be used to extract air for processing from

Table 1: Conditions affecting choice of dehumidifier				
	Operating temperature range	**Best efficiency**	**Worst efficiency**	**RH conditions suited**
Desiccant dehumidifier	−40°C–+40°C	Conditions outside the refrigerant's capability range	Extracts moisture in all expected UK conditions	Colder or drier air
Refrigerant dehumidifier	1–35°C	15–35°C	Below 20°C efficiency declines markedly	Prefers warm and humid air – RH 40% or above
Low grain refrigerant dehumidifier	1–35°C	15–35°C	Below 20°C efficiency declines markedly	Extracts moisture from air at lower specific humidity than standard refrigerant

various locations, or to direct processed dry air to several positions where it would help drying.

Desiccants are necessary when temperatures are very low, or humidity low. This can occur in the winter months.

Air movers

When you visit a property being dried after a natural or domestic flood, you will usually find two types of equipment operating: dehumidifiers and air movers.

'Turbo driers' are commonly used. A turbo drier has a snout to which various accessories can be added, such as manifolds, so the air can be directed into numerous tubes (useful for drying cavity walls). Standard axial fans are often used – the type of unit housing a propeller blade protected by a cage. An axial fan does not focus outgoing air in the same way as a turbo drier. The snout of the turbo drier is used for example to push a current of air under a carpet (termed 'floating' the carpet).

How to dry cavities and voids

Cavities and voids are collecting places for flood water. Making holes in finishes and internal or external leaves of cavities can allow the release of water. This can be a useful strategy if there is a level of water that can exit by gravity, or sometimes by use of pumping equipment.

Modern technology allows the damage management contractor to dry out hollow construction using psychrometrics. The key principle is usually to force warm, dry and of course 'thirsty' air into the voids through holes. Warm air takes on board the wetness within the void, and the movement of air encourages efficient evaporation. This is a much less destructive method than removing finishes wholesale, which could incur considerable reinstatement cost.

Figure 9: In the ground floor of this Great Yarmouth house, 2 refrigerant dehumidifiers and 8 airmovers have been installed to dry out the house for a second attempt at replastering. The property suffered a flash flood, was dried, replastered and given a concrete ground-bearing floor to replace the original timber suspended system. However the new dry-lining soon showed circular damp stains as brickwork was subject to a long standing damp problem. The plan now is to replaster using ventilated membranes and to install a suspended concrete floor incorporating a drained oversite.

Walls – injection drying

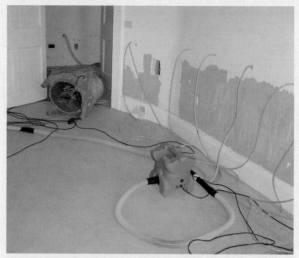

Figure 10: You are looking at one of three Sheffield apartments, that have suffered water damage from leaking central heating pipes in the upper flat. The partition being dried is a hollow timber stud partition without any insulation fill. Water from the leaks ran down three floors within this partitioning. Taking off plasterboards could be one way of drying it out. You certainly cannot delay the drying, or secondary mould will set in. A system for injection drying has been set up, which only needed 12mm holes boring in the plasterboard, to allow entry of numerous feeder hoses run off a manifold. Dry, warmed air is pumped into the wet void to encourage a rapid and efficient evaporation of water. An air mover is sited in the room corner to assist evaporation from wet plaster. Photo © courtesy Action Dry.

Floors – injection drying, insulated floor slab

Figure 11: A high-pressure fan sucks free-standing water from under the screed via a water separator. Warm, dry air from a desiccant dehumidifier is then forced into large holes drilled into the floor screed. You may note four tubes from a manifold with terminals that neatly seal into the floor holes. Dry air will be pushed across the voids between insulant and concrete/screed, to exit via the floor edges or other exit holes drilled for the purpose. The air leaving the slab void will be wetter than the air entering it via the tubes – this difference will be an indication of the amount of water being removed.

- Or the insured? The devastation caused by the flood now escalates! Once plasters are hacked off, the building (and former home) becomes very much a building site. Drying might be faster, but additional reinstatement works may extend the contract period for the remediation. Yet more and as yet unfamiliar contractors will now move in. At least the insured is not paying directly for the hacking off and replastering. The plaster removal could damage joinery and any other finishes or fittings attached to the plaster removed.
- The insurance company? An increased pay-out for the flood damage. Increased payouts mean higher insurance premiums for others. Insurance premiums escalate.
- The nation? Scarce economic resources may be misallocated on work that might not be necessary.

So decisions to take off wall plasters in conjunction with drying after flood must not be considered lightly, and the following factors may need to be considered.

Drying a building: should plasters be removed?

Key questions to consider:

- How long has water been in contact with walls or been able to soak into walls from an adjacent element?
- Is the plaster a *barrier* which would inhibit drying of the substrate?
- Is removal of an impervious paint finish or the wall covering sufficient preparation to allow efficient drying?
- Has the plaster been contaminated significantly by foul water?
- Is the plaster significantly contaminated by salts?
- Would taking off hard solid plasters cause significant damage to the substrate, e.g. pulling off masonry faces, etc?
- Has it been confirmed from tests that the substrate is very wet at depth?
- Will taking off the subject plaster involve significant associated reinstatement costs, e.g. the refixing of radiators, plumbing, rewiring, refixing of attached joinery or other fittings, finishes, or components?
- Are there monies available (e.g. from insurance policy) to fund replastering and associated works?
- Are there any 'conservation issues', e.g. would replastering in a historic building be extremely expensive, or would hacking off existing plaster-constitute a damaging removal of historic fabric?
- Is the wall plaster part of a waterproofing system that might be guaranteed?
- Will removal of plasters cause significant loss in structural integrity of the subject wall?
- Has the plaster been irreversibly damaged by the flood water?

The BRE[3] make the point that you may only need to remove plaster from one side of a wall to enable the wall to be successfully dried.

If plasters are contaminated by hygroscopic salts it would mean that even if the wall could be dried, some time after the drying, the plasters might again become damp by attraction of moisture from the air by hygroscopic salts. Plasters that are contaminated by salts are very difficult to check for dryness, as the presence of salts tends to magnify readings by electronic moisture meter (see Chapter 8).

It is probably true that as well as reducing the overall wall thickness, by taking off plaster, a greater surface area of substrate is available on a *rough* brick substrate, as opposed to the smoother plaster finish. The greater surface area could be a factor in encouraging evaporation and thereby hastening drying time.

Should wall linings be removed?

There is likely to be a strong and in most cases irrefutable case for taking off wall linings and wallpapers to aid drying, as these finishes may well already be flood damaged. Some wall linings, e.g. vinyl and washable papers, are quite impervious, so if left in situ they would inevitably impede drying of the plasters and wall. Such linings can allow moisture to build up unseen for some time, until it finally appears with gusto! It may be wise to avoid using impermeable/vinyl-type washable paper during reinstatement works.

Should plastic floor tiling be taken up to promote drying?

If there has been standing water for some time, there is the likelihood that floodwater will have wetted a floor screed below a plastic tiled floor. The floodwater will have at least been able to soak into the floor at the perimeter, and in a solid floor situation would have often soaked quite high up walls. But there will be cases where flood water has not actually significantly wetted a solid floor under an impervious floor finish, so there may not be a case to take up the floor finish just to aid drying.

It is possible to check whether the solid floor is dry by removing one or two tiles, scraping off the adhesive, and checking floor humidity by a 'humidity box' – see *Diagnosing Damp*[1], page 83. You may in some cases be able to refit the lifted tile, or replace it with a similar tile. If the plastic tiling is to be covered over by carpet, one or two tiles of a different shade should not be a problem. Alternatively you could drill a hole in the floor, straight through the tiles – as long as you are convinced no pipes or cables or membrane would be damaged. You could then carbide test the drillings to ascertain moisture content, and also insert a humidity sensor to obtain information on the humidity condition of the floor. The sleeves that are used to house the electronic thermo-hygrometer may be left in situ, so at any time afterwards you can simply insert an electronic sensor attached to a moisture meter to take readings of relative humidity, temperature and specific humidity. (See Chapter 8.)

Wholesale tile removal can be extremely risky, as plastic floor tiles commonly contain asbestos. The removal of tiles must then be carried out or overseen by a specialist licensed asbestos-removal contractor. Materials would be carefully taken up and sealed in bags, by operatives wearing the necessary PPE (personal protective equipment), and the subject room sealed off. Thus you may appreciate the common sense of finding out if the solid floor has been significantly wetted by the flood, before engaging in tile removal. Replacement of tiles will of course be additional costly reinstatement work.

Before engaging in drilling of floor screeding it is often useful to excavate a trial area of screed in a place likely to cause the least inconvenience or damage – this might be within a corner cupboard or an out-of-the-way room corner. You will then know more about the solid floor make-up and can make more informed decisions on its preparation for drying.

Where can the chartered surveyor find a role in the drying process?

There is a surveying window, but it is quite a small one.

There is a considerable advantage, of course, to be gained in commencing drying as swiftly as possible. There is a risk, for example, of secondary mould development, necessitating prompt control of humidity conditions in the immediate aftermath of the flood. But the first day or so must be regarded and used as the *surveying window* – when independent advice might often be useful in assessing the moisture condition of the elements and finishes of construction, so the drying contractor can target the drying more efficiently.

Without independent advice at the early stage of remediation, decisions may be made on drying that:

- suit the drying contractor – who is keen for a straight forward, easy and *quick* drying phase;
- suit the loss adjuster – least cost of reinstatement work;
- suit the insured – maximum replacement of plasters, carpets, personal effects, balanced against the competing desire for minimum time of drying and reinstatement;
- ignore the needs of the building!

There may also need to be confirmation concerning the cause of the flood, if there is any doubt at all on this. There may for example be a need for a rethink of design regarding building services – if a failure has caused a flood event. There is no point in just replacing a mains water pipe fitting with the same component that has already shown itself to be vulnerable.

Can a drying contractor know when the building has been dried to its pre-loss state of dryness?

The short answer here could be a simple 'no'.

Firstly, it is unlikely there will be any reliable record of the building's state of dryness, pre-flood.

Sometimes just part of a building suffers the flood, so you can compare damp meter readings in the flooded to un-flooded zones. In buildings subject to flood over the whole floor plan, contractors tend to rely heavily upon moisture meter manufacturers' published risk bands for damp meter readings – typically these are risk, safe or unsafe. (See *Diagnosing Damp*[1], Chapter 7.) Standard damp meters give an indication of dryness at or very near a surface. If humidity sensors are inserted into walls or floors, contractors tend to consider the wall or floor material acceptably dry once RH has dropped to 75% – but from personal experience I know for sure that walls and floors of older buildings can often be acceptably dry when RH within the floor or wall element is 85%, or sometimes even a little more. (Please refer to Chapter 8.) And of course some buildings can never be fully brought back to a satisfactory state of dryness, as they were suffering damp problems before the flood event. You may have some previous survey reports to give you clues, or perhaps the occupier will tell you of previous damp stains. And remembering too that as a rule, newer buildings record lower damp readings in plaster and timber than older examples. So all I would say is that experience is needed to know when a particular building has been dried sufficiently for walls and floors to be refinished/decorated.

CASE STUDY 1: DOVER – CRISIS? WHAT CRISIS?

Mrs A has been through much worse than this. She lived through the Second World War, when her Folkestone home was under attack from the air. She is now surrounded by the paraphernalia of the drying trade. Can you spot the moisture meter case? But Mrs A seems to be very cool, calm and collected in what would for many be a crisis. Not for Mrs A the imperceptible upward climb of a hidden capillary movement of damp – but the rush of a torrent of water into her home through the back door ... real damp!

The story

Calm after the storm. You can't hear it – but a whirr comes from the large blue machine in the foreground. Note too the humidity and temperature sensor on top of the dehumidifier. This will hopefully tell us the room air is quite dry, so a suitable drying chamber has been created. And low relative room humidity will also tell us there should be no risk of secondary mould.

Figure 22: Triumph over adversity.

The damage management contractor has been able to achieve quite effective closed drying, as the door at the top of the central stairway can be shut to compartmentalise the building for efficient drying. No point in attempting to dry the whole house.

Things were certainly not under control as Mrs A came downstairs on Sunday night, 28 September 2003, to find standing water. She was not alone, other Dover properties were also flooded. The storm drains apparently just couldn't cope with sudden high rainfall.

Luckily help was at hand, as Mrs A's daughter was staying for the weekend. She was soon at work mopping up water and helping to save family treasures – irreplaceable photographs stacked near the dresser were the first things to be rescued. Water had cascaded down the garden over the concrete terracing, and straight in under the back door, over the solid kitchen floor and into the living room.

The wet carpets were quickly removed, or there would have been a secondary mould problem. And the damage management contractor was in there quickly, by Monday morning. Like any emergency service, the contractor is ready for action 24/7. Soggy carpets, too heavy to move, were cut up and carried out. Some short sections of floorboard in the living room were taken up to assist the drying. A refrigerant dehumidifier, three turbo driers and two axial fans were soon powering away to promote a swift evaporation of water. Silt was removed and the ground floor sanitised.

Luckily the green three-piece suite sat on feet 75mm above floor level, and the standing water was not quite high enough to get to it. The dresser too, traditional and on firm feet, helped keep its contents dry. It was just stacked papers on the floor that got wet.

During our visit on 2 October, the contractor turned off equipment for a few minutes so we could chat to Mrs A. She had lived in the house for 45 years and had been through air raids in Folkestone, so this was not really a crisis to her! She is a resilient woman, and probably more resilient to flood than the building fabric that surrounds her.

She was confident and happy with the contractor. Drying, while quite 'technical', is also very 'human'. Damp remedies are instigated during what is for most people a highly traumatic life event. The first impression the victim has of the drying professional will be important – just as the first impression a client may have of a house surveyor. A subtle blend of confidence without arrogance is the key, and sensitivity in communication with all parties involved.

The contractor took moisture meter readings in the timber floor as we chatted, and amazingly the floorboards and joists were already recording quite dry readings of 12–14%, which just goes to show how quickly things can get back to normal. Actually everything was satisfactorily dry after three weeks of drying. The kitchen solid floor would never be completely 'dry', as it was formed directly off the soil – and there were pockets of pre-existing 'damp' in some external walls, but you would have to jack the building up and rebuild it from the ground up to solve this.

CASE STUDY 2: SOMERSET – DIGGING FOR VICTORY

Figure 23: The residents of this Somerset farmhouse seem to have found their rural idyll . . . or have they?

Figure 24: You begin to become suspicious, when you see a canoe tethered and ready for action at the back!

The owners showed me the survey report they had commissioned before purchase of the farmhouse, entitled 'Inspection Report', by a very diligent architect. In a final paragraph there is mention of a flood risk:

'The property is attractive but once in a while may be subject to flooding' – possibly a great British understatement!

Copious advice could be found in the lengthy report, from how to fix the roof to mending a loose WC pan.

The buyer took on the house knowing there might be flood problems, but probably not knowing how often, how inconvenient or how serious. The outgoing householders were not very communicative in this regard. Prospective purchasers might have been better informed from a chat at the local riverside inn.

The author helped take levels. We transferred levels traditionally using a long levelling board, duly reversed regularly to eliminate unnecessary errors,

and transferred levels all the way from the front door threshold to a tree at the bottom of the never ending garden. We painted a white mark on the tree, corresponding with the back door threshold level. If water rose up the tree towards the white mark, it would inevitably soon be on its way to the house. This tree was significant. It stood next to a brook.

The main threat is towards the centre of the gardens. Water that runs down in torrents from the higher ground to the right swirls back along the right side boundary, trying to seek a way down to the lower ground on the other side of the garden. The lawns near the house gradually fill. The occupier became very familiar with the condition of his turf, and came to tell by its relative sponginess when ground water was welling up underneath. The owners almost developed a sixth sense, being able to know very accurately when rising waters were due to threaten their home. This happened the very first winter after moving in. The initial reaction was more defensive

Figure 25: View from half-way down the garden looking down towards the copse, where you would find a low bridge and a tree, just visible from the house. You could view our white marker using binoculars. The land to the right of the garden slopes upwards. The garden is a peninsula of higher ground that obstructs the movement of floodwater from the higher ground to the right down eventually to the River Exe.

Figure 26: Quaint as this old stone bridge is, when the stream fills up during flash floods, the bridge abutments act as a brake to stop the outflowing water, which backs up onto the owner's land along the right side garden embankment. Rising water here warns of potential problems for the house perhaps only hours away.

than attacking. That first winter flood, back in 1987 prompted the owners to adopt a stance which they termed their 'minimum damage posture'. This is more feasible when your home has two floors – as sensitive and valuable items can be stored on the first floor.

Stage 1 Flood defences internally

Keep vulnerable items and services well away from advancing water (the minimum damage posture) or able to be carried to safety.

Kitchen units were raised up on blocks after that first winter. The living room carpet was divided into two sections, so that each was light enough to be rolled up quickly and carried upwards to safety. The furniture selected for the ground floor sitting room was light and with high legs. Electric sockets were raised up high. Water rose in that first winter flood to 5mm over the whole of the ground floor, not very deep, but just imagine 5mm of water in your own home, look in every room and visualise which items would be ruined.

Figure 27: Lightweight furniture that can be quite easily carried upstairs when the flood season approaches. The rugs are easy to take up and drag to safety. The solid floor will not be damaged significantly by flood water.

Figure 28: As a home inspector or building surveyor, you would have to be suspicious here. Sockets 900mm up off the floor, no timber skirting board, and salt damage from flood water. Once wet, the thick house walls will never dry out completely – the salty plaster will prevent evaporation, as moisture taken in by the hygroscopic salts re-wets the wall in cycles. Water comes up from the ground as well as flowing laterally into the house from the garden.

Figure 29: The heavy pine kitchen base units are extremely resilient, seemingly able to suffer repeated floods – but need to be raised a few inches up off the stone farmhouse floor – the pragmatic timber blocks are a bit of a give-away for any surveyor.

This defensive furnishing arrangement helped the owners get through without much damage the first year of their occupation. But a flood warning on New Year's Day 1989 was really the final straw.

Stage 2 Flood defences – landscaping

The owners studied very carefully the lie of the land. Devising flood defences is all about levels. The gardens were really behaving as a dam. Water from the adjacent hillside just couldn't find a way through to the lower land on the left side – so the remedy was logical enough – dig!

Figure 30: John takes a well-earned rest from the digging! Earth will be moved across the garden and piled high to create protective banks along the right boundary – to divert the backing water towards the central drain channel. We will boss the water!

Waterproofing contractors tend to adopt quite a cautionary approach, and assume they are in every case designing waterproofing to withstand hydrostatic pressure as per BS 8102. Whether or not a basement is actually subject to a head of water or a percolating ingress of water will often only be appreciated once internal finishes are hacked off during substrate preparation (see figure 117).

Importantly for us surveyors, BS 8102 is relevant not only to cellars or basements which are obviously wholly or partly below ground, but also to building walls subject to an *external raised ground level.* When you find dampness caused from external ground levels having been raised above horizontal damp-proof course level, installing internal waterproofing to BS 8102 requirements could be one way to remediate the dampness. BS 6576: 1985, *Code of Practice for Installation of Chemical Damp-proof Courses*[14] does not apply to below-ground *water*proofing.

If early clauses in the British Standard are applicable to waterproofing of existing basements, then it has to be said that strictly speaking, waterproofing contractors rarely comply with the standard, at least in local domestic waterproofing contracts. BS 8102 (clause 3.1.1) requires that designers and installers carry out a thorough site investigation (to BS 5930) prior to design of waterproofing. BS 5930 is a very extensive standard covering all aspects of site investigations. Waterproofing contractors, as indeed many damp-proofing companies, often carry out surveys for free. A BS 5930 site investigation would require time-consuming and costly testing of soil samples and groundwater samples for sulphates, etc. and determination of water table height.

Basement waterproofers would argue that their designed system could cope with any aggressive groundwater encountered or any significant rise in water table. Aggressive sulphates can be countered by external membranes, or use of sulphate-resisting cements in concrete or screeds, etc.

THE THREAT OF RISING GROUNDWATER

Basements are considered by the BRE to be energy efficient, as a greater proportion of a property's outer walling is insulated against heat loss by surrounding ground. But set against the undoubted advantages of utilising below-ground space is the considerable risk of flooding from rising water tables. Due to a lack of good building plots, we are turning to inferior building land that was given a wide berth by our forebears – even using flood plain sites.

We are also facing problems from rising groundwater levels in several major UK cities, e.g. parts of Birmingham and London. Major cities have experienced a retreat of industry, resulting in less extraction of water from deep wells. During the years of water extraction, the water table in London gradually lowered, until around 1965; from then on we have seen a continuous rising of groundwater. This really is rising damp!

Rising water threatens the continued use of below-ground space, and could damage building structures and services. The new British Library was built with pumps to protect the building and its contents.

WATERPROOFING AN EXISTING BASEMENT – GENERAL CONSIDERATIONS

Faced with a damp basement, first thoughts will naturally be directed on how best to keep out penetrating dampness. But bear it in mind that other issues will need to be addressed too.

A means of reducing or eliminating condensation needs to be designed in. No matter how well you succeed in combating moisture from outside the habitable space, the condensation *enemy within* could defeat all your efforts to create a dry living space. Design standards for basement waterproofing flag up the need for condensation control to eliminate dampness. Suitable heating, ventilation, insulation and lifestyle can eliminate or reduce the risk, as well as help provide a more comfortable and enjoyable living experience. With a lack of openable windows it is most likely that mechanical ventilation would be needed – almost inevitably, if the basement incorporates kitchen, bathroom, WC or utility room space.

A structural engineer's advice at an early stage is advised if you plan to increase existing basement ceiling height, or carry out any alteration with structural implications. Work near to property boundaries could require preparation of a Party Wall Award under the *Party Wall Act* 1996.

Means of escape in case of fire (or even flood) must be designed for – and the relevant Building Regulations and codes of practice consulted and complied with. There will need to be consideration of lighting – and how to use both artificial and naturally available light to best advantage. These are some of the important design issues to address for a good quality of basement space to be achieved.

Basement damp patches

I have lost count of the number of occasions I have stood next to a client, both of us locked in concentration studying basement damp patches. That damp patch may often look nothing more than a £50 plaster repair, but a damp patch in a basement is a little more ominous and expensive, and going down the localised repair route could damage your professional reputation, rather than impress the client.

So a site meeting might not end on a good note. Instead of suggesting a localised repair, you will more often than not have given the client the painful truth: that the basement needs gutting!

The client will need to make a decision to 'manage' the dampness (i.e. fire-fighting damp) or install a comprehensive waterproofing scheme, i.e. a 'cure'.

Managing could just mean making good damp patches as they arise and redecorating. However, that could be a risky route to take, as there could be an underlying development of rot or mould that would be best tackled sooner rather than later.

Ten reasons why basement damp patches demand our respect

1 Defective areas of waterproofing are notoriously difficult to make good.
2 If an area has failed, there may be a considerable water threat from behind.
3 A failed patch of waterproofing could be indicative of a general lack of substrate preparation, or worse still an unsuitable substrate.
4 If waterproofing has failed in one place, the remaining work could be substandard or fail in time.
5 The patch of plaster/render may be damp because it is not a specialist waterproof mix/specification, and nor then is the remainder of the wall finishing.
6 The damp patch may be caused by an as yet unidentified cause – requiring funds to investigate and funds to remediate.
7 It could mean external conditions have changed, e.g. the water table has risen, meaning the water-proofing could be of inadequate specification.
8 Even if a defective area of waterproofing is suc-cessfully repaired, the water could find another route in.
9 There could be yet more damp areas presently hidden by built-in cupboards, bathroom suites, wall or floor finishes or storage, etc.
10 A contractor who has already shown poor work-manship first time round may not have the skill or diligence to carry out a repair effectively on a revisit.

Typical basement waterproofing works

- Decanting of occupiers.
- Removal/storage of all furnishings, personal effects, etc.
- Strip out of bathrooms, kitchens, services.
- Removal/adaptation of internal partitioning.
- Hacking off/general preparation of walls and floors.
- Removal/setting aside joinery items.
- Formation of drains/sumps as necessary.
- Application of waterproofing to walls and floors.
- Application of any loading coats/walls/slabs.
- Refitting kitchen/bathroom/WCs.
- Final finishes/decorations.
- Associated external works.

The scope of waterproofing required will depend to some extent on the degree of 'dryness' required in the subject basement. Obviously, where valuable archive material is to be stored, a totally dry controlled environment will be required. In a cellar under a house, used only for storage of non-valuable items, we may be prepared to suffer limited dampness. Table 3 is an

Table 3: Guide to level of protection to suit basement use. Based on Table 1 of BS 8102[12]

Grade	Basement usage	Performance level	Form of construction
1	Car parking, plant room, workshop	Some seepage and damp patches tolerable	Type B
2	Workshops and plant rooms requiring drier environment, retail storage	No water penetration but moisture vapour tolerable	Type A, B
3	Ventilated residential and working areas including offices, restaurants	Dry environment	Type A, B, C
4	Archives and stores requiring controlled environment	Totally dry environment	Type A, B, C

excellent starting point for waterproofing design. It nicely illustrates how waterproofing strategy might need upgrading if we change use of the basement – e.g. from occasional storage to residential use – Grade 1 to Grade 3. Seepage of water into the habitable space, or damp patches, would not be tolerated in a Grade 3 basement.

The concept: you may design basement water-proofing to meet a desired grade, or alternatively upgrade a basement from one grade to a higher grade. Certain forms of construction are more suited to upgrading. You could for example upgrade a Grade 1 environment to Grade 2 by installing a drained cavity system or by application of internal waterproofing. An existing Grade 2 basement could be upgraded to Grade 3 by additional ventilation, heating or insulation – or by dehumidification.

What constitutes a 'dry' environment?

What exactly is a 'dry environment'? CIRIA Report 139[15] offers useful guidance on how to interpret Table 1 of BS 8102. In section 2.2.3, 'Quantifying the required internal environment', each grade of base-ment is considered with respect to 'environmental parameters'. Table 2.2 of the CIRIA Report extends the limited information contained in Table 1 of BS 8102.

For example, for a Grade 3 basement (habitable space) we should expect RH 40–60% when the air temperature is at 18–22°C. Such conditions could be achieved from appropriate waterproofing, heating and ventilation. Regarding dampness, CIRIA recommends that materials at the surface of the completed interior should be air dry – and in CIRIA's terms this would mean an environment of RH less than circa 70 per cent.

It is clear from BS 8102 that the required grade of basement is achieved by a combination of water-proofing and heating and ventilation measures. Waterproofing contractors should themselves be aware of the need for correct heating, insulation and ventilation to achieve the required internal environment (i.e. to satisfy the standard's clause 8.4 'Control of Condensation'). You cannot just waterproof a basement and expect a dry interior. You may well consider monitoring the basement space after refurbishment, so a check can be made in the months that follow of internal air temperature, humidity and surface temperature. At least then if problems arose you would be better able to advise your client on causation.

It is very common for waterproofing contractors to be called back to a property suffering dampness once occupied and used. Condensation could be the cause, rather than a failure of waterproofing. In section 8.4 of the BS 8102 we find cross-reference to another major British Standard, BS 5250: 1989, *Code of practice for control of condensation in buildings*[16]:

> 'Whichever method of waterproofing is selected, arrangements should be made to minimise subsequent dampness from controlling condensation (see BS 5250). When natural ventilation cannot be provided in condensation prone areas, e.g. bathrooms and kitchens, mechanical ventilation should be specified.'

Permission to reproduce extracts from BS 8102: 1990, Code of practice for protection of structures against water from the ground, is granted by BSI. British Standards can be obtained in PDF or hard copy formats from the BSI online shop: www.bsigroup.com/Shop or by contacting BSI Customer Services for hardcopies only: Tel: +44 (0)20 8996 9001, Email: cservices@bsigroup.com.

WATERPROOFING – DAMP CONTROL PRINCIPLES TO APPLY

I strongly support the rationale adopted by Peter Bannister[17], explaining how you can stop or control moisture in three ways, and possibly four:

- by barriers
- using drainage; and
- from evaporation.

> 'There is a case for adding "**sheltering**" – perhaps more relevant though to above ground damp management. Just adding a canopy over a doorway can eliminate rain penetration through defective door seals or threshold detailing. Older buildings seem to make more use of sheltering, a "support measure" that can reduce rain load on vulnerable external detailing…'

If you look closely at all the available methods on the market to waterproof a new or existing basement, you will see one or more of the above clearly evident. To achieve reliable waterproofing or damp-proofing it would seem sensible for more than one of the above strategies to be used, so creating a second line of defence.

TYPES OF WATERPROOFING – AS PER BS 8102

The standard classifies waterproofing protection into three distinct structural types:

Type A – structures requiring protection against damp penetration

Such as concrete or masonry. These structures are not *in themselves* able to prevent damp penetration (of either water or water vapour) below ground, but need to be waterproofed by application of waterproofing materials internally or externally.

Such structures, if in reinforced concrete, would meet the requirements of BS 8102. Waterproofing would be by barrier materials, e.g. mastic asphalt, waterproof sheet, waterproof render or polyurethane resin tanking.

Type B – structures in watertight construction

Reinforced concrete designed and built to withstand damp penetration as well as to be structurally sound.

Type C – structures with internal drainage

Usually by means of wall and/or floor cavities.

The drained cavity in the basement collects groundwater that has entered through the building fabric from outside in the ground. This water is usually drained to a sump and then removed by pump.

Waterproofing to existing basements commonly falls under category A – where, for example, concrete or masonry elements below ground are waterproofed directly internally by applied finishes or membranes – or category C – when a cavity drain waterproofing system is applied inside the structural walls. Either of these waterproofing methods can achieve basement waterproofing to Grade 3 or 4 standard.

KEY WATERPROOFING SYSTEMS AVAILABLE

In the domestic market, cavity drain systems seem to be growing considerably in popularity, and probably at the expense of multi-coat render systems.

The following waterproofing methods will be described:

- cavity drain – Type C;
- multi-coat render – Type A;
- cementitious coatings –Type A;
- liquid applied membranes –Type A;
- mastic asphalt systems –Type A; and
- bonded sheet membranes – Type A.

It is no doubt possible to design in (using inner walls or linings), a drained cavity to work in combination with any of the above waterproofing materials.

When devising remediation of basement dampness, a waterproofing system will need to be selected, carefully considering at least the following criteria:

- ability to cope with hydrostatic pressure;
- loss of internal space (loss in room width and ceiling height);
- requirement for sound substrate (e.g. for good bonding);
- extent of substrate preparation required;
- ease of application;
- provision for post-installation fixings (for services, joinery, etc.);
- decorative options available;
- ease of repair/maintenance;
- value for money (e.g. cost versus expected life and performance of system).

Reputable systems will be designed to meet current building regulations, be supported by BBA certification, and be installed by trained operatives. The selected system should be supported by an insurance-backed guarantee, although the honesty, reliability and professionalism of a reputable contractor will always be your most important 'guarantee'. Any system must also enable the required grade of basement to be achieved. Systems selected must meet Health and Safety and COSHH (Control of Substances Hazardous to Health) requirements.

The selection criteria listed could of course be extended to help you make optimal decisions for particular contracts.

- It may be necessary to install waterproofing using methods that minimise disruption, dust or noise.
- Hacking off hard renders can cause untold damage to a substrate, especially a softish brick or stone, and sometimes walls will have been very seriously damaged from multiple hackings-off of renders from repeated attempts to damp-proof/waterproof over the years.
- Perhaps there are time constraints and the quickest methods must be used.
- In historic buildings you may need to install waterproofing that causes least damage to existing building fabric, or could be removed at a later date (i.e. is reversible). Any hacking-off of stubborn finishes which damages underlying substrate might be deemed unacceptable for a valued historic property.

Producing a dry living space from a previously damp and wet cellar really asks questions of designer and contractor – there is no place to hide. This is why you need to employ the best waterproofing contractor you can find. Remember that remedial waterproofing is not considered by the remedial damp-proofing industry to be very long-lasting – an expected life of 20–30 years is suggested in the BWPDA Code of Practice[18]. Let us bear it in mind too that remedial treatment contractors so often only provide a ten-year guarantee.

Waterproofing needs to be installed pretty near perfect, and to remain pretty near perfect, to keep water out over the years.

CAVITY DRAIN SYSTEMS

Many of you will at some time have discovered 'newtonite lathing' when stripping out an old building. The lathing comprises a black corrugated bituminous impregnated sheet, usually fixed with galvanised nails. It is the forerunner of the modern plastic dimpled sheet waterproofing membranes we use today. Most surveyors consulted talk very positively about the original newtonite lathing, which used 'air gap technology' to manage dampness in traditional walls. Newtonite lathing was last used in 1991. The original company, John Newton and Company, pioneered the modern cavity membrane systems used today to damp-proof walls – both above and below ground, which can incidentally also be used for external render systems in new and existing buildings. This category of waterproofing falls within Type C in BS 8102.

Things have really moved on here. There are now quite a range of patent cavity drain systems – and this type of waterproofing seems to be growing considerably in popularity. In the BRE Good Repair Guide 23 *Treating Dampness in Basements*[19] you will see mention of the 'drained cavity' method, and in figure (a) you will find a traditional detail of a drained system – where an inner block wall, tied to the main outer wall by wall ties, creates the cavity. The cavity is shown 50mm wide – so we lose 150mm for each perimeter wall around the basement space using this method, in addition to the thickness of the solid plasters. The BRE advises two alternative drained floor options – firstly the use of triangular drainage tiles (which may be difficult to obtain from mainstream builders' merchants), and alternatively the use of dimpled sheet (obtainable from all the manufacturers of drained cavity waterproofing systems). The drain at the base of the wall cavity is formed using a screed to falls – not easy to execute, and shown linked to a drain outlet. The bottom course of the inner wall is built of engineering bricks. In principle this system should work and be serviceable for many years, especially if the cavity drain can be rodded out periodically.

But nowadays there are cheaper ways of forming a cavity drain system, using dimpled sheets for the walls as well as the floor. Such sheets incorporate studs to create an air gap between substrate and sheet of typically 8mm. The outer face of sheeting is meshed so a wet plaster finish can be applied if desired. The concept is very simple. By placing a dimpled sheet against the external earth retaining walls, an air gap is created between external wall and the lining. This kills off at a stroke hydrostatic pressure that in other systems would act to push waterproofing off a substrate. Any water ingress is dissipated over an area, rather than impinging on waterproofing at a single pressure point.

Water ingress is therefore dealt with very easily. Any physical water trickles down the inner face of the external wall, and is drained away by perimeter drainage channels, either directly out of the building, where levels allow, or to sumps where it is pumped away. Servicing of pumping equipment is an ongoing maintenance outlay, as is rodding out of perimeter drains.

Modern systems using plastic dimpled sheeting take up little room space – as the sheets are quite thin – saving width and height of space internally.

In some respects, cavity drain waterproofing systems for basements perform like masonry cavity walls – any water ingress runs down the inner face of the outer leaf to either drain out of the cavity via weep holes, or to evaporate away by ventilated cavity.

There are strong arguments for continuing the membrane for full height up subject walls, even if the floor level is not very far below external ground level. Firstly, you then have the opportunity to take the membrane up into the ceiling void, which then offers a top ventilation opportunity, and secondly you will not face the difficult problem of merging new plaster to existing plaster thicknesses. Original plasters may be no more than 20mm thick, and the finished thickness of the plastered membrane a little more – meaning you could find perfect merging of new to old a problem, possibly requiring a dado rail to mask it. It is also difficult to avoid a tiny shrinkage crack at the join of new to existing work – which could create a decoration problem.

The BRE Guide[19] also shows a 'ventilated dry lining' option in figure (f), where a dimpled sheet is shown affixed to an external wall in conjunction with a cement/sand screed. However, no drainage provision is provided at low level. The BRE rightly comment that such a system will cope only 'if the dampness is slight'. Where no perimeter drain exists, in conjunction with a solid floor as per figure (f), there is nowhere for any water ingress to drain. The BRE detailing shown is potentially risky, as quite a high external ground level is actually shown. Risk of water ingress could of course be reduced by installing an external land drain – which is not shown or mentioned by BRE.

We must offer here some words of caution: *cavity drain systems need to be well maintained so that any water ingress drains away efficiently.* The dimpled lapped sheets are not designed in themselves to cope with direct water penetration and should perimeter drains silt up, water ingress could occur. The sheets themselves cannot on their own cope with hydrostatic pressure. Silting can build up under dimpled floor sheets, damming up any draining water.

There have been failures of cavity drain systems when for example the subfloor has allowed ponding of draining water, or deposits of lime have built up. While a perimeter drain should incorporate rodding points, the gap under a ventilated membrane would be difficult to access. It is common for back-up pumps to be installed, sometimes powered by a separate power supply. This aspect of drainage design needs to be carefully thought out.

The exclusion of penetrating dampness from external ground to habitable space depends not just on the cavity drainage on the inside wall face. The BCA Design Guide[20] reminds us that an external

Advantages and disadvantages of modern cavity-drained waterproofing

Advantages

- Hydrostatic pressure is dissipated, as the system does not attempt to stop water at specific positions.
- Good bond to substrate is required only at specified spacings of fixings, rather than over entire substrate area.
- Modern systems using plastic membranes take up relatively little internal space.
- It is not always necessary to hack off or remove existing finishes and coatings – unless they are friable and likely to affect the efficiency of the cavity drainage.
- Modern systems use comparatively cheaper materials and components than traditional waterproofing techniques.
- The system does not rely on a single means of combating dampness or moisture ingress. Evaporation from a ventilated air gap, perimeter drainage and the cavity membrane work together to prevent and control dampness.
- Damaged waterproofing may be accessed and repaired.
- Modern membrane components are quite easy to position and fix to substrates.
- Manufacturers offer a comprehensive design and specification service.
- Waterproofing may be extended.
- Once dry, plasterwork can be decorated normally.
- Wall, floor and ceiling membranes may be finished in variety of wet and dry plaster and board options.

Disadvantages

- The sheets themselves are not designed to cope with hydrostatic pressure, so if they are forced to, e.g. when a cavity drain blocks, they might not stop water entry.
- Dimpled membranes are flat and fairly rigid – making it difficult to line complex shapes or surfacings.
- Dimpled sheets cannot be laid flat under soffits, as they could collect water. Minimal falls are recommended.
- Some sheets are quite opaque, and it would be difficult to ensure that drill holes for fixings are made in the most appropriate positions.
- Post-installation fixings need to meet manufacturer's specification details.
- Flooding could occur if pumps fail or drainage silts up or blocks.
- The system could rely on adequacy or condition of the associated drainage system, e.g. a soakaway, cesspool or main drainage, itself requiring maintenance.
- Installation of a sump requires excavation below a floor, which may not be desired.

Figure 41: A skilled plasterer applies a cement/lime/sand mix to a ventilated membrane – in this case applied to the soffits and walls of a London basement. Such a membrane is fixed using patent plugs sealed with mastic, and the plaster keys to a mesh welded to the room face of the membrane. Photograph © courtesy of J. Newton and Co., www.newton-membranes.co.uk

Figure 42: The cavity membrane in this case links to a studded floor membrane, together with a perimeter drain. We see here a sump built into the basement floor, complete with inlet and exit drainage pipework and an electric pump activated by a float switch. The system must be 'flood tested' to make sure it works. Photograph © courtesy of J. Newton and Co., www.newton-membranes.co.uk

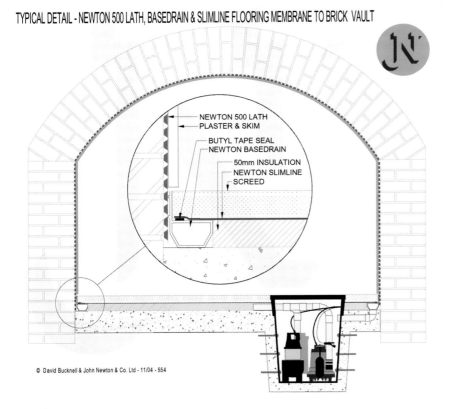

TYPICAL DETAIL - NEWTON 500 LATH, BASEDRAIN & SLIMLINE FLOORING MEMBRANE TO BRICK VAULT

NEWTON 500 LATH
PLASTER & SKIM

BUTYL TAPE SEAL
NEWTON BASEDRAIN

50mm INSULATION
NEWTON SLIMLINE
SCREED

© David Bucknell & John Newton & Co. Ltd - 11/04 - 554

Figure 43: Basement plastering in action. Brick vaulting is waterproofed using ventilated cavity membranes, linked to perimeter 'base drains' with sumps. This system can be used below or above ground. In an above-ground scenario, the damp threat could be from above, e.g. a converted railway arch. Detail sheet courtesy of J. Newton and Co., www. newton-membranes.co.uk

basement wall should resist water ingress sufficiently to ensure that the cavity only has to cope with a controlled amount of water or dampness.

MULTI-COAT RENDER SYSTEMS (INTERNALLY APPLIED)

Cement renders may be applied to the internal faces of walls or as screeds onto floor substrates. The renders act as a barrier to wetness or dampness from the substrate.

Cementitious renders used for waterproofing typically incorporate waterproofing agents which are added in prescribed quantity to the mixing water.

How successfully a multi-coat render system is in below-ground waterproofing will depend on a number of critical factors:

- Is the substrate suitable for application of a cementitious render system?

- Is the substrate correctly prepared for render application?
- Are the render materials of suitable type and quality?
- Are the render materials mixed appropriately?
- Are the render coats applied correctly?
- Are renders correctly detailed at junctions, intersections, service entries?
- Are the renders cured suitably?
- Is the integrity of rendering compromised by any subsequent construction or fixing activity?
- Is the performance of the render system compromised by application of unsuitable building finishes/paints?

You will appreciate that achieving reliable water-proofing requires considerable attention to design, detail, application and usage.

Multi-coat render systems are not designed to withstand structural movement. For example, Sika Ltd clearly state in their technical literature[21]: 'Sika-1 waterproofing system is a rigid membrane and will not accommodate movement in a structure to which it is applied.' So only specify this type of waterproofing when you are sure the building will not be subject to any movement cracking that could compromise its integrity. If you see cracks in basement walls during your pre-design inspection, you would need to assess the cause of movement, and whether a multi-coat render system of waterproofing could be designed to accommodate it.

The BRE supports multi-coat cementitious render systems for waterproofing: 'correctly mixed render or compound, properly applied to a stable background, should last for many years'[19]. Note the words: *stable background*.

There will be situations when a substrate is too friable to permit good bonding of cementitious renders or coating, but might be capable of being deep-drilled and plugged to support a cavity membrane.

Since around 1995, Sika Ltd, one of the leading suppliers and designers of waterproof render systems, has supplied mixed aggregates, pre-bagged and colour-coded. It was discovered that even pre-bagged and graded aggregates from mainstream builders' merchants were not always graded suitably for use in below-ground waterproofing, where strict quality control of materials used is necessary.

The pre-bagging of aggregates in a controlled factory setting removes risk common on the building site. Sika Ltd also run training courses for recommended contractors to help maintain standards on site.

Below-ground corner beads can compromise effectiveness of waterproofing if they themselves corrode or affect continuation and thickness of coats at an external corner or return. Check returns with a metal detector – if metal is flagged up, you could have a potential waterproofing weakness at that position, if a corner bead is in-situ and most particularly any kind of bead that could corrode or deteriorate in damp conditions.

Pre-bagged aggregates are visible stacked to the left side, so there is a good chance this waterproofing application will be successful. Make sure those carrying out multi-coat rendering application know the correct specification for the materials and know how to apply them. Always refer back to the product manufacturer for specification information.

Figure 44: To help reduce the risk of cracking of rendering at the junction of wall and floor, you can see how a patent combiflex joint reinforcement system is positioned. The combiflex system helps accommodate movement and is also an additional water seal. The Sika Combiflex tape system can also be used to seal cracks and seal around services penetrations. As a surveyor inspecting a waterproofed basement, you would not be able to actually see this reinforcement system once it had been rendered over. Image © courtesy of Sika Ltd, www.sika.co.uk

Figure 45: Here we see a skilled tradesworker applying waterproofing render at a corner. Note he builds up the corner without the aid of a corner bead. I can tell you from first hand experience that building up a rendered corner without a bead to help support render and produce a neat plumb guide is a painstaking operation! Corner beads are more acceptable in above-ground scenarios, and wherever there is no risk of dampness to damage metal beads – stainless steel is probably the best material for them. Image © courtesy of Sika Ltd, www.sika.co.uk

Typical render application for Sika 1

Key stages for floors:

1. Hack off existing finishes.
2. Fill holes, apply fast-acting sealers to stop water ingress.
3. Wet the substrate.
4. Apply splattered spritz coat.
5. Apply second render coat.
6. Apply finishing render coat.

The spritz coat is not 'laid on' using a trowel, but spattered on using a throwing action. This is not a standard plastering technique.

Fixings

As mentioned earlier, a well-executed waterproof render system can fail if there is lack of care in designing and installing fixings.

One method is to affix a softwood batten to the render finish, into which fixings could be screwed or nailed. Sometimes it is possible to use struts wedged between wall and floor to produce the necessary rigidity to hold components in place. Heavy fixings may require the formation of deep pockets cut into the substrate. In all cases, the manufacturer of the render system must be consulted.

Skirtings and other lightweight linings can simply be glued to the render system.

It is important that only adhesives recommended by the manufacturer are used.

You could of course build an inner wall to solve the fixing problem. The BRE in *Understanding Dampness* (figure 6.52)[12] show how this can be carried out. Obviously building an additional inner wall takes up space, that could be limited, and will be an additional cost. But should the below-ground space be intended for use, for example, as a gym – requiring heavy equipment to be fixed off a wall or floor – then it may benefit from an inner wall and perhaps an additional loading floor over the multi-coat waterproof screed.

Considerable care is needed in fixing joinery, particularly skirting boards. Standard nail or screw fixings can defeat the waterproofing –most specialist contractors use strong contact adhesives for joinery fixing.

Penetration by services

The trick is to minimise the number of points where pipes or cables penetrate through waterproofing. You may need to consider rerouting services, so penetration of a waterproofing system is unnecessary.

Patent methods and materials are available from manufacturers to seal existing or new service entries, and the advised detailing must always be followed.

Curing

Once the render has been applied, careful curing is essential.

In the writer's experience, often too little attention is paid to careful 'curing' of renders, either from lack of awareness or lack of care. Typical symptoms of unsatisfactory curing are cracks in the renders, which can compromise performance.

Curing of cement renders does not happen quickly. Maximum strength is achieved after around 28 days. Renders must not be allowed to dry out too quickly, i.e. before curing has been fully achieved. This means that in hot and windy weather, renders should be sprayed with water occasionally, or covered by plastic sheeting, etc. In the old days we used hessian. Sika advise that in hot, dry or windy conditions, covering or spraying the render may need to continue for up to seven days. If water evaporates out of the render mix too rapidly, the render might not achieve maximum strength and performance.

You may be called upon to check a waterproof system exhibiting cracks. It is important to note that in some systems, surface 'micro-crazing' in the top layer might not be so significant as to compromise waterproofing performance. It may be that the top layer serves as a protection for the main waterproofing layers. Micro-crazing must not be misinterpreted as curing shrinkage, drying shrinkage or substrate bond failure.

We need to control cracking. If too much water is used in the mix, the render can suffer cracking from drying shrinkage. Cracking may be reduced by allowing the render to properly cure, using a water-reducing agent in the render mix, making sure the render is well bonded to a sound substrate, using sands with a low water demand, and limiting any 'dubbing out' to 10mm maximum thickness. Cracks, if they do form, fall more or less into two classifications: surface cracks that can simply be filled, and cracks that could reduce the strength or waterproofing quality of the render.

As a general rule, cracks greater in width than 0.25mm can allow passage of moisture and would not be acceptable in waterproofing renders. Cracks will be more significant if they affect more than one render coat at the same position. The greater the hydrostatic pressure, the more likely it is that a crack will allow the passage of water. The implication here is that if you find cracks that for the moment do not allow water to seep through, in the future, if water pressure increases, the same cracking could fail to keep water out. Waterproofing performance always needs to be assessed over its expected design life.

Multi-coat renders are what they say they are – *multi*-coats. If the crack under investigation is limited to the top skim plaster coat, it may be nothing more than superficial – a crack to fill before painting. But if the crack is found to continue through successive layers of waterproofing, things become progressively more serious. A crack that is found to extend through all the render coats is in effect a complete puncturing of the waterproofing. So to assess cracking, first check that the crack is limited to a surface skim coat crack. Permission and site conditions allowing, you can then investigate to greater depth.

Decoration

Paints should not be applied until the surface is dry.

If a multi-coat waterproofing system has been finished by a skim coat of plaster, for example 'multi-finish', you might find it useful to inspect the bagged plaster, as the applied finish will not be dry until it lightens to the powder colour. The author is not convinced that a 'multi-finish' skim coat is ideal in a basement or ground floor application – or indeed anywhere where it could be affected by moisture – as such a finish is gypsum-based and not very tolerant of damp. It also contains sulphates, and unsightly efflorescence can form on the plaster surface from drying out. You should consult the render mix manufacturers regarding appropriate finish, as there may be patent plaster preparations available.

An earth-retaining wall behind a tanking system will never dry out. As waterproof render systems are themselves vapour permeable, you must not allow the decorative finish to act as a vapour check. This means that you should use vapour permeable paints on tanking plasters – certainly a paint that is no less vapour permeable than the tanking itself. Only use paint recommended by the contractor and checked out in consultation with the paint manufacturer. Also, agree the timing of the paint application with the waterproofing contractor – or again, the contractor might argue that it was applied too early. Better still, commission the waterproofing contractor to decorate. Assuming that defects can happen, **never give the contractor the opportunity to *blame the paint*!**

There must have been thousands of disputes where chemical injection damp-coursing above ground has failed, but the damp-proofer has escaped liability when associated plastering was carried out by others. Damp-proofing, if actually needed, depends more than anything else on the standard of internal remedial plastering which acts to mask damp behind. (We can never assume that chemical injected dpcs actually stop damp.)

It is wise to avoid using multiple contractors for specialist remediation of damp. As for above-ground damp-proofing, *multiple contractors could mean multiple blame* – so always make sure there is a single point of responsibility from a main contractor for work carried out.

Advantages and disadvantages of multi-coat render system

Advantages

- Take up relatively little internal space.
- Traditional plastering and render skills can be used, albeit with some adaptation to meet particular mixing and placing requirements. Key between coats must not be achieved by 'scratching' coats.
- Patent render systems can withstand hydrostatic pressure.
- Renders can be applied satisfactorily to complex shapes, including soffits.
- Renders can (according to manufacturers) be satisfactorily repaired.
- In domestic basement applications there is no need for sumps and pumps internally for discharge of collected water.

Disadvantages

- The system relies for success on carefully selected aggregates.
- The system relies for success on meeting stringent specification of successive render coats.
- The waterproofing could fail if applied using standard plastering and rendering techniques.
- Renders need to be carefully cured.
- A cementitious render system may suffer cracking from building movements, reducing the water-tightness and structural integrity of rendering.
- The system needs to resist water pressure at specific locations.
- The system relies on a satisfactory bond to substrate over its entire area, as it is located on the negative pressure wall side.
- Existing wall and floor finishes will usually need to be removed and the exposed substrate primed and keyed/prepared.
- Early decoration after render application is usually limited to breathable water-based emulsion paints.
- It is difficult to extend multi-coat render waterproofing.
- Fixings need to be carefully designed and executed to avoid careless damage to waterproofing.

CEMENTITIOUS COATINGS

Cementitious coatings are quite thin, from 1–3mm, and so have little integral tensile strength. It follows that they must be applied to a sound substrate, or a prepared render base coat. So brickwork, unless in excellent condition, would need a render coat first before the coating application. Some manufacturers recommend use of a mesh (e.g. stainless steel) to strengthen the coating. Cementitious coatings can usually be laid directly onto a concrete substrate, following priming and sealing of cracks. At the very least, brickwork would require flush pointing and any holes and imperfections making good. Certainly brickwork with many spalled bricks would need to be rendered first prior to application of coating. Cementitious coatings can include additives for improved elasticity and flexibility.

Coatings are pre-mixed, comprising cement, graded aggregates and chemical additives. There is therefore not the risk of contractors using unsuitable sands that often occurs when multi-coat renders are used in waterproofing.

Sovereign Chemicals Ltd (Hey'di system) recommend removal of unsuitable (e.g. hollow) renders prior to coating application, and in some cases would recommend application of a new render coat before coating.

The fact that a render base coat would often be needed when applying a cementitious coating to say brickwork or stonework, means there is then of course a substantial additional cost in the waterproofing application. Some savings in space can be gained by using a cementitious coating due to its potential very limited thickness. The BRE, in their Good Repair Guide 23[19], do not specifically mention the thinly applied type of coating available in today's market.

Cementitious coatings are commonly used for waterproofing underground car parks, swimming pools and service tunnels.

Product literature by Sovereign Chemicals Ltd claims the Hey'di system can cope well with hydrostatic pressure (having been tested to 65m hydrostatic head of water). To achieve reliable waterproofing to withstand hydrostatic pressure, Sovereign specify a 'special system application'. Where there is a significant head of water we must be sure the basement walls have sufficient structural integrity to sustain the applied loads.

BONDED SHEET MEMBRANES

Any sheets need to be lapped or joined in some way – a potential weakness and opportunity for water ingress. Sheet materials are likely to be fairly rigid, and therefore require considerable skill in application over complex or non-flat substrates. However, a sheet material is of manufactured uniform thickness and reliability.

Sheets are cold applied or heat bonded to the substrate. On the positive (i.e. outer) side of the structural wall they may successfully withstand pressures from soil and water, but on the negative (i.e. inner) side of the structural wall, may need a loading wall for stabilisation against applied forces. Bonded sheets would be better able to cope with minor movement than more brittle multi-coat render systems. The substrate would need to be free of surface water for a good bond to be achieved. This kind of waterproofing would mostly be used for new works.

Modern products include toughened polyethylene carriers with polymer modified bitumen coatings, supplied in rolls and used internally or externally. Standard sheets are between 1.5 and 3mm thick. The sheets are used in combination with standard pre-formed units to waterproof at corners and details. This kind of membrane is designed to cope with 'normal structural movements'. Light torching enables a continuous weld to be achieved at laps. Bonded membranes can achieve all BS 8102 basement grades 1–4.

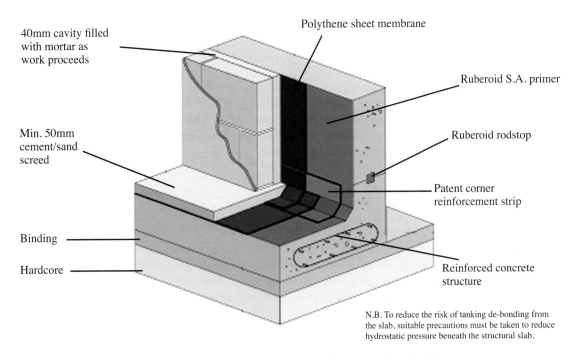

Figure 46: Internal tanking floor wall junction. Diagram courtesy Ruberoid Building Products, www.ruberoid.co.uk

The sheets link neatly from wall to floor, if needed, to create a 'tanked' waterproofing.

As for all waterproofing methods, preparation needs to be carefully executed. You would need, for example, to flush point all exposed brickwork and then prime before application of sheets.

The downside of using bonded sheets is the requirement for loading of sheeting by internal loading walls and screeds – where room width and ceiling height will then be sacrificed. Modern systems may be protected by patent boards, rather than walls and screeds. Once loaded, or hidden under protection boards, it will be difficult to repair bonded sheeting due to lack of access. We find similar issues in flat roofing, where a ballasted roof finish prevents inspection of the waterproof membrane. You would need to make sure of the shelf-life of sheeting rolls, as the performance of the adhesives must surely reduce over time stored.

LIQUID APPLIED MEMBRANES

Liquid applied membranes are a potentially effective means to waterproof a basement.

Most surveyors will be familiar with Synthaprufe – the most common liquid applied waterproofing material. It is a strange liquid, in that it is brown in the tin, turns black once applied, but then returns to brown if it fails. It is a bituminous emulsion containing natural rubber latex, which dries to a waterproof and vapour resistant black flexible film. Synthaprufe is resistant to sulphates and other salts from the soil. Synthaprufe bonds well to other materials, but needs to be protected to ensure long life and effectiveness.

Synthaprufe can withstand 'normal building movement'. Once applied correctly, a seamless waterproof membrane is achieved, and it can be applied to damp surfaces – a great asset when waterproofing basements, for obvious reasons.

Synthaprufe is applied using a disposable brush, with coats applied to build up a finished thickness of minimum 1mm. But here lies a problem – on a surface which is not totally flat and uniform, it might be difficult to be certain that the correct finished thickness has been applied over the whole area.

The manufacturers recommend that a floor waterproofed using Synthaprufe is covered by a 50mm 1:3 cement/sand screed. On walls, and in 'conditions of mild dampness' a 'finish of a minimum of 12mm of gypsum plaster should be applied before decorating'. In more severe conditions an inner loading skin of brick or block may be required. In conditions of hydrostatic pressure, or if it is to be used below ground or where anything more than 'mild dampness' is expected, the manufacturer should be consulted. Technical details are available from the manufacturer which show three coats of Synthaprufe used for tanking, protected by an inner wall of brick or block and a 50mm screed protection to the synthaprufed floor.

In BRE Good Repair Guide 23, a detail is shown of a liquid applied membrane used together with a blockwork loading wall and cement/sand screed topping. The BRE describe such a waterproofing option as 'durable', but with a 'space penalty'.

Other materials are used for liquid membranes, such as elastomeric urethanes or epoxies. Epoxies can be very useful for floors as they can act as a vapour check and wearing coat when laid on a sound substrate.

MASTIC ASPHALT TANKING

Mastic asphalt tanking must surely be the method with the longest track record.

Asphalt is one of the best waterproofers we have available, but it is expensive to use as it requires skilled labour. Traditionally, basements were often waterproofed externally using this material. It is applied in at least two staggered coats – meaning that a defect in one coat would be masked by another. It is supplied in blocks which are heated up to produce the hot molten asphalt ready for applying – so of course there are health and safety risks in its use. You will find a detail of asphalt tanking in most construction textbooks, showing asphalt built up in two coats, with an angle fillet at the wall/floor junction and a 50mm thick cement infill placed between vertical asphalt and an inner brick or block wall. Horizontal floor asphalt in three coats is protected and loaded by a cement/sand screed, sometimes augmented by a concrete slab.

Such waterproofing, costly, durable and incurring severe space penalties, is not often carried out for existing buildings. But it is certainly an option, and where space allows, and budgets permit, is extremely reliable. However, if the building were to be subject to significant movement from settlement or subsidence it could fail, and once cracked or damaged, there would be no second line of defence in a traditional asphalt tanking system, unless a perimeter drainage system was built in. Failed asphalt tanking would also be difficult to repair, being concealed behind loading walls and under floor toppings.

The BRE supports asphalt tanking as a basement waterproofing option, but points out the 'significant space penalty, in terms of area and usually height as well'[19].

HYBRID SYSTEMS

In any basement there will be both vertical and horizontal zones to be waterproofed, perhaps sloping areas too. Horizontal zones could include ceilings, soffits and floors.

The suitability of the chosen waterproofing system needs to be considered with respect to *all* of the different wall and floor characteristics as found. So could we mix and match? Can we use combinations of

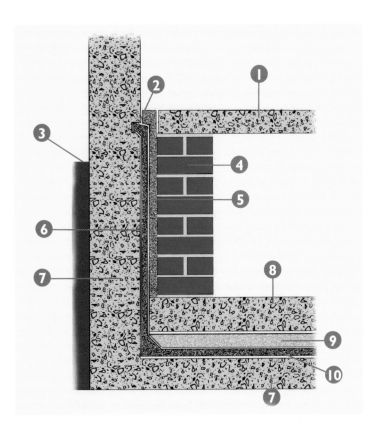

Figure 47: Internally applied mastic asphalt tanking.
© *Courtesy MAC Ltd.*

1) *Reinforced concrete structural floor slab.*
2) *25 × 25mm chase cast in concrete.*
3) *Ground level.*
4) *Loading and protecting brickwork.*
5) *40mm space flushed up with mortar (course by course).*
6) *20mm three coat mastic asphalt.*
7) *Reinforced concrete structural wall and floor.*
8) *Concrete loading slab.*
9) *50mm protective sand and cement screed.*
10) *30mm three coat mastic asphalt.*

waterproofing to cope with a variety of substrates or inclination/configuration of substrate? There seem to be opposing schools of thought here.

The BCA Design Guide[20] advises against mixing hot and cold systems, stressing the risk of incompatibility when using hybrid systems. The guide advises that 'continuous horizontal, sloping or vertical waterproofing [should] be specified, and executed, in one proprietary waterproofing system'.

But it is common to find combinations of approach in remediation work as varying conditions or configurations of the subject building are addressed. In retro-fit application of cavity wall ties, we might choose to use a resin-fixed tie where areas of the inner leaf are found to be friable, but use standard expanding tie fixings elsewhere where a sound substrate allows. In overcladding a tower block you might often come across a rainscreen cladding to upper floors, but note a wet system used to the ground storey – comprising insulation over-laid by render reinforced by meshing – offering improved fire protection against rubbish or accidental fires.

This issue has been discussed with some industry experts who support, for example, using a cavity-drained floor system in combination with a multi-coat render waterproofing to the surrounding walls. Such a remedy might be an option if the configuration of walls makes it difficult to use a relatively rigid studded membrane.

But there is an issue concerning guarantees, when the manufacturer of the cavity drain floor system might not approve of the detailing at the interaction of the wall renders and cavity-drained floor. You would in such a case mainly rely on the expertise of your professional adviser. There would also be problems concerning the meeting of British Standards or Agrément certificates, where hybrid systems of waterproofing will not be described.

IMPORTANT EXTERNAL SUPPORT MEASURES

External support measures should always be considered when remediating a damp basement.

Where a basement or cellar is only used for car parking, storage of non-valuable items or perhaps just as a casual work area, you might only need to implement external support measures to produce a suitably dry internal environment. You might be prepared to use the space as long as it does not flood too often, suffer too much water ingress or damp patches.

The concept of 'total waterproofing' is used in the BCA Design Guide – *Basement Waterproofing*[20]. It's all about how the success of waterproofing might depend not just on the applied waterproofing, but also on how we control moisture conditions inside and outside the building envelope to produce an acceptably dry space.

We have already touched on the importance BS 8102 places upon suitable measures to control the internal environment – to beat the dampness enemy within by careful control of heating and ventilation. But what about wetness from outside?

Turning to section 3.2 of BS 8102, we find a useful section on 'preventative measures'. Our total waterproofing approach can include control of surface water and ground water. The more we can assist the waterproofing, the greater the chance of success.

In section 3.2.2 'Exclusion of surface water', it is recommended that adjoining ground should slope away from the structure for three metres, and should not be open-jointed. Open-jointed pavings can trap and hold moisture and allow it to drain towards the property. But remember too that jointed pavings collect and drain off considerable volumes of surface water, which can't be allowed to impinge on the property perimeter. Cut-off drains are advised for adverse ground slopes.

Section 3.2.3 then offers measures to improve or maintain subsurface drainage, e.g. by preserving existing land drains or laying new roddable drain pipework in straight lines. The subsurface land drainage could discharge by pump or gravity, with open-jointed or perforated pipes protected from silting by graded filters.

One basic principle needs to be mentioned here. Coarse soils, e.g. coarse gravels, chalk, rubble, rocks, etc. offer good drainage, and are not likely to significantly shrink or swell to cause heave or subsidence from changing moisture content. However, fine soils, e.g. silts, clays, very fine sands, peat, etc. drain poorly, and are very often likely to significantly shrink or swell with changing moisture content. Soils that shrink or expand markedly can threaten waterproofing systems that are unable to cope with the resultant movement stresses. Such soils also drain inefficiently, and thought should be given to incorporating perimeter subsoil drains to reduce the water load impinging on perimeter basement walls below ground.

Water may impinge on basement walls around and below ground level where surface water drainage around a building has been ill thought out. Rainwater must be diverted away from the building perimeter, or directed efficiently into underground drains.

Hard surfacings may allow rainwater to splash against porous walling at low level to penetrate into external walls – causing damp patches in basement rooms – typically at high level where the internal floor level is well below external finished levels.

Gary Branson devotes considerable advice for home owners on reducing perimeter damp penetration at low level[22]. In a sketch entitled 'Common Sources of Wet Basements' we see a rainwater downpipe discharging water very close to an external wall, with water percolating downwards to soak into basement walls. He shows us how a 'splashblock' could help here. A splashblock is a chute located under the rainwater shoe (i.e. final bend at base of rainwater downpipe) which diverts rainwater away from the wall. An alternative is to extend the bottom section of the rainwater pipe away from the building.

These methods are of course unnecessary if the rainwater downpipe links properly to the gully. But too often, especially in heavy rain, water tumbles down inside the rainwater pipe to gush out in profusion, some

of it missing the gully. (See figure 48.) The gully needs to be large enough to accept the rainwater discharge, and ideally the rainwater pipe should feed into the gully by a patent connector. The gully may need to perform two functions. It could be accepting rainwater from a vertical pipe, as well as surface water from a path or yard – in which case the gully must be seated at the correct height.

External support measures summarised

- From a walk-round survey, identify and specify remediation to any potential damp penetration threat around ground level.
- Install external surfaces to slope away from the building.
- Install a cut-off drain where ground slopes down towards the building.
- Install subsoil drains, or upgrade/clear/repair/maintain existing drains, including provision of adequate outfalls, sumps, pumps and other drainage facilities and equipment as required.
- Check water mains and repair or renew as necessary.
- Check adjacent drains, repair or improve as needed.
- Rod all drains and clean out all drain gullies.
- Check all rainwater, soil and waste pipework and repair/renew/upgrade as necessary.
- Make sure external finished ground levels are set the required 150mm below the existing dpc.
- Make sure the walling below dpc height is suitably water resistant by virtue of correct materials, condition of jointings and pointings or adequacy of applied finish.
- Make sure rainwater is suitably directed away from the building perimeter and pipework is properly fed into gullies or drain rest bends.
- Test gullies to make sure they actually hold water, otherwise cracks and holes could be allowing water penetration from the gully into adjacent masonry at or just below ground level.

Figure 48: Surely just making sure this gushing rainwater actually goes into the gully would help keep the wall dry?

Table 4: Basement waterproofing – considerations for selection of waterproofing

Criterion	Cavity drained	Multi-coat render	Cementitious coating	Traditional mastic asphalt	Liquid applied membrane	Bonded sheet
Defence against hydrostatic pressure	Good if drainage maintained. Cavity thwarts hydrostatic pressure.	Good	Average. Improved on positive side.	Good with loading coats.	Good with loading coats.	Good with loading coats.
Ease of repair	Repair possible during and after installation.	Defects can be located but reliable repair not easily achieved.	Good.	Access to waterproofing a problem.	Access to waterproofing a problem.	Access to waterproofing a problem.
Requirement for sound substrate	Good fixings required at specified spacings.	Sound substrate required.	Base render coat needed if substrate unreliable. May be applied on a damp substrate.	Substrate must be dry before application.	Some liquid membranes can be applied to damp substrates.	Substrate must be dry before application.
Running maintenance	Drain to be cleared and sumps/pumps serviced.	Nil, but check render not compromised by fixings, hole drilling, etc.	Nil.	N/A	N/A	N/A
Loss of internal space	Average for waterproofing.	Average.	Minimal if applied directly to substrate.	Needs screed plus loading slab on floor, and loading wall on walls.	Loading coats cause loss of internal space.	Loading coats cause loss of internal space.
Ease of application	Skilled operatives needed.	Use pre-bagged materials, trained operatives.	Skilled operatives needed.	Skilled operatives needed.	Skilled operatives needed.	Skilled operatives needed.
Cost	Average.	Average.	Average.	High.	High.	High.
Substrate preparation	Minimal substrate preparation needed. The substrate does not need to be dry.	Good preparation essential to achieve good bond.	Good preparation essential to achieve good bond.	Good preparation essential to achieve good bond.	Good preparation essential to achieve reliable thickness of waterproofing.	Good preparation essential to achieve good bond.
Provision for fixing	Some point fixings need pre-planning. Can be curtain-fixed from top.	Mechanical fixings can cause problems, adhesives are preferred method.	Mechanical fixings can cause problems; adhesives are preferred method.	Fixings easily made as waterproofing behind a loading wall or slab.	Fixings easily made as waterproofing behind a loading wall or slab.	Fixings easily made as waterprofing behind a loading wall or slab.
Decorative options	All available. Dry finishes can be used to produce fast installation times.	Can be decorated directly. Use only vapour-permeable paints for at least six months.	Can be decorated directly. Use only vapour-permeable paints for at least six months.	Loading wall typically plastered and painted.	Loading wall typically plastered and painted.	Loading wall typically plastered and painted.
Ease of application to complex shapes	Sheets fairly rigid, cannot be applied flat to soffits.	Easily applied to complex shapes.	Easily applied to complex shapes.	Asphalt can negotiate complex shapes on any plane.	Liquid waterproofing can negotiate complex shapes on any plane.	Sheets need careful application to negotiate details.
Effect of building movement	Can cope with some movement/cracks to substrate.	Affected by movement/cracking of substrate.	Can cope with limited movement/cracks to substrate.	Can tolerate only limited building movement.	Can tolerate only limited building movement.	Can tolerate some building movement.
Loading coat	Not required.	Not required.	Base render coat sometimes needed.	Loading wall and slab needed.	Loading coats needed.	Loading coats needed.

The 'Design Assessment Guide' published in the BCA Design Guide *Basement Waterproofing*[20], shows the suitability of the various waterproofing options under differing water table positions.

It is useful to note that Type C drained cavity waterproofing systems offer a low-risk waterproofing option for low and high water tables. Other options, such as Type A waterproofing, may not achieve a Grade 3 or 4 environment, even if drainage is incorporated. For a greater understanding of the guidance graphs, please refer to 'selection procedure' in the BCA Guide.

The BCA advise that design of basement waterproofing can be determined from a systematic appraisal. You would firstly decide upon basement usage, then gather site information, decide upon a form of construction, and finally select the waterproofing most suited. In an existing basement, construction form would be there to inspect as found – and you would need to determine the materials used and thicknesses, etc. from site inspection.

The BCA are well aware, as indeed we are, of just how carefully basement waterproofing should be designed and implemented, and advise early contact with suitable specialist installers. We also see the merit of seeking advice from specialists, but realise too that the more knowledge you yourself acquire, the better able you will be to appraise the specialist's recommendation.

CASE STUDY 1: DOWNWARD AND UPWARDS

Figure 49: This building had not been built that long, but was already about to be altered quite substantially.

The educational building could not have been more than 25 years old. The outer walls are of brick and block cavity work, with intermediate floors of concrete beam construction.

Background

The sports wing had a number of shortcomings at this school – the lack of ceiling height for use as a fully-fledged gymnasium was the most pressing.

The alternatives were to raise the ceiling or lower the floor – or both!

It was decided to lower the floor. Walls previously above ground now need to perform as below-ground walls.

The first task would be to remove the existing suspended concrete floor, which would involve cutting concrete beams where they were built into perimeter cavity walling.

The brick and block cavity walls would be strengthened to take additional lateral loads. The method used was pure cunning! Access holes were cut in the inner cavity wall skin, and concrete pumped in – changing the wall to a solid wall with increased strength.

Lateral damp penetration would be excluded by applying an internal multi coat render system.

Figure 50: The project is well advanced, with a new concrete slab in situ, and the perimeter walls already waterproofed to around 1500mm height.

Figure 51: A clever technique for maintaining continuity of waterproofing at a wall intersection.

New chemical injection
dpc level

Current yard level

Plastic horizontal dpc

Likely yard level
when newly built

Figure 52: The classic damage sandwich of raised ground levels. Yard-dpc-yard-dpc, and so on.

An opening has been cut through the internal blockwork, so waterproofing just carries on through!

The bulge in the waterproofing is where the new waterproofing carries over the slight projection of the old cut-off floor beams. The render is reinforced with a patent 'combiflex' strip at this position. Combiflex is also used to strengthen rendering at the wall/floor junction.

When this building was built, the external yard levels would have been much lower than they are today. It is not just old Georgian, Victorian and Edwardian houses that suffer from raised land putting the wall base at risk from damp damage. Any building can be threatened.

The new gymnasium floor level is six or seven brick courses (i.e. 450–525mm) below existing yard level along this elevation. But before the floor level was lowered internally the original physical dpc would have been two courses below yard level. This may or may not have been causing a low-level damp penetration problem.

Looking at the lowered door opening reveal, there looks to be a good height of new waterproofing protection, as the new waterproofing extends easily a full metre above the external finished yard level. For added protection, the contractor has installed a chemical injection dpc, using a gunned silicone cream, to provide in my opinion a support measure to help control dampness. The internal waterproof render coats will be the mainstay.

In order to produce an attractive interior finish, the rendering internally would need to be covered by panelling. It was decided to form a decorative dado detail, which would require expert fixing methods.

CASE STUDY 2: DAMPNESS WILL OUT!

Figure 53: A problem at the White House! Perhaps 30 or more years back, it would have looked very much like the right-hand property, a traditional red brick London town house.

Houses that are rendered will offer great opportunity for rising dampness if they do not possess a reliable horizontal damp-proof course. A veritable lobster pot for dampness: *once in rarely out.*

What any surveyor would consider 'damp stains' were apparent in the lower ground floor at waist height. Surveyors will invariably find themselves heading downstairs to a lower ground floor or basement to survey a damp problem.

Most brickwork begins to be significantly damp when its moisture content is 1–3%. So at A and B the wall is *definitely very damp,* at 5.2–6.9%.

At height C the brickwork only contains a marginal amount of moisture (0.5%) – the amount of moisture the brickwork would pick up from typical British dampish air, i.e. not from damp penetration, rising damp, a plumbing leak, etc. So at C we could refer to the wall as 'air dry'. This is in effect the control reading for the wall. See *Diagnosing Damp*[1], page 89, Table 3.

But why stains at waist height – please look closely at figures 56 and 57. All is revealed after a little plaster removal.

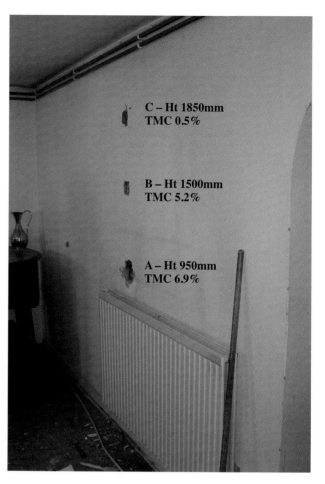

C – Ht 1850mm
TMC 0.5%

B – Ht 1500mm
TMC 5.2%

A – Ht 950mm
TMC 6.9%

Figure 54: Damp damage at around 900mm height.

Figure 55: More of the same – damp damage marred the beautifully furnished sitting room off the hallway, visible just above the light flex, near the grand piano, at exactly the same 900mm height.

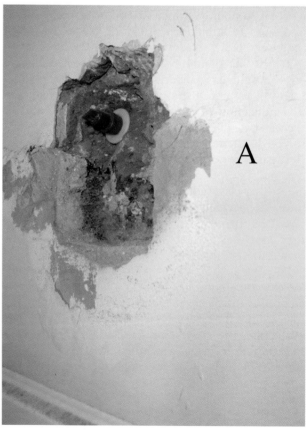

Figure 56: At 'A' the decision was taken to cut out a square of plaster not far from the front room grand – in an attempt to find out why plaster is failing to contain dampness at this height above floor level.

At A, where we cut a square of plaster, figure 57 shows how dampness within the wall is finding a way out. The damp damage coincides with the junction of two different waterproofing systems.

Diagnosis

Before cutting out a plaster square, you might have expected you were witnessing rising dampness – that has just managed to climb a little above a waterproof render system that was applied from floor to 900mm height. However, it can be dangerous to limit rising damp in our minds to the common 1m rise!

As carbide test results of drilled samples showed, dampness seems to be rising within this dividing wall (between the two main lower ground floor rooms) much higher than the oft-quoted 900mm. As you can see from carbide meter tests, the walling was very damp to a height of 1500mm.

The truth was that moisture seemed to be finding a way out at the junction of two quite successful waterproofing coatings. Electronic moisture meter readings were taken vertically up the walling from floor to ceiling on the line of the plaster cut-outs. The readings were always low, except at the junction line of the two plaster types, where high readings were recorded.

Looking at the plaster cut-out at A, the bottom half of the exposed substrate was black. This is *synthaprufed* brickwork. In the 1980s, the existing cementitious rendering was hacked off up to a height of 900mm. The walls had originally been cement rendered to full height.

The walls from floor to 900mm height were then 'waterproofed' with three coats of Synthaprufe. A

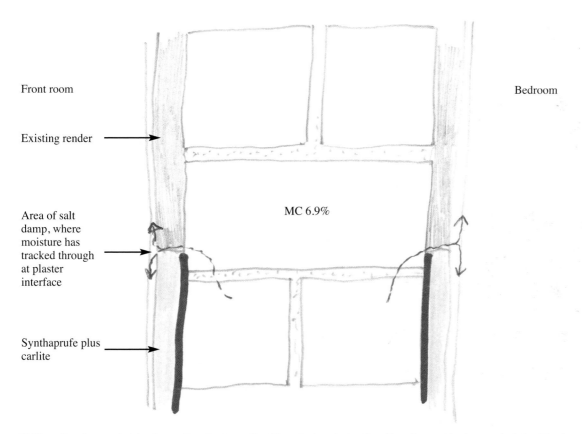

Figure 57: The wall section – typical detail at top line of waterproofing. The author's understanding of how damp patches have resulted at position A.

Table 5: Vertical analysis of damp readings and symptoms at test position (see figure 56)						
Test	**Height**	**Plaster type**	**Carbide MC**	**Search mode**	**Pin probe**	**Salts**
C	1850mm	Existing cement render	0.5%	154	16 R/R	
B	1500mm	Existing cement render	5.2%	171	17 R/R	
A	950mm	Existing cement render	6.9%	1000	60 R/R	Nitrate 75mg Chloride positive
Plaster join	900mm			1000	100 R/R	Salt damp
	150–850mm	Synthaprufe + Carlite		200–210	11–20 R/R	
	Skirting				10.2%	

gypsum-based undercoat was then applied onto the Synthaprufe, finished with a gypsum skim coat. (Many surveyors may take a deep intake of breath here – gypsum plasters are always considered unsuitable for below-ground walls. However, applying gypsum plasters to three coats of Synthaprufe has proved a successful waterproofing method at many properties over the years, as long as gypsum plasters make no contact whatsoever with any damp floor or (more importantly, whether chemically injected or not) the wall surface, to create a bridge.)

According to Synthaprufe technical literature, the method of waterproofing at the subject property would not be considered suitable for below-ground situations. At this property the lower ground floor was around 500mm below ground (probably not deep enough to really feel like a basement), so below-ground basement waterproofing requirements would apply.

Three coats of Synthaprufe plus gypsum plaster = 'damp-proofing' rather than 'waterproofing'.

The problem lay in the presumption that dampness would not defeat a 900mm wall barrier.

Key point: inner walls that are waterproofed on both sides really feed dampness upwards if there is no effective horizontal dpc present.

Here we also needed to consider the fact that the external ground was around 500mm above the internal floor level. The least you would need to do would be to add 500mm to the 1m (standard assumption) – so we could expect dampness to rise *a minimum* of say 1500mm up the basement wall. Safer still to give the dampness a 2m high jump challenge.

The damp inside the wall actually petered out at around 1700mm. Dampness reaching to ceiling height or thereabouts would be a concern, as this would be where ground floor timbers would be located.

Remedy options

Extending the Synthaprufe coating would prove practically impossible, as the Synthaprufe peels away as plaster is hacked back.

You would need to hack off the existing waterproofing as well as the render coat above, and apply a new waterproof system, probably to full height in all the rooms exhibiting damp patches. This would be expensive, but a guaranteeable option.

Whether the route is a multi-coat render system or a cavity membrane air gap system, the cost of producing a reliably dry decorative finish for this flat would not be cheap.

The water threat requires a belt and braces approach. Before you begin to question the wisdom of hacking out three squares of plaster, sometimes invasive investigation of buildings can cause very little disturbance or aggravation to occupiers. In this case, the occupier had agreed to some invasive investigation – as long as the cut-outs were behind one of the large wall paintings!

Figure 58: Invasive investigations nicely covered up by a re-hung wall painting.

Alternative basement waterproofing scenarios

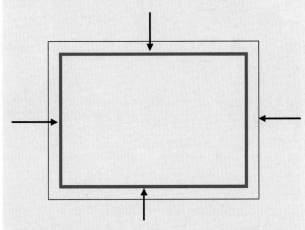

Figure 59: The ideal basement: no internal dividing walls, simple plan shape, no changes in levels.

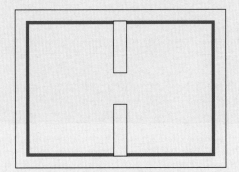

Figure 60: Basement with dividing walls, waterproofing discontinuous.

Lateral penetration is likely at the junctions of earth retaining/dividing walls.

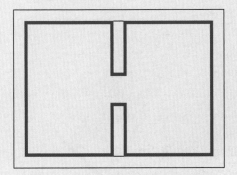

Figure 61: Waterproofing continuous around dividing walls.

There is a good chance of success, providing door frame fixings do not compromise the waterproofing. Any subsequent internal alteration would compromise waterproofing integrity.

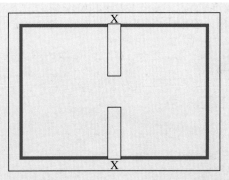

Figure 62: Waterproofing discontinuous at dividing wall intersections to earth retaining walls.

Vertical chemical injection at X would be doomed to fail, as chemical injection is designed only to withstand moisture movement by capillarity. Water below ground can be under much greater hydrostatic pressure.

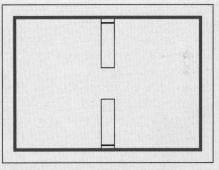

Figure 63: Difficulties of waterproofing junctions of dividing walls and earth retaining walls solved – the dividing wall is physically separated from the earth retaining wall.

This may be by a partial height removal of wall material, or by connection of dividing wall to earth retaining wall by a restraint joint after waterproofing – where the divider is tied to the outer wall by sleeved connectors set into sealed pocket housings in the outer wall.

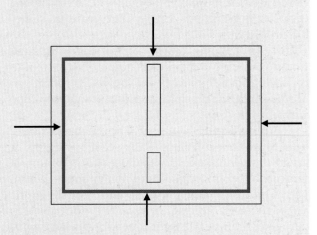

Figure 64: Internal partitions are removed, and structural support provided over if necessary. This opens up the basement space and would offer a good chance of success for waterproofing with less junction and intersection detailing required.

CASE STUDY 3: GETTING IT RIGHT DOWN UNDER

Figure 65: A rather attractive Islington residence – said to be the oldest house in Islington. All may well look presentable above ground – but below …?

Figure 66: Standing water – not that you would wish to stand anywhere in this basement without wellington boots.

Figure 67: No need to take samples for moisture content checking by carbide meter in this basement. The masonry is visibly saturated. You can appreciate the task of creating a dry habitable space as you cast your eye over the mixture of loose and friable brick and stonework either side of the exit steps to the garden area.

Figure 68: As we hack off some of the wall finishes we uncover the story of previous attempts to waterproof this space. Under the finish plaster is a grey-coloured slurry coat that did not keep the water out. Preparation is the key. This render coat must now be removed and the exposed substrates made good as necessary, to receive new waterproofing coatings or fixings.

The hydrostatic pressure can be alleviated by improving land drainage around the building – as an external support measure. The more lateral damp penetration can be reduced, the greater the chance of success for any waterproofing installed. It will simply have less water load to deal with.

For this building, water ingress under pressure would not be an 'event' for a waterproofing system to cope with, but a day-in, day-out *continuous occurrence*. Maybe a little too much for pumps and sumps to cope with.

There was also a height issue. The ceiling as existing from solid floor to ceiling was a scant 1.9 metres. A cavity-drained floor could take up 125mm of thickness (i.e. from the cavity membrane – 20mm, plus screed of 65mm, plus allowance for falls in the screed – much needed to drain the floor towards perimeter drains). So height counted against a cavity-drained floor system in this particular case.

The original waterproofing must have been installed by less than fully conscientious waterproofers. It comprised a waterproof slurry, dry-lined with plaster-boarding, fixed by adhesives. Needless to say plaster-boards and adhesives offered very little resistance to the dampness that had defeated the slurry-coating defence. There had been no linkage of any sort between the less than substantial floor slab and the wall waterproofing, and no perimeter drainage at all. The brick substrate had not provided a good enough

Figure 69: Note the position pointed out well below the water table, where water actually spouts into the basement. Such an entry point can be dammed very rapidly by applying fast action powders.

key for the slurry coating, and there was no evidence of brush hammering (a common method to key-up masonry). The current contractor feels that on the evidence of substrates as they appear now, brush hammering would have probably caused more damage than the rather friable substrates could tolerate, in any case. Much water was found collecting under the slab. Some of the concrete reinforcement was found to be damaged by pitting. A new concrete slab would be needed, independent from the perimeter walls. Some limited differential movement may be accommodated by the wall/floor junction of new waterproofing.

Remedy selection

If we refer to Table 4 on page 47, we could scan down the key selection criteria of a waterproofing system. At Islington, as can be seen from the rather dramatic pictures above, we were faced with pretty evident hydrostatic pressure. How would the various potential waterproofing systems cope? Not only is there a very definite water entry, but the substrate looks rather unpredictable, to say the least, and we need to effect substantial brickwork repairs to achieve the desired standard of substrate on which waterproofing may be fixed or applied.

Now let us weigh up the relative merits of a cavity-drained waterproofing system versus a multi-coat render system. These are two of the favoured systems on offer from the selected contractor.

Looking first at cavity-drained waterproofing:

- good fixing positions are needed at minimum spacings;
- the system is vulnerable to hydrostatic pressure if pumps fail; and
- it can suffer problems if drain routes block from silting (under-floor membranes, etc.).

On the plus side, the air gap should dissipate hydrostatic pressure before it can build up to impose on the membrane system.

Multi-coat render systems are designed to withstand hydrostatic pressure, and will do so as long as the renders can be well bonded to their substrate, are mixed and applied carefully using suitable materials, and, importantly, a really reliable substrate needs to be achieved by good attention to preparation.

No doubt either system potentially could succeed – but which has the least risk of failure? The contractor needs to be convinced of the method about to be used, or costly and commercially damaging reparations could follow. The contractor decided to carry out some destructive testing to clarify the floor slab construction.

In order to decide on the best waterproofing approach, the contractor needed first to know the strength and stability of the existing solid floor. So the floor was core-drilled, and found to comprise a 50mm concrete slab, topped by a 100mm cement and sand screed. The slab was reinforced by steel bars, and a plastic damp-proof membrane was found underneath the slab. Membranes under slabs can sometimes be damaged quite early on in their life, e.g. the membrane can be accidentally damaged during concreting, or may be subsequently punctured by sharp aggregates or hardcore underneath.

The hydrostatic pressure was such that within the first day after drilling the inspection core, 25mm of water had collected over the floor slab, having seeped up via the test hole and from perimeter water weeping along the chimney breast brick coursings.

The sheer amount of water continually entering the basement space was thought by the waterproofing consultant to be too much for a sump and pump to cope with.

There was also a concern that the water collecting or draining under cavity floor membranes could be contaminated, as there were known to be underground drains in the vicinity. The waterproofing consultant began to veer away from a cavity-drained waterproofing system – contaminated water could not be tolerable under drained floors of a habitable space.

Looking at the exposed masonry underground at Islington, you would not be able to immediately apply cavity drain membranes with any confidence. First, quite an intensive preparation would be required, as the existing failed slurry coat should be removed down to a sounder substrate. De-bonded finishes cannot remain in situ, or you risk accumulation of debris in the air gap. Like any cavity wall, the gap serves a function, and has to be maintained. The exposed brickwork would almost certainly be uneven, and probably damaged by removal of previous attempts to waterproof, so at the very least the uneven and damaged substrate would need to be 'dubbed out', using a 3:1 sand and cement or 1:1:6 cement:lime:sand mix, to produce an acceptably flat finish for accepting the membrane sheets. This of course would add to the cost of a cavity membrane installation.

In this case the contractor opted for a thorough preparation, and the application of a multi-coat render waterproofing system. Remember too that cavity-drained systems have not been used in the UK for much more than ten years, so we are still learning about their installation and in-use performance. Waterproofed renders have a longer track record, although failures have not been that uncommon – but probably arising more from unsatisfactory application and substandard materials than inherent short-comings of the method. Some old buildings have suffered foundation subsidence, which a rigid water-proofing has not been able to cope with, and so multi-coat render waterproofing has cracked and failed. Some cracking, at the wall/floor junction could now be designed out by installing patent reinforcing strips at the abutment.

Remember too that there can be *hybrid* solutions. You could, for example, apply cementitious renders to walls below ground, and add for good measure an inner drained membrane system. Sumps can be waterproof rendered and pumps incorporated as a belt-and-braces or further line of defence against water ingress. As mentioned in the main chapter, it is quite common to render walls but install a cavity-drained floor system. It is often the walls that present the difficult shapes and configuration for the relatively rigid cavity membrane sheets, but the floor will usually be flat (or perhaps at a slight incline!).

The contractor had definitely decided to go down the multi-coat render route to waterproof the basement (see the virtual pond in figure 66). For this contract, pre-bagged aggregates would be used, and manufacturers' specifications strictly adhered to, so there would be a very good chance of the render system succeeding. Nothing underground is perfect, but the finished space was attractively finished and furnished – and thankfully dry!

4 Plumbing problems

INTRODUCTION

In *Diagnosing Damp*[1] sources of moisture in buildings are divided into the following categories:

- air moisture condensation;
- penetrating dampness;
- internal plumbing leaks;
- below-ground moisture;
- site-specific source, e.g. natural flooding, water from fire-fighting; and
- others, e.g. cleaning, construction moisture, etc.

There has been an over-emphasis on rising damp, condensation and penetrating damp. Leaks from internal plumbing or underground drainage commonly cause damp damage, and require remediation. The same plumbing leaks crop up time and time again, so time spent describing the common causes shall be time worth spent.

It would be interesting to calculate the total length of pipework in a three-bedroom semi. Could it add up to more than 100 metres? And how prolific too are the joints – every one a leak waiting to happen. A further calculation would also be revealing. Just how much of this myriad of pipes is visible for inspection, and how much is hidden from view behind panels and ducts or, worse still, embedded within screeds and plasters?

It would take a whole book to describe in detail how all the components of the various plumbing systems might sprout a leak, a seep, a trickle or a drip, but from experience, the author will highlight a few of the more common causes.

COMMON CAUSES OF PLUMBING LEAKS

Water mains

Beads of condensation on cold pipes can be frustrating and difficult to remedy. If there is moisture in the dwelling air (which there always will be), and the mains cold pipe is cold (which it always will be), a film of moisture or chains of watery beads will appear on the pipe surface. Remediation may be to replace a metal pipe with plastic, insulate the pipe or reduce the amount of moisture in the room air, so that the amount of condensate forming reduces too.

In a recent kitchen refurbishment, the author was dismayed one morning to find water droplets in profusion over cold feeds under the sink … and this pipework had been executed most diligently. It was the day after ceramic tiling had been carried out. The kitchen air must have become very humid from water evaporating out of adhesives and grouts. Thankfully, once the evaporation had ceased and air had returned to its normal relative humidity, the droplets disappeared and never again re-appeared. It was a considerable relief, as droplets of water in a chipboard kitchen cabinet can cause considerable damp damage. Water can settle on the horizontal base boarding and trickle towards the board intersections.

Water mains are often rather ignored as a potential cause of damp problems in buildings. Leaks can cause problems both inside and outside the building. A fierce water main breach can displace ground soils to destabilise a foundation, causing not just damp but a structural problem. Leaked water collecting on a pathway can ice up to form a slip hazard.

It is becoming much easier to detect a mains water loss as more properties are fitted with a water meter. For properties without a meter, more traditional means of confirming leakage, such as listening sticks, may be employed. Water mains can leak for a multitude of reasons:

- bi-metallic corrosion between different metals breaks down a joint;
- pipes can be accidentally punctured;
- pipes can corrode;
- pipe joints can just pull apart; or
- joints can weep that were poorly made.

Some copper pipework produced in times of copper material shortages is of inferior quality and could have been installed with latent flaws, meaning its service life would be very much shortened. The consequences of a water main leak can be severe, as there is a limitless supply of water from the water mains to escape via the flaw. See Appendix H.

More and more properties are dispensing with storage facilities for water, as evidenced by the number of old tanks you see piled up in skips. Central heating systems are run directly off combination boilers, with no need for feed and expansion tanks. So more and more kitchen and bathroom taps are fed directly by mains supply and there are fewer tank leaks from the loft.

Water main leaks feature in several of the case studies. It is worth dwelling on a few pointers to good joint-making so we might avoid the predictable leaks.

The dripping stop valve

Valves that shut off water commonly use two basic methods. Some valves incorporate a washer (usually a replaceable component), whilst other valves will shut off water by closing of a metal gate (e.g. a 'gate valve') or the revolving of a metal ball with an aperture through its middle (the valve successfully turning off water by virtue of a meeting of two accurately machined faces). Valves that use rubber washers are more often able to *completely* turn off water. Gate valves nearly always allow a small dripping of water to continue, even when the gate is really tightly shut

Two common valves are used in the domestic setting. The mains stop valve most of us are familiar with is a brass inline valve fitted with a standard tap, and often fitted with identification label like a parcel! Many textbooks advise us all to label stop valves, but few heed the advice. Such a valve is usually turned off by hand and has a capstan head fitted to a spindle that is threaded at the end that houses a 'jumper' fitted with the washer. Turning the tap gradually pushes the spindle downwards and eventually the washer fully seals off incoming water from the mains side. This type of stop valve is designed so that should the washer remain stuck to its seating, water pressure will force it off, so a no-flow situation cannot arise. So it is important that the valve is fitted the correct way round, with the marked arrow in the direction of flow.

Nowadays, 'service valves' are becoming more widely used. They are ball valves.

The ball has a through hole, and when the hole is in alignment with the direction of flow, water can pass through the valve. The valve is usually turned by a straight bladed screwdriver.

Traditional stop valves are used to turn off the house supply. They are a very real damp threat. The problem is the gland packing. The spindle is sealed by compacted material, and drips commonly develop around it. Sometimes the packing gland nut can be tightened to solve the drip, sometimes the gland packing needs to be replaced. Some plumbers use PTFE tape, some use wool compacted with petroleum jelly, and some hessian and plumber's pipe jointing paste. However, many stop valves are in inaccessible places, and drips may continue for weeks, months and even years. Timbers can rot from the persistent weeping of these valves.

Occupiers and managers of property need to know where stop valves and service valves are located. An emergency, when the supply needs to be isolated quickly, is not the time to explore the complexities of your plumbing. Mains shut-off keys need to be kept where needed, but few householders seem to keep one

handy. If water cannot be quickly turned off inside the property you may need to access the OSV (outside valve), usually located in the pavement in front of the house wall or fence. Use a large screwdriver to lift up the flap and the mains key to turn off the supply. Older valve chambers will include a pear shaped flap with the letter 'W'. If the pit is not filled with debris, you will see either the capstan head of the stop valve or an extension rod of square section. Use the mains key to turn the valve clockwise till it has turned the

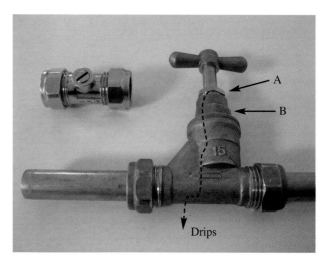

Figure 70: On the left a 'service valve', suitable for isolating the mains supply to a WC cistern or perhaps a bathroom tap. They are not that likely to drip. To the right a traditional stop valve – that can turn off the mains. Usually found under a kitchen sink or under the stairs.

Figure 71: Undo nut B and the whole inner guts of the tap can be taken out, and the rubber washer levered off from its holding rivet and replaced with a new one. If the valve's seating looks rough or corroded, you can screw a reseating device onto the same female thread and 're-seat' the tap. Such a stop valve costs just a few pounds to purchase – so you can just replace it and repair the old one at your leisure.

water off. This whole operation may be quite straightforward in a single occupancy property, but you may see in some pavements an absolute gaggle of water main flaps – and which one relates to the subject property may be very difficult to work out.

Modern water meter chambers can be opened to reveal a vertical plastic rod, for which a special shaped plastic key may be needed … an emergency may not be the time to order one!

In the author's experience, the number one culprit for water main leaks does not hit the headlines, as drips from a stop valve are not dramatic events. But steady drips in concealed voids from around the spindle can amount to substantial water escapes over prolonged periods. You so often find stop valves under floors, over timber joists, and drips have seeped into the timbers and caused wet rot. Sometimes a stop valve next to a WC cistern, installed with the best intentions, may be causing rot to floorboards below as it weeps and drips, as well as damaging the floor coverings. Stop valves near kitchen units drip, and chipboard cabinets cannot usually withstand being wetted for long.

Once you have fitted a traditional stop valve, it pays to *ever so slightly* tweak the packing gland nut A. This will prevent drips seeping from around the spindle. Eventually, after a few years' service though, tightening the nut does not stop a drip.

COPPER PIPEWORK GENERALLY

Central heating leaks

Central heating distribution pipework running off a boiler will usually be under significant pressure, created by feeding mains supply into the network when topping up. A pressure gauge on the boiler will tell you if the central heating system is up to pressure or losing pressure from leaks. As a guide only, typical central heating circuit pressure may be from 1–2 bar (lower when cold).

Leaky copper compression fittings

A proliferation of compression fittings under a bath or sink usually looks ungainly and unprofessional, and each one is a potential leak. Professional plumbers are more likely to use soldered 'Yorkshire fittings', or the even more professional 'end-feed fittings'. Yorkshire fittings are pre-soldered, whereas the end-feed fitting is sold without integral solder.

Visual inspection of copper pipework can mislead you into thinking all is well. On one occasion the author stripped out some old central heating pipework and was amazed to find one section of pipework fell apart as it was removed from its brackets. One 15mm copper tube end had been fed into its straight connector by only

2–3mm – just enough to somehow remain intact until it was disturbed.

To avoid this plumbers should place a pencil check mark on the tube to be fitted into a connector, so they can be sure the pipe end is fully home before firing up the joint. Soldered joints are, in the main, less likely to cause leaks than compression fittings. For a compression fitting, the end of the tube is fitted with an 'olive' (a metal ring), and a nut forces the ring against the mating surface of the straight connector, elbow bend or 'T' fitting. Professional plumbers tend to make the connections without using any jointing paste. However, jointing paste helps make a watertight and reliable joint, and when it hardens up actually helps bind the joint. But there have been cases when plumbing installations e.g. in hospitals, have failed at the snagging stage – as paste in compression joints was deemed a potential health hazard. Pipework needs to be carefully set out, or compression joints may fail. Pipes need to enter the fitting in line with the fitting, or a good joint may not be achievable. Pipework should not be under any tension or there could be a tendency for the joint to spring apart. If you need to physically pull the pipe towards and into the fitting you have a problem – the pipe was cut too short!

Is this end cap reliably fitted? Would you be prepared to walk away from the property for a long weekend with the pipe mains pressure live?

An end cap such as the one in figure 72 was used to terminate pipework to a shower undergoing maintenance. The owner departed for the annual summer holiday. Disaster struck. A neighbour, intending to be a good neighbour, turned on the property mains stop valve so that the garden tap could be used to water the owner's back garden plants. As the neighbour watered the plants, she heard the sound of trickling water in the neighbour's house. Water was indeed cascading down the stairs and through the first floor ceiling. She realised there was a problem and turned the pavement stop valve off. She had meant well of course, but the owner had turned off the house stop valve before going on holiday, realising that the shower cold water feeds had been left in a risky state with only end caps to hold back water. By turning on the mains stop valve in the pavement, the neighbour had caused the end cap to be forced off by the sudden change in pressure.

Figure 72: This is a 15mm compression end cap. It could be used where a cold or hot feed is temporarily out of use, or perhaps during plumbing work when connections to a bath, basin or sink are not yet completed.

Figure 73: Fittings that cannot be used with spanners are less easy to tighten, and there is less control.

Considerable experience is needed in tightening nuts – it is more likely you would under-tighten than over-tighten.

Fittings needs to be locked on the pipe by a very tight olive, or you risk a flood. If you are at all unsure here, consider soldering on an end cap while the pipe is dry. And if you turn off the water main in the pavement, tell your neighbour to leave it well alone!

Water main connections using modern plastic tube may fail if there is lack of attention to detail. You should not attempt to tighten up a compression fitting to a plastic pipe without first fitting an inner thimble.

Leaky push-fit connections

Plastic push-fit pipework is becoming more commonly used for mains, low pressure hot and cold distribution pipework and central heating. This pipe system is not suitable for gas!

Those of us who have for years painstakingly bent, prepared and soldered copper plumbing are perhaps a little suspicious of new technology. We might associate plastic pipework with the lesser skilled in the industry,

but this can be unfair. There are some very clear advantages in this plumbing option, as set out below. Well-executed joints will not leak, and one manufacturer is sufficiently confident in their push-fit system to offer a 50-year guarantee on pipe and fittings.

The connections of the range the author tested is 'idiot proof'. Integral O-ring seals are even pre-lubricated, and there are guidemarks on the pipework to ensure that the end of the pipe is inserted sufficiently into the fitting. However, in spite of the exhaustive instructions from manufacturers, leaks could occur for any one of several reasons:

- the fitting is not clean when used, e.g. when fittings collect site dirt, through careless storage or handling;
- the O-ring is displaced due to insertion of a very roughly cut pipe end;
- the pipe has not been properly inserted into the fitting;
- chemical breakdown of plastic fittings, due to use of oil-based plumber's sealing pastes;
- pipework affected by heat/fire: temperatures over 125°C cause damage;
- pipework damaged by rodents/vermin;
- pipework damaged by UV light;
- fittings used on unsuitably sized pipework, e.g. non-metric copper (i.e. ½″ imperial);
- fittings used to connect unsuitable pipe material, e.g. stainless steel or chrome shower pipework: the fitting can be pushed apart as the internal plastic gripper will not function correctly;
- pipework or fittings drilled, cut or otherwise damaged accidentally or by vandalism in use.

Failures of construction components will nearly always occur from poor installation and misuse of the product. You really do need to read the product guidelines.

Figure 74: A new plastic pipe is to be connected to copper pipework. See at the end of the plastic pipe the metal rim of the stainless steel thimble, which must be fitted into the pipe's end before the 15mm compression straight connector is fitted and tightened up.

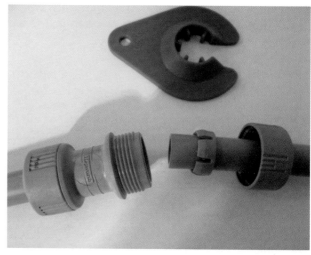

Figure 75: A modern push-fit straight connection, suitable for mains, hot and cold water distribution. See above the fitting a special grab wedge for pulling off olives when re-using a fitting. Dedicated pipe cutters should be used and spray joint lubricant is sometimes needed. Tube and fittings courtesy Hepworth Building Products, www.hepworth.co.uk

Figure 90: Sitting in the bath, you would observe such an overflow fitting, to which the plug is attached. You are looking at a sham: not chromed metal but just cheap plastic.

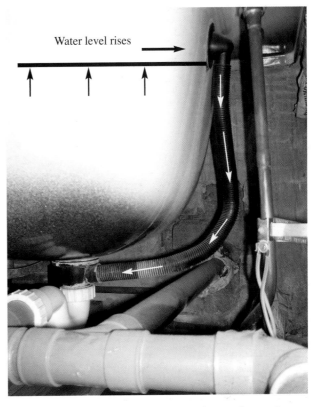

Water level rises

Figure 91: Bath overflow. To the left you can see where overflow travels – out of the bath high up via the overflow fitting, down the crinkly pipe and into a black plastic fitting to which the bath 'P' trap fits underneath.

have the capacity to deal with a bath that is seriously filling up from both taps turned on. The bath water level will just keep rising until it overflows onto the bathroom floor. The real test is to turn on both hot and cold taps, fit the plug in the bath, sit back and observe. As the water level gradually rises up the side of the bath, the bath of course gets heavier and heavier. If the bath is acrylic it might flex, putting considerable strain on the edge seals – and once the water begins to gurgle through the overflow outlet, do not be one bit surprised if the water level continues to rise until you finally decide to turn the taps off! Overflow pipes will rarely cope with a full-blown rise in the bath water but would just deal with a less serious escape, such as getting into a bath which has been filled too high. We dare you to test your own bath!

Because the overflow pipe enters the waste system above the trap connection, if the bath trap is blocked, so too will be the overflow! The potential for flood damage is obvious. See figure 91.

An overflow should really be serviced by a separate pipe that bypasses the trap – and should really not even be linked to the same waste pipework system. Such an overflow pipe just needs to exit through an external wall and ideally feed down to a yard gully, where its splashing outpouring can be spotted.

Basins commonly leak underneath, where waste fittings have been poorly installed.

Frequently kitchen and basin traps can be found completely mummified by all manner of tapings and bandagings. Such an approach can never cure a leak. Plumbing fittings need to be taken apart, carefully

inspected for flaws, cleaned, washers and seals replaced if need be, and reassembled. Not an expensive or difficult job for a householder to tackle – and very straightforward for a plumber.

RADIATOR VALVE PROBLEMS

Many internal floods are caused by decorators or DIY enthusiasts who fail to realise how a thermostatic valve operates.

Figures 92–94 show you how a thermostatic radiator valve can be reliably capped or shut off when the radiator is taken off for decorating.

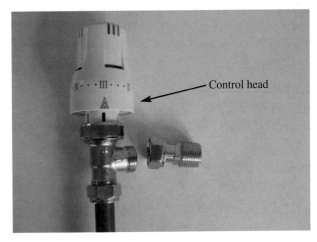

Control head

Figure 92: A modern TRV with its radiator coupling.

Figure 93: The same valve, with the control head removed. Now screw down the plastic shut-off cap, which will depress home the valve plunger.

Figure 94: Or you could fit an end blank to the radiator connection coupling thread, as shown here to a standard radiator valve.

Clogged basins cause havoc after a Sandwich party

Figure 95: Yet another flood causes havoc over a bank holiday weekend in Sandwich, Kent – the lit room being the office that suffered the flood damage.

At Sandwich, we will witness the aftermath of a staff party over a public holiday. One luckless partygoer had blocked a wash basin after just a little too much over-indulgence. She quit the Ladies leaving a tap still running, and running, and running!

Figure 96: The basins are missing an overflow! A blocked sink, taps still running, the building locked up from Friday until Tuesday – that's an awful lot of water …

Figure 97: The floor covering detailing does not help. True, the carefully crafted upstands are designed to contain spillage. But looking closer, the radiator pipes are routed through the carefully crafted floor covering without any sealant to plug up the gap round the pipes. This is where the pooling water found a way through.

'lockshield valve', is used when balancing the system. So take off both caps, and to make sure both valves are off, use a spanner if necessary to tweak them tight.

But a 'thermostatic radiator valve' (TRV) is fitted with a heat sensor. Such a valve senses the temperature in the room, and allows the valve to open, allowing hot water to enter and heat the radiator. You cannot reliably isolate such a valve by just turning down the temperature control. You will need to take off the temperature sensing head and secure the pressure pin with a dedicated manual locking nut. Otherwise (especially if you plan to remove the radiator for some time), you might have to consider taking the valve off and fitting a 15mm compression cap in its place. If you do not fit the locking nut, or safely cap off the pipe feed using a compression cap, you run the risk of the valve opening when there is a temperature drop in the 'subject room', which would cause a water escape. Some thermostatic valves actually have an 'off' position, which may be safe in theory, but it is still a good idea to cap off the radiator connection or even drain down the system and cap off the supply. You also

need to protect the valve from dust and dirt during the redecorating. You can either fit the patent dust cover, or fit a plastic bag around the valve, secured with tape.

But sadly, the Clapham household in our case study had not received this advice.

You might notice the inline *service valve* below the TRV. The plumber originally fitting the TRV had thought ahead – it would be possible to isolate the TRV with just a small turn of a screwdriver to turn off the service valve. But whoever took the radiator off did not realise the point of the service valve, and by failing to turn the on-off screw had caused thousands of pounds' worth of devastation.

Manufacturers of TRVs are well aware of the risks of not properly shutting them down when a radiator is removed, and typically offer advice such as: 'If the control head is used to close the valve, there is a danger of water damage if the temperature falls and the valve reopens unexpectedly.'

Thousands of pounds' worth of damp remediation for the cost of one radiator blanking-off cap.

Figure 114: **Somebody** *removed a radiator, but didn't realise that this type of valve cannot be simply shut off before the radiator is detached.*
See figures 92–94 for the correct methods to isolate radiator valves.

Service valve
(now OFF!)

Figure 115: Now take a look at some of the damage a misunderstanding about radiator valves caused. First and second floors: tiles fall off after a good wetting of the backing plasters; middle floor: plasters are removed to aid the drying.

Figure 116: On the ground floor, what used to be a strip-floored reception room is now in a very sorry state. Little is left of the oak strip flooring, which suffered serious water damage from the floods above.

Figure 117: The leaks from the (TRV) central heating valve three floors above seemed to have caused the worst water damage to the bottom storey, where not only the strip flooring was ruined, humped up like a big dipper, but also plasters needed to be hacked off to help dry out the walls and ceiling linings which had peeled and blistered from the saturation had to be removed.

5 Wall base damp-proofing

INTRODUCTION

There are probably more questions asked by surveyors on the subject of damp coursing existing walls than any other area of surveying – probably because there is a dearth of published advice, apart from information supplied by those marketing patent damp-proofing systems!

IS A NEW DAMP-PROOF COURSE NEEDED?

Let us remember that over-emphasis on this question diverts attention from several others that really should precede it, such as:

- Is the dampness present 'significant' (see Glossary, and also *Diagnosing Damp*[1], Table 3, page 89).
- Where exactly is the wall base significantly damp?
- Where is the dampness likely to be coming from?
- What are the available remedy options to control, stop or mask the dampness?
- How should the preferred remedy option be detailed and installed for best effect?

It is not that difficult to measure how much moisture there may be in a wall at low level. But confirming the source can be difficult.

Even if you confirm that 'ground salts' are present in low-level wall plasters, this does not mean dampness is coming from down in the ground. Nitrate or chloride salts may be present from an historic damp problem. Nitrates are also found in fertilisers spread over the top surface of flower beds. See *Diagnosing Damp*[1], Chapter 7 – 'Salts Tests'.

Many wall base damp problems are due to low-level damp penetration, when the wall has been unable to cope satisfactorily with the moisture load from leaky drain gullies, pooling yard water or splashing rainwater. And there may be additional moisture from below ground.

You can sometimes remedy wall base damp by improving perimeter surface water drainage, or the condition and detailing at the wall base to prevent damp-bridging or the wall soaking in too much moisture. The insertion of a damp-proof course may sometimes be a measure to consider. A horizontal dpc will prevent or control dampness that is soaking into the wall base and travelling upwards, but will not on its own prevent lateral movement of dampness through a wall.

In traditional buildings where there is good height between the wet wall base zone and vulnerable decorations, finishes, timberwork, etc., wetness may often be controlled by natural evaporation from the masonry. However, in buildings where this alone cannot deal with the low-level dampness load, perhaps because wall finishes are too impervious or there is insufficient evaporating wall surface, then a damp-proof course may be needed help control or stop damp.

Sometimes combinations of the following remedies can be very effective.

Surveyor's checklist – remedies for wall base damp

A – Damp-proofing of the subject building

External applications

1) Measures to protect wall base from low-level damp penetration – application of plinths and protective coatings.
2) Measures to improve breathing of wall – removal of impervious coatings/renderings externally if deemed a hindrance to evaporation.
3) Repairs to masonry, renderings, etc. to reduce/control damp penetration.

Integral applications

4) Physical damp-proof course.
5) Chemical damp-proof course.
6) Electro-osmosis damp-proof course.
7) Evaporation improvement methods.

Internal applications

8) Evaporation improvement methods.
9) Internal barriers.
10) Internal barriers with ventilation and/or drainage.

B – Support measures – work not actually carried out to the building structure and fabric

11) Reduce subsoil moisture content – e.g. by drainage.
12) Improve surface water drainage around the property.
13) Repair, make good, renew or improve adjacent suspect underground and above-ground services, such as rainwater disposal arrangements, drain connections, gullies, drains, water pipes, waste and foul drainage, leaky inspection chambers, etc.
14) Reduce perimeter ground or finished yard level.

The remedies above can be considered in the light of two key requirements:

i) Speed of building response

Some remedies would act to *gradually* help dry a wall base, e.g. improving perimeter surface water drainage, but it could take *months and years* for this to noticeably reduce dampness internally. See Chapter 8 for monitoring advice.

ii) Ease of remedy application

Some remedies applied to faces of walls or floors internally necessitate a considerable initial strip-out of internal fittings, obstructions or wall finishes. Others involve external work, creating far less internal disruption. External remediation is more likely to be feasible to detached property, as semi-detached or terraced property usually offers no access to the neighbour's side of party walls.

Damp-proofing that is introduced into the thickness of a building element (such as chemical injection damp-proofing) suffers from a number of difficulties. You cannot easily know whether the chemicals have fully impregnated the wall or bed joint thickness. Also, it will be difficult to know whether the wall thickness above the treatment is becoming suitably drier from the damp coursing, and especially when an internal wall face is replastered.

ALTERNATIVE REMEDY APPROACHES FOR WALL BASE DAMP

Three key means to stop or control dampness were eloquently explained by Peter Bannister[17], as follows:

- barriers;
- evaporation opportunities; and
- drainage opportunities.

These mechanisms can act as stand-alone dampness strategies, or be used working together.

But I would wish to add one more to the three:

- sheltering.

I have seen many cases of damp penetration, particularly to door openings, when the penetration could have been remedied merely by shielding the door opening by a well-designed canopy or porch.

As a general rule, you will achieve more success in stopping or controlling dampness if more than one of the above four strategies are used. In the case studies you will see examples of remedies using combinations of strategy.

EXTERNAL APPLICATIONS

Measures to protect the wall base at low level often encompass a combination of remedy elements. In Case Study 1 of this chapter we see the running of a new wall base plinth together with new floor ventilation arrangements. In Case Study 2, the wall base is shielded by a protective cementitious plinth, and new perimeter drainage installations help guide water away.

When elevations suffer deterioration, whether damage to masonry units themselves or erosion of the jointings, too often the decision is taken to coat the elevations with renders. A quick, clean wall finish can be achieved, but a dense wall finish whose prime function is keeping dampness out could also keep dampness trapped within – as the balance may or may not be right. Once walls are cement rendered or painted, the finish will nearly always be very difficult to completely remove. However, there will be cases where the removal of impervious coatings might be the only way to return the property to its original functioning state. Sometimes cement plinths are applied far too high – so as well as shielding the wall base from low-level damp penetration, they act to hold dampness within the wall, where it can no longer efficiently evaporate out.

External walls can be simply repaired where damaged brick faces or missing pointing allows damp penetration. Stones or bricks will of course need to be carefully matched, and it will take time for the new bricks to blend in with the existing as they weather over time. Where matching bricks are difficult to obtain, weathered bricks are sometimes cut out and reversed – the inner face may well be in good order.

INTEGRAL APPLICATIONS

Physical damp coursing

Brick replacement method

Softer bricks are traditionally cut out at the damp course level, and new harder (e.g. engineering) bricks inserted as replacements. Two courses of engineering bricks would sometimes be used for damp coursing non-habitable buildings, e.g. electricity substations, bus shelters, etc. This can be an advantageous method, as modern plastic damp-proof courses can provide too much of a slip plane (some free-standing walls have literally been knocked or blown off their damp-proof courses).

Saw-slot method

In the past, slots have been cut out at damp course bed joint level, and metal sheet dpcs installed. Today, plastic and occasionally lead sheet is more commonly the preferred damp-proof course.

Massari method

A polyester resin is introduced into the full thickness of the subject wall to form a dpc bonded to the masonry above and below. This could well be an effective method, providing the resin damp course is not prone to cracking if the wall settles or subsides.

Physical damp course insertion – saw slot method

If a building is detached and *needs* a damp-proof course to control or stop dampness above ground level, then a physical damp-proof course would probably be the most suitable option. Most of us would feel reassured seeing evidence of a physical dpc in a wall, such as a line of plastic or lead edging.

Physical insertion of a damp-proof course is often given a rather negative vote of confidence in the industry. It is usually deemed to be too expensive and disruptive.

A 1962 edition of BRE Digest 245 (numbered back then Digest 27[23] devoted several pages to physical dpc insertion. There are black and white images of cloth-capped workers handling specialised grinding equipment or chain saws. Grinding masonry poses significant health and safety risks from the dust created, causing silicosis (a serious lung condition).

More recent editions of BRE Digest 245 (1981)[24] contain less information on physical dpc insertion, although their value is very much emphasised, for example:

'The only certain way in all circumstances of introducing an effective dpc into a wall is to insert a new physical membrane. Techniques for doing so have improved over recent years and the cutting of an old lime/sand mortar bed joint through the entire thickness of a 225mm (9 inch) solid wall should, in most cases, present no problems.'

In the 1981 Digest[24], chemical injection is termed a non-traditional approach, whereas physical dpc insertion is considered traditional. The chemical dpc option appears to be more forcefully promoted than in earlier digests, for several reasons:

- Chemical injection is advised when physical insertion is not possible
  (e.g. to random coursed masonry).
- Very thick masonry walls were considered too difficult to physically damp course (but see next section, 'Advantages and disadvantages of physical dpc insertion').
- Agrément certificates were by then available for tested chemical dpc products.
- The presence of settlement cracks in structures could mean it was dangerous to attempt physical dpc insertion.

However, BRE 245[24] further adds the point that:

'The advantage of the physical techniques is that the membrane can be extended internally to form a vertical dpc between any solid floors and the horizontal course.'

Cutting methods have developed from the early days in the 1950s, when circular and hand-held saws were used. Disc cutters have been used incorporating dust extraction, but caused problems if the masonry was excessively damp, clogging of the vacuum bag[25]. The efficiency of hand-held power chain saws improved during the 1970s, making physical dpc installation more competitive.

Nowadays, low-density polythene is commonly used for the dpc, a distinct improvement from the 24 or 26 SWG copper that was once used. The polythene can either be linked to a solid floor damp-proof membrane or, for a timber-suspended floor, simply tucked down between walling and floorboards

As equipment for cutting slots in masonry walls improves, greater speed and ease of installing a physical retrofit dpc must surely tip the balance more towards this method. One of the biggest problems, however, lies in the lack of expertise in the UK in installing physical damp-proof courses. The author has to date made contact with just one company based in London that is able to install a physical damp-proof course.

Advantages and disadvantages of physical dpc insertion

Advantages

- Easier to link with other physical damp courses. (See figure 119, diagram B.)
- Suited to coursed brick/stonework.
- Only damaged/defective internal plaster needs renewing.
- Uses more traditional building skills.
- Can be visually inspected (but not entirely).
- Can be expensive to install, but a long-term remedy.
- Backed by BRE.
- Method can be used to repair a section of existing dpc very visibly.
- The physical damp course can be linked to floor damp-proof membranes by simple lapping.
- Materials used for the damp course will usually have a very long expected life.
- Specialised cutting machines can be used to cut slots in thin jointed masonry – even when engineering bricks are present.
- The plastic damp course material is available in 900mm width rolls, making it versatile and able to be installed to masonry of changing alignment and thickness.
- Masonry walls up to 700mm thick are commonly (and successfully) physically damp coursed.
- Once installed, the dpc should last for many years, making it unlikely that a later reinstallation of a failed retrofit damp-proof course will be necessary.
- If hard and stubborn plasters and renders can be retained, there will not then be the need for potentially damaging hacking off.
- No need to introduce large volumes of water-based treatments into the masonry.

Figure 118: A 1½ B brick wall shown with a new physical dpc, which links to an existing solid floor dpm. The floor screed has been renewed along the wall perimeter to help achieve a reliable dpc/dpm linkage.

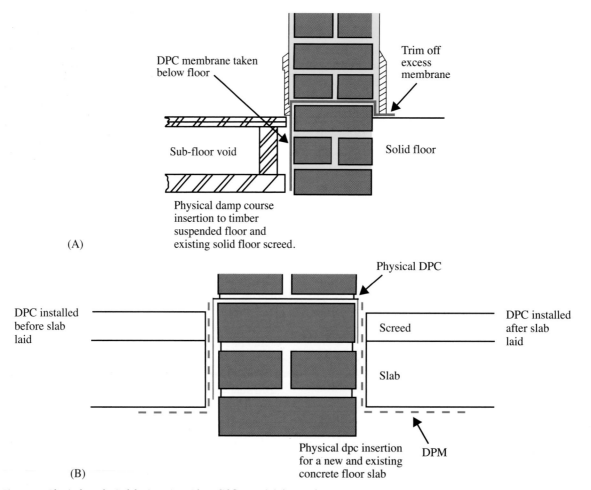

Figure 119: Plastic sheet physical dpc insertion with a solid floor. In (A) the new dpc is tucked well down the wall, before a new concrete slab is laid with its own dpm lapping up over the wall dpc. In (B), we see a shorter downward lap, where there is an existing concrete slab, with its visqueen membrane lapped up over the new dpc, and a new finishing screed laid after. Sketches courtesy Dampcoursing Ltd, www.dampcoursing.com

- Suitable for historic framed buildings, where an effective physical damp course is needed under the timber cill plate, typically on a dwarf support wall.
- The physical damp course material is manufactured to British Standards.
- There are less likely to be problems of split responsibility, as a physical dpc does not rely on specialist replastering (especially by another contractor) to work.

Disadvantages

- Physical dpc insertion will cost more than chemical injection per metre run of wall. But see also Table 7 – as chemical injection dpcs become less competitive when both sides of a wall need to be plastered.
- There are potential structural risks, e.g. of wall settlement, as a mortar course is cut out in stages.
- Due to the staged insertion there will be numerous laps in the damp course.
- Cutting a mortar joint could damage services.
- Access is usually required to both sides of a wall to be damp coursed.

- Additional means of damp coursing will be required if the property adjoins other property (i.e. there are party walls) and where vertical damp coursing is needed to proof below-ground sections of walling.
- There can be a lack of local specialist installers.
- Best suited to detached properties, or needs to be installed in conjunction with other less reliable damp coursing methods.
- Unsuited to some walling materials (e.g. flint or granite, which being hard damage the chain cutters).

General comments on the physical dpc insertion method

If the dpc membrane is inserted carefully, an extremely effective barrier to upward movement of moisture is created. The operation is not as expensive as many believe, although the actual damp course insertion is a fairly slow and labour intensive method (i.e. around 10 metres per day for a 225mm thick wall by two operatives) and therefore can be quite expensive, say, £90 per metre run of wall.

Figure 120: A dedicated power saw with tungsten carbide toothed chain cuts a chase to the third brickwork bed joint. Photo courtesy Dampcoursing Ltd, www.dampcoursing.com

Figure 121: A low-density polythene damp course is carefully inserted into the bed joint following removal of debris by a clearing hand saw. The membrane, installed in lengths lapped 150mm, is soon wedged up using slate slips and subsequently pointed up. Photo courtesy Dampcoursing Ltd.

Stages: Physical damp course insertion:

1 Cut chase, usually in one-metre lengths, by tungsten carbide chain saw.
2 Clear out debris, etc. using a clearing hand saw.
3 Cut membrane to size – commonly low density polythene.
4 Insert damp course sheeting.
5 Fill void above membrane with cement/soft sand 1:3 or 4.
6 Plug chase on each side of wall using slate slips.
7 Point up as far as 150mm from end of membrane section (to allow lapped joint).
8 Proceed to work on next bay. Bays may be staggered in the same way as underpinning bays, to ensure the wall is at all times adequately and safely supported.
9 Make good defective plasters after dpc insertion.

Note that cutting usually begins to the wall's outside face, so a neat joint can be cut and later pointed up – with less likelihood of damage from cutting from the inside. It is possible for the cutting to negotiate rainwater pipes, etc. Skirting boards would usually be taken off and refixed on completion.

Only salt-damaged plaster would be hacked off as a matter of course. Some making good of plaster might be required once skirtings are re-fixed. It is sometimes possible to simply remove plinths to kitchen base units, allowing just enough access for internal making good, thus saving the need to refit the kitchen.

Only small patches of wall plaster would normally be removed, as there should be no need for an internal specialist plaster masking system, unless of course there was a significant lateral damp penetration to address. The physical dpc does its job very reliably. If movement of moisture is stopped, transportation of salts will cease once water already above the dpc has found its way out of the wall by natural evaporation and moisture transfer within the solid material. The drying out of the wall can be monitored using modern moisture measuring equipment. In some cases, salt at the plaster surface could simply be scraped/washed off, or the salts neutralised prior to redecoration.

Firms that undertake physical dpc insertion may also install chemical dpcs. This may be because some walls can be very difficult to damp course physically (such as a party wall – where access would usually be required to both sides of the wall during physical dpc insertion). Apparently there are ways to insert a physical damp course from one side only, but a contractor would often chemically inject a party wall (although it is important to remember that a Party Wall Agreement may need to be obtained before drilling begins).

Physical insertion may often be a suitable technique for historic buildings. In a timber framed building, for example, a physical dpc can be inserted under a sole plate. This will mean a highly effective dpc will protect that timber member from further rotting from underneath. Internally, important historic fabric, such as wall plasters or timber panelling, can remain in situ where physical damp course insertion does not require any accompanying specialist plastering.

There are some great opportunities for dpm linkage with physical insertion, as the new dpc can be cut extra wide so that a substantial flap remains available for linking to, for example, a floor dpm. This option is not available with a chemical dpc insertion. If a wall is to be left unfinished, and certainly unplastered, chemical injection would be a risk! Without the second line of defence, i.e. the plaster, the chemical dpc may not be adequate on its own.

Chemical damp coursing

Sometimes a band of masonry will receive the chemicals, and sometimes a targeted mortar course.

Chemical injection damp-proof courses are usually injected into walls about 150mm (or two courses of brickwork) above ground level. By injecting chemicals into walling, usually silicones or siliconates, a band of masonry is produced that has water repellent qualities. The chemicals used cure to act as pore liners, preventing capillary movement of moisture through the tiny pores of the brick, stone or mortars. The chemicals are either solvent or water-based solutions. The solutions are applied at high or low pressures by dedicated pump equipment linked to multiple lances.

Evaluation of physical dpc option

Let us evaluate the physical dpc option in relation to the remedy feasibility factors listed earlier in this chapter:

- **Cost** – usually higher per metre run than chemical injection dpc. (See Table 7).
- **Disruption – externally and internally** – minimal disruption from actual dpc insertion, but providing the access may necessitate stripping out fixtures along walls to be worked on.
- **Durability** – the dpc should last the expected remaining life of the building.
- **Skill availability** – availability of specialist contractors currently restricted
- **Aesthetics/appearance** – little effect on damp-coursed masonry– just a newly pointed bed-joint visible after installation.
- **Reliability** – if installed correctly, completely reliable in preventing upward passage of moisture through an above-ground wall not subject to hydrostatic pressure.
- **Method of damp control/prevention** – the physical dpc is a barrier, but being able to retain traditional soft plasterwork also gives an evaporation opportunity of walling above the dpc.
- **Maintenance/repair** – relatively easy to repair, just entails inserting new dpc material lapped to existing.
- **Access required to install internally** – access to both sides of the wall required.
- **Dampness managed or cured?** – rising dampness from ground or base of wall *cured*, usually once and for all.

The lances incorporate special pressure-tight seals to help force the fluids into the substrate.

Many older properties have at some time had walls drilled to accept the chemicals. So you will see lines of drill holes at the base of masonry walls on a regular basis during survey work. If there do not seem to be any injection drill holes present, the property may have been injected from the inside faces of walls. Some properties have been treated on multiple occasions, as the original chemical damp-proof course may have been deemed to have failed, or a new chemical damp-proof course with the guarantee attached is required by the client for procedural reasons.

The presence of holes does not guarantee that anything has been injected into them, so be careful how you word survey reports. You can insert a pencil to find out the drill angle and some indication of hole depth. Holes for chemical injection have often been drilled downwards at an angle to allow the chemical to soak into masonry and jointing material. This is a risky operation, as existing slate damp courses have been known to be damaged in the process.

On entering a property, look carefully for surface irregularities of the plaster finish at around one metre above floor level – this will nearly always be evidence of replastering. Chemical injection dpcs are most often part of a *combined remedy approach*, with plasters hacked off and replaced along damp-proofed

otherwise a moat is created to help soak water into the subject wall – exactly the opposite of what you are trying to achieve. A channel also reduces the effective width of a pathway.

The remedy proposed

The chosen remedy, to install a new suspended timber floor, independent of the perimeter walls, and in conjunction with skirting ventilation, had not previously been suggested to the client, who agreed to this innovative remedial option after being shown the existing and proposed sketches and given a full explanation of how the proposed strategy should perform.

I have not yet come across a lay client who could not understand carefully explained principles of construction.

A client who understands the key principles, and the pros and cons of alternative remedies, is better able to make the final decision on remedial approach, with an understanding of the relative risks of the available options.

Advantages of a suspended timber floor:

- A timber floor would be in keeping with the traditional architectural style of the building.
- Although now partly rotted, the original floor had performed well, lasting nearly a century.
- Installing a timber floor would be a relatively clean and efficient method of construction.
- It would be a simple matter to lay pine boarding over the floor joists, and so produce an attractive floor finish.

- It would be easy to run cables and pipework under the floor.
- A timber floor of traditional design would not be too costly.
- A timber floor would help ventilate, and hence keep drier, the base of perimeter walls.
- The installation would be non-invasive.
- The construction is accessible and repairable.
- Such a floor installation is 'reversible' i.e. easily removed or changed without risk of damage to the existing building fabric.
- Thermal insulation could be incorporated if requested.

Factory treated timber would be used for the floor structure, to reduce the risk of insect damage in the floor.

A compromise solution was needed, as ideally we would either reduce external levels or raise the floor height to deal with the low-level damp and floor ventilation conundrum. But neither option was available.

Finding reducing the flank pathway problematic, it was necessary to devise a way of ventilating the subfloor. It is possible to use mechanical ventilation systems, but I favour natural ventilation pathways where possible – they are reliable and virtually maintenance-free.

The ventilation solution devised, shown in figure 126, was not an entirely new approach. If we refer to Chapter 5 of *The Repair and Maintenance of Houses* by Melville and Gordon[30], in Figure 62F we see a similar method to ventilate a subfloor subject to high external levels using 'skirting ventilators' – with routes for ventilation provided by ducts. Those authors also suggest that the ventilation may be tested by 'holding a

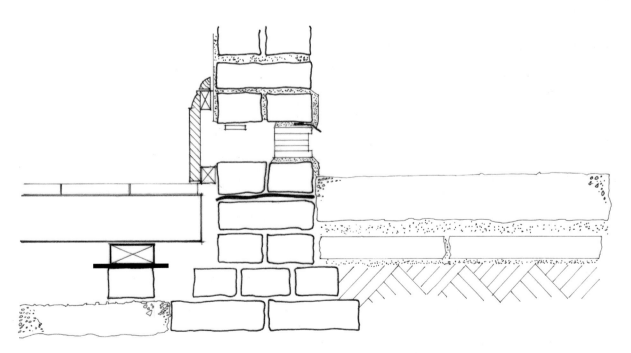

Figure 126: Proposed detail RH.

lighted match against the air vent' – probably now considered a health and safety risk, but fun all the same.

The detailing devised isolates the timber floor from potentially wet perimeter masonry – a key requirement. Ventilation is provided by three terracotta air vents to each flank, as well as existing ventilation below the front step and to the rear end of the floor internally.

The need to provide adequate ventilation cannot be overemphasised, and is flagged up by the BRE[31], who consider it to be a prime requirement for durability of roof timber. The BRE states also that 'the measured moisture content of timber must be maintained below about 22%, and preferably below 20%' to reduce the risk of dry or wet rot development. But woodworm can be a threat to builder's softwood at even lower moisture contents. Woodworm prefer to inhabit damp timber, and larvae have been able to survive in timber with a moisture content as low as 8–10%, although optimum conditions may be within the moisture content range 26–50%[32]. Using pretreated timber, just a little more expensive than the untreated, would reduce the threat of woodworm attack. For health and safety reasons I would always advise the use of pretreated timber, rather than the application of preservatives on site – although cut ends of softwood should be liberally brushed with a suitable general purpose preservative. Wallplates are to be protected by damp courses.

As discussed earlier, low-level masonry seems to have become very damp, due to a low-level penetration, rather than dampness from a below ground source – so the cementitious plinth shown on the sketch proposal should help to reduce this, by providing a barrier at the base of the wall and sealing the gaps between brickwork and concrete path – where water was seen trickling through. The skirting board is spiked onto treated softwood battens, which should last a good many years, and could be quite easily replaced anyway. You may wish to isolate the pre-treated batten from low-level brickwork using a damp-proof membrane. The skirting is easily accessible and would be relatively inexpensive to replace in say 40 years' time if need be.

Skirting boards are a key feature in the control of low level dampness. In many traditional buildings, high skirtings spiked to timber grounds offer an efficient damp control solution. Air pathways behind the skirting help evaporate out any developing dampness, and the plasters, commencing at some height up from the floor are less likely to be affected by low level damp.

Maybe this time round, with an improved specification, the floor could even last for *two* centuries!

Teething trouble?

Soon after floor completion, we discovered distortion to floorboarding to the rear part of the floor. Could leaks be finding their way into the subfloor and creating high humidity to distort floor boards?

Site works

Having cleared out the old sleeper walls, new sleeper walls were built incorporating numerous quarter brick sized openings between bricks for cross-ventilation, with a new damp-proof course bedded on top after filling of the brick frogs with mortar. The floor rests on the sleeper walls sheerly by its weight. Joists are spiked to wallplates, carefully cut back approximately 25mm from the brickwork. Textbooks nearly always show an angled cut to the joist end, which might reduce the chance of debris lodging between joist and wall.

After building the sleeper walls and bedding in the wallplates I gave the client some advice on fixing the floorboards, explaining the importance of using a pair of flooring cramps to squeeze the boards tightly together, to reduce the risk of unsightly gaps developing between boards from shrinking after fitting. The floorboards were nailed down using floor brads, to finish a fraction below the board surface using a nail punch. Always drill small pilot holes before driving in the two nails to each end of a board, to prevent splitting. One or two boards were left un-nailed in order for me to access the subfloor void (where plastic sleeves had been fitted in low-level brickwork) to monitor the moisture condition of brickwork and structural timber after the remediation work.

Three airbricks were installed to each flank. In addition to the flank vents, some opportunity existed for installing floor ventilation along the building frontage. The more traditional terracotta brick offers rather restricted ventilation openings, but I refuse ever to fit a plastic vent into an old building – they just look out of place! You may sometimes need to incorporate support to the ventilation opening cut through the brickwork – traditionally this was done by means of a strong slate bedded in over the air brick.

A cement plinth was run along the flank side of the building to help reduce lateral water penetration.

Figure 127: A straight edge laid across the boards confirms distortion of boards at the rear end of the floor.

A close scrutiny of the boards confirmed 'crowning'. Crowning occurs when a floorboard has expanded to its *upper* surface – as opposed to 'cupping' where boards would appear to have turned upwards towards their edges.

My mind was put at rest. The client explained that just after the skirtings had been installed, the fixed light at the rear end of the room had been replaced, and during the work some rain had got in! The flooring had become wet *from above*. I could breathe again – and hope the boards would return to their original shape once normally 'dry'.

Evaluation and monitoring

The client was extremely pleased with the finished result. The floorboards have been varnished and the finish is attractive and appropriate for an art studio. Because of its modest size, the studio is easily heated by a single electric radiator.

Figure 128: A happy client!.

At the time of publication monitoring is still in progress. This is required:

- to assess whether the structural floor timber remains satisfactorily dry, to reduce any risk of rot or beetle infestation;
- to evaluate the wetness in the brickwork below floor level, where the new plinth should hopefully reduce wetting from collecting rainwater.

Step by step guide: diagnosis – remediation – monitoring

Step 1 – Assess floor condition.

Step 2 – Transfer levels using a straight edge and spirit level.

Step 3 – Pour water to check surface water drainage and likely entry points for water.

Step 4 – Draw up a scaled sketch of the wall base to aid diagnosis and remedy formulation.

Step 5 – Formulate a remedy and identify key site supervision issues.

Step 6 – Install the new timber floor.

Step 7 – Install support measures – air vents and cement plinth.

Step 7 – Install ventilated skirting, leaving key sections available for easy removal for monitoring visits.

Step 8 – Monitoring.

CASE STUDY 2: TRICKY BILLERICAY – TO MANAGE OR CURE? THAT IS THE QUESTION!

Figure 129: Not the kind of property you would expect to have wall base damp problems. Surely they knew how to install a dpc 30 years ago?

You will know about 'bridging' of cavity walls by wall ties that hold blobs of fallen mortar from careless bricklaying, and may have heard of or even seen examples of lintel problems, when metal cavity wall lintels collect water from rain penetration, and allow it to track sideways towards the lintel ends, to cause damp patches either side of a window head.

Figure 130: *A perfect pristine living room, white walls, no stains, no mould, so 'no apparent defects' – but did the modest pin probe readings in the skirtings of 12–15% alert the surveyor to a damp problem? In this age of house you would expect lower readings and would have obtained them in the 'dry zone'.*

But the Billericay defect you are about to savour has not yet received the attention it deserves. Perhaps it is too often mistakenly labelled as 'rising damp', with the remedy an internal masking of dampness by waterproof plasters. Once masking of dampness is planned, there will be less effort to fully understand where the dampness came from and how it got where it did.

The aim of this case study is really three-fold:

- to explain what symptoms low-level cavity wall bridging could present in a house survey;
- to assess how the dampness got to where it did; and then the tricky bit …
- to devise steps to remedy the damp problem.

The wall base damp we describe in this case study was not flagged up by the homebuyer surveyor, who surely noticed the marginally high damp meter readings I picked up. This was partly because ground floor rooms were nicely decorated, and the surveyor may have been reluctant to use the damp meter pins because the house owner was present. The surveyor may also have failed to realise the significance of marginally high damp meter readings. If you are not allowed to use damp meter pins, as much as you'd wish, make sure you explain in any survey report *the implications* of not being allowed to do so. If damp meter readings are even just a little higher in one part of a building, or maybe higher up or lower down on a wall – you need to find out why – or recommend 'further investigation'. The homebuyer surveyor paid my fee for the dampness investigation!

At Billericay, the damp problem first came to the attention of the owner some months after moving in, when skirting boarding was removed during alteration works. The owner was surprised to find rot and insect damage on the back of the skirting. Various remedial treatment companies came to quote for work. Remedies varied in scope, and the owner became confused. An independent investigation was needed to clarify the cause of the damp problem and how best to deal with it.

The author's subsequent diagnosis was very much in line with two of the three remedial treatment companies – but the approaches to remedy diverged somewhat!

Contractors tend to look for substantiation to install the remedy they are geared up to provide. So never ask a damp-proofer to inspect a leaking gutter – because you may receive a quotation to chemically inject it! Often the route is to mask dampness, rather than carry out external building work, hard landscaping, etc. for a longer-term cure. Masking dampness often involves a new plaster system that can quickly become dry and be decorated. This may, of course, be a suitable approach on some occasions – but not as a matter of course.

Symptoms presented inside and outside the building

Internally, the walls and joinery are visually perfect! So be on your guard. Even in a thorough dampness investigation, I was finding it difficult to take as many damp meter readings on walls and skirtings as I would have liked – the new owner was watching closely over my shoulder, wincing as metal prongs pricked the pristine walls. The skirtings were chamfered and offered no useful concealed rebate to insert the pins.

EMM readings were noted on a floor plan to assess any patterns. Pin probe readings recorded to timber skirtings clustered in the mid-20% range – sometimes as high as 30% – along both external and some internal solid walls. Wall plasters recorded pin probe readings again of a maximum of 30R/R, but the readings tailed off to about 12–16 at a height of 300mm above floor level. This damp reading profile was very consistent along the walls, but there was no evidence of plaster deterioration, e.g. salt damp. If salt

Figure 131: *Where the wall base seemed most affected by lateral low-level damp penetration, along the north flank, a section of skirting was taken off and was clearly damaged by wood boring weevil. Much of the skirting in the house may well have been a little damp – but probably not quite damp enough to have succumbed to this particular insect's tunnel boring. Typical weevil damage is a shredding effect of the timber along the grain.*

dampness was present, moisture would be derived mainly from below ground, and we would expect to find much higher damp meter readings, often 100R/R and salty stains, blistering plasters, etc.

The readings were indicative of walls and skirtings *just* damp enough to deteriorate slowly over time. The flank was probably suffering the most dampness – it was along this wall that the skirting degradation was found by the home owner.

In the rear dining room, the two remedial treatment companies had carried out some destructive examination – a small section of masonry had been removed from the base of the internal cavity wall skin in two positions, and some floor screeding taken up, and interestingly a hole broken through the concrete floor slab. A thin dpm was found at the base of the floor inspection hole.

It was possible to see a very *dark and damp* mortar bed between the dpm and dpc of the inner cavity skin. See figures 133 and 134. The damp mortar bed later carbide tested at 6.5% AMC –very damp!

The cavity was viewed via the two brick openings – and it was possible to actually see wet mortar debris at the base of the cavity wall.

On the morning of my survey it had rained, and the owner informed me that the mortar bed had definitely darkened after the rain. Low-level damp penetration was quite clearly at least one of the sources of moisture causing a damp problem. Was it the lead source?

The wall plaster had been originally applied down to the concrete slab – therefore the plastering had been carried out *before* floor screeding.

Externally, it was immediately obvious that the base of the cavity wall was subject to damp penetration. The damp-proof course was a mere 60mm above paving level along one wall run, with the average perhaps one brick course. The wall base appeared darkened from direct damp penetration, with the flank wall showing also classic green staining up to three courses up the external cavity skin.

Horizontal damp courses can control or stop dampness passing them vertically, but cannot prevent dampness tracking through the wall laterally below or above them.

The fact that the cavity wall dpc was situated less than the Building Regulations minimum of 150mm above ground level, may not be significant in terms of the resistance of the wall base to low-level damp penetration, but could mean the wall base is subject to rainsplash above the dpc. It will also usually mean that there is an unsatisfactory relationship between level of external finished yard level and cavity wall detailing at low level. When yard levels are too high, dampness that does penetrate the wall base can cause more problems once in the cavity zone. Bricks splashed by rain often suffer more frost damage directly below the outer skin dpc, as water soaking up brickwork stops at the dpc level.

Figure 132: This flank is dank! Wetness hugs the pavings and seeps into low-level masonry. There is little sunlight to dry things out on this north-facing elevation. Pity this pathway wasn't distanced from the house wall. The damp-proof course is just above paving level, surface water is soaking into the cavity wall – note the dark wet patches. A higher dpc would not stop the lateral low-level damp penetration. The fact that the outer skin dpc was visible just a course of bricks above paving, could mean wetting of the wall base by rainsplash could cause water penetration and especially so if the cavity wall is full of debris and able to offer a bridging route across for penetrating damp.

Pavings were levelled on 'dabs', so joints would be likely to be open and water would be able to collect underneath. This in effect creates an external perimeter reservoir of water that could feed into an unprotected wallbase.

Note how the cavity fill had been terminated only one course below the dpc level. Mortar droppings could therefore easily provide a bridge for wetness to soak upwards, and in this case directly to a very soft and sandy mortar course between floor dpm and inner skin dpc.

Dampness could also soak through the brickwork just below the floor dpm, as the polythene dpm was trimmed short of the cavity face of the inner cavity skin.

While tamping concrete, probably with a long timber board, the plastic floor dpm would have probably been holed and chafed along the sharp brick arris at 'X' – so wetness in the brickwork could easily soak through to the soft sandy mortar bed above the dpm.

Imagine the outer skin dpc a course higher – would this affect lateral damp penetration? Probably not. But *once inside the cavity*, with dpcs only a course above the wetted-up cavity zone, moisture has but a short distance to soak up and cause a lot of problems.

Remedy

Efforts to *isolate* plasters, skirtings or screed from a wet mortar bed joint above the dpm are **management.**

Efforts to clear the cavity of debris, which would certainly help reduce or completely stop moisture tracking through to the internal plasters, screed and skirting – are again really **management**. The cavity debris has *only become a route for moisture* because of unsatisfactory paving installations that feed wetness into the wall. If we cleared the cavity, the wall base

would still become wet within the cavity from low-level damp penetration. Low-level masonry would be wet from adjacent surface water, and masonry would be likely to suffer frost damage up to dpc height. So masking would allow some of the adverse damp effects to continue unabated.

A **cure** is a more fundamental remedy, and in this case would address the poor relationship between external pavings and the cavity wall base detailing. If pavings were lowered sufficiently, the cavity wall would take in less surface water. Just removing pavings and creating flower borders would help, as rainwater would percolate down into the soil rather than collect, pool and splash against low level brickwork. Later we show how, instead of lowering pavings wholesale, we might just locally lower external yards by forming a drainage channel. Forming drain channels is not uncommon, but such remedies for damp have until now not been fully explained in published works.

A cure should be more successful over the longer term. It not only creates dry conditions at the decorative

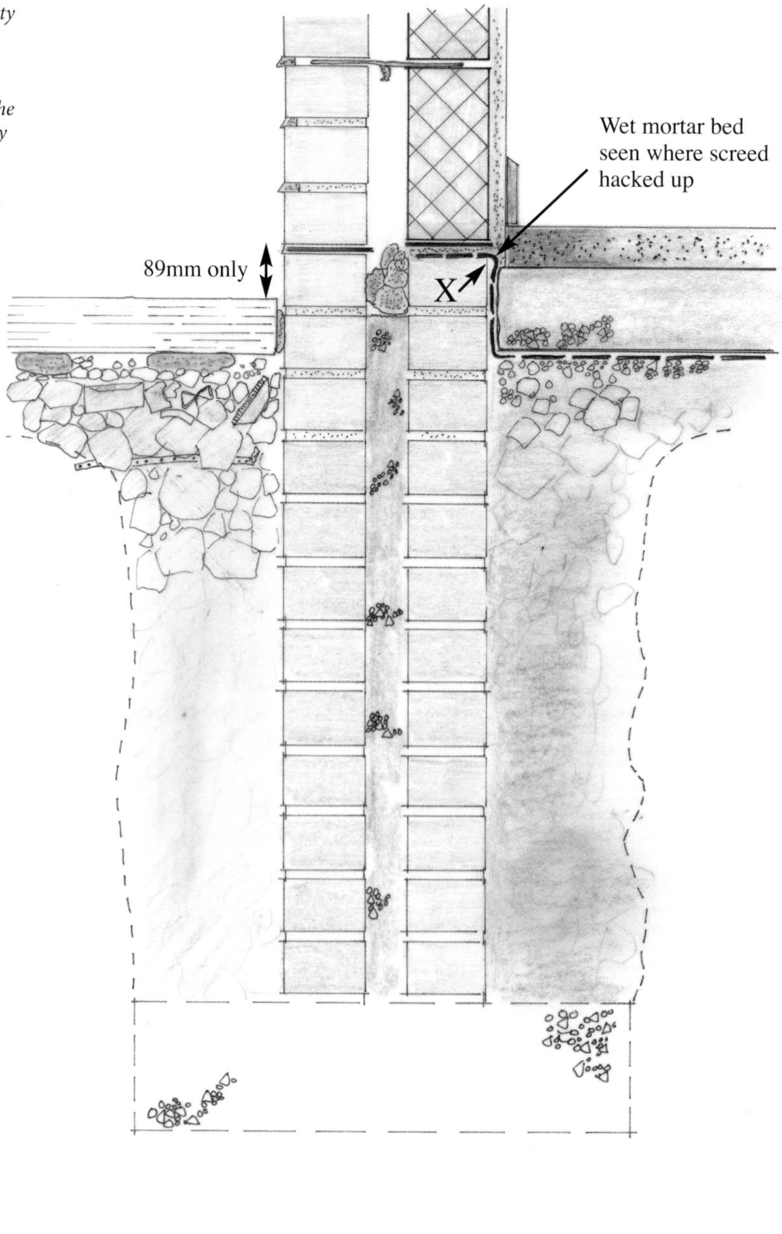

Figure 133: Billericay 1970s cavity wall – as found. 1972 Building Regulations stipulated that the cavity should extend to not less than 150mm below the level of the lower dpc. At Billericay the cavity wall infill extends upwards too far – creating the potential for accumulated debris in the cavity to create a damp bridge.

Wet mortar bed seen where screed hacked up

89mm only

X

6 Rot and woodworm

INTRODUCTION

If you are a general property surveyor and find rot or an insect infestation that you may be unsure of, this does not mean you need to always pass on *all* responsibility for remediation to a 'specialist'. Rot or woodworm damage is nearly always a signal that there has been too much dampness at position X in the building. Standard building repairs will often suffice, coupled with measures to eliminate the moisture ingress.

There are many informative texts on wood rots and insect infestation. They range from those written robustly supporting the chemical treatment industry, to those seeking to remedy rot and insect damage by a 'holistic' approach to moisture management.

The chemical treatment approach is well-known to surveyors. Surveyors tend to pass on rot and insect damage cases to the remedial treatment industry – and chemicals feature strongly in guaranteed remedies.

In the chemical treatment approach, existing organisms are more or less killed off, and preservatives remaining in or on the timber or masonry act as a defence against future rot outbreak or colonisation by insects. Chemical treatments are either 'blanket treatments' of a whole building element, or are targeted to a specific zone of the building.

In the holistic approach (sometimes referred to as the environmental control approach) the main aim would be to manage dampness more effectively in the building, so conditions that favour rots, mould and insect infestations do not develop or persist. This requires a good working knowledge of the building as a whole.

And there are remedies that combine use of chemicals with management of dampness. Using chemicals can help speed up remedial works. In assessing the extent of a rot outbreak, the amount of stripping out can be reduced if optical instruments such as borescopes are used to check condition of voids/concealed areas.

Rot and insect damage is really nothing more than a signal that there is a 'damp problem'. So eliminate the damp, and you more than often eliminate the rot or insect threat. Every life form on this planet needs water to survive.

DRY ROT

Key issues

We look for as many field marks as we can to correctly identify the fungus causing timber degradation, in the same way as we might identify a tree by leaves, buds, bark or flowers. Less experienced surveyors have been known to state in reports that cobwebs or even plant roots are conducting strands – i.e. evidence of fungal decay! This would happen far less if surveying students had been shown examples of timber decay, either on a site visit or in the classroom.

To confuse matters, some wet rots also produce quite thick conductor strands (e.g. the rather feathery rhizomes of the white pore or mine fungus, *fibroporia vaillantii*). These strands are whiter than dry rot strands, and remain flexible when dry. So it could be foolhardy for anybody but a mycologist to identify a rot from rhizomes alone. However, although general house surveyors may not be fully competent in identifying a rot or beetle infestation, they can have the advantage of an open mind concerning remediation – and may be more inclined than a remedial treatment surveyor to specify traditional building repairs.

So exactly what is 'dry rot'?

It is said that dry rot accounts for £400 million pounds' worth of damage annually[33]. In essence, dry rot is a fungus, it has a life cycle that requires a spore to germinate. It is a brown rot. It destroys wood's cellulose, leaving the lignin.

The spores are more or less everywhere. Although we commonly describe the life cycle as fruiting body-then-spore, you could rightly ask how this tiny spore came into existence without having been released from the fruiting body – which of course developed from the fungus which grew from a single hypha sprouting from the seed – the spore! It is very much a chicken-and-egg life cycle. Although you would find it hard to single out a spore sized at 1/100mm, collections of dry rot spores form a *reddish dust* and would confirm the presence of a fruiting body. The spore would need to be deposited on timber in the right conditions for germination. The spore germinates, producing a small tube-like thread (the hypha), which resembles a fine root. Ultimately a mass of hyphae forms and is then called *mycelium*. You can see an example of this growth in figure 173. As hyphae multiply, timber gradually decomposes and loses its strength. The fungus can produce conductor strands to support or spread growth, and sporophores or fruiting bodies to produce spores to further spread the fungus. The fruiting bodies are a rusty brown colour with white margins. They seem to be produced particularly when the organism is threatened or suffers change in its environmental living conditions, which it prefers to be stable.

Key requirements for fungus development:

- a viable spore;
- damp or wet wood – for germination, moisture content close to fibre saturation, 28–30%, RH 95–98%; for growth, optimum 20–55%;
- suitable temperature – optimum for growth: 15–22°C; and
- oxygen – in confined spaces the fungus can use up oxygen in the air – making it dangerous for humans to enter.

Predictions vary about the rate of spread of dry rot , from 2.25mm/day to 5mm/day to 11mm/day. Similarly, decay rates quoted may differ.

For basic requirements and biology, see Chapter 7 in *Timber Decay in Buildings*[32].

Dry rot seems to thrive where calcium is present in addition to the basic timber food source. This could be why dry rot is so commonly found in timber close to or embedded in lime mortar based brickwork or lime plaster ceilings using timber laths for support. It is thought that dry rot uses the calcium in lime to 'control acid-mediated degradation'[32]. Dry rot is also said to need iron.

Dry rot treatment and timber repairs – issues of remedy selection

The source of moisture causing a dry rot attack must be stopped; just doing this will *eventually* kill it off. The remedial treatment industry has long-standing experience in researching and eradicating woodworm and rots – although having perhaps rather a bias towards chemical treatments. The guidance offered in the chemical treatment manufacturer's handbook: *Dry Rot and its Control*[34] stresses the need to firstly stem any water ingress, pointing out that this in itself may be sufficient to 'eventually control and eliminate the activity'.

These words of wisdom might have come from a source promoting the environmental control of dry rot, rather than a chemicals supplier! However, in practical terms this approach on its own is not always an option. Few surveyors would be confident to just starve the

fungus of moisture, and few house surveyors would have the monitoring skills or the equipment to know for sure whether the building was actually drying out after primary repairs and maintenance. The biggest problem is just the sheer time it takes for masonry and the associated components and finishes to dry back down to a safe moisture equilibrium, after perhaps years of water ingress. However, the oft-cited drying time of 'one month for an inch thickness of masonry' does not take account of the fast drying times that can now be achieved using modern drying regimes and equipment. (See Chapter 1.)

Be under no illusions concerning those who support the 'environmental control' of dry rot. They are certainly not just theorists or academics, but practical researchers who try out new methods in real buildings. Their aim is not to bring down the chemical treatment industry, but to simply find the best way to deal with dry rot, with the starting point a greater understanding of the organism's biology, and most particularly the conditions it needs to grow and thrive. Their approach may be viewed as that of avoiding a *misuse* of chemicals, rather than never ever using them. Misuse means using too much chemical, applying it incorrectly or where it presents a risk to the building or its inhabitants or users, including animals, pets and plants.

Sadly chemical treatment is too often a substitute for careful detailing of construction elements, components and materials. More 'natural' approaches to dry rot eradication require closer supervision of site works and a greater understanding of how to control the built environment to deny dry rot the niche it seeks to grow and thrive.

We also need to realise that close supervision of construction work means regular site visits which create fees, perhaps not within the client's budget. More often than not, supervision of refurbishment by surveyors is sadly little more than contract administration – in other words a paper chase. So surveyors may choose to rely on a quite heavy-handed chemical treatment of the dry rot and the legal security guarantees provided. The costs of the dry rot treatment will usually be but a small proportion of the total refurbishment outlay, so will be lost amongst much larger figures.

A more conservative approach to dry rot treatment is more likely when minimum intervention is a prime consideration (e.g. when there is a need to avoid damaging or disturbing as little building fabric or finishes as possible, such as in a listed or historic building). The BRE[35] advises 'rapid drying' of the structure. This would involve specialist drying techniques and monitoring, but may be a useful strategy.

Whichever approach or combination of approaches is decided upon, it is important not only to starve the relevant zone of the building of water ingress by repairing or renewing roofing, upgrading rainwater goods, repairing external brick pointing, etc., but also to help as much moisture as possible that is already within the fabric to escape out. The less water we apply to the fabric during dry rot treatment, the better. The longer we delay replastering, the more time we give the brickwork to dry out.

We need to consider how we might ventilate the structure, to prevent a build-up of moisture in the future and help any lingering water find a way out by evaporation or drainage. We could consider using less dense internal plaster finishes, that might help the wall breathe. Although more costly, traditional lime plasters might be worth considering, to help maintain a breathing wall. Certainly application of hard and dense cementitious renders internally can only trap moisture within the wall's thickness. Allowing masonry to remain too damp or wet for too long could be providing the much-needed moisture for any lingering dry rot to re-establish.

Dry rot treatment used to be more chemical-based, with large areas of masonry flooded with fungicides. The timber remedial treatment industry uses chemicals more conservatively these days

Many of the more dangerous chemicals have now effectively been banned for use as in situ remedial treatments, e.g. PCP (pentachlorophenol), TBTO (tributyl tin oxide), dieldrin and lindane. Active ingredients in common use for remedial treatment of timber today are permethrin and borates – chemicals considered safe enough to use in sensitive wildlife sites where nesting and roosting barn owls or bats might be at risk. Chemicals used for remedial timber treatment must be approved by the Health and Safety Executive (HSE) in accordance with the *Control of Pesticides Regulations* 1986. Products displaying an HSE number will be listed as safe.

It was once common practice to blowlamp masonry in the vicinity of an outbreak. Many surveyors today will never have held a blowlamp, and fewer still will have used one in anger. I can assure you they are wonderful. Rideout makes the point that using a blowlamp for treating dry rot could start a fire, so it is not altogether surprising that this practice has pretty well ceased[32]! Rideout also points out, however, that a blowlamp is only likely to have an effect on the surface. Interestingly, in the 1920s Blake[36] advised the use of a blowlamp to help dry out damp masonry.

WET ROT

Wet rot does not promote the same kind of fearful reaction as dry rot – yet it causes the most damage inside and outside our homes and businesses. We have all seen rotting window cills, when perhaps external decoration had been delayed too long, or perhaps skirting boards that have sucked up too much moisture from damp walls or floors. It is usually considered that timber with a moisture content of 20% or more might succumb to the fungus. But beware: thicker

skirtings or framings registering only marginal damp meter readings could actually be much damper – and even rotting unseen behind. Take wet rot seriously – Case Study 2 of this chapter shows us just how much havoc the fungus can wreak.

The commonest wet rot fungus is *coniophora puteana* – the cellar fungus. It causes brown rot that consumes the cellulose in wood. Unfortunately for us surveyors, the fungus breaks down timber, producing cracking both along and across the grain, so the damaged can be confused with the cuboidal cracking of timber typical of dry rot. However, there are other clues to help us.

Fruiting bodies of this particular wet rot fungus are according to the BRE rarely seen, whereas the fruiting bodies of dry rot are more common. But beware! Rideout informs us that 'the fruit is relatively common in buildings and when it is found it is invariably called dry rot'[32]. Colour Plate 14 of Rideout's text shows wet rot fruiting bodies on a timber soffit. They are olivey green, and have white edges, and I must admit, they do look a little like dry rot sporophores!

Dry rot tends to damage timber to produce cubes, with the timber damaged for its full thickness, whereas wet rot damaged timber so often has a veneer of seemingly sound timber. This wet rot fungus produces brown branching surface mycelium. The timber darkens as it rots.

Wet rot outbreaks tend to be more localised than those of dry rot. Perhaps the cause is faulty plumbing. Maybe a very damp wall or floor produces joinery damage from wet rot.

The BRE Guide[37] will give you yet more useful pointers to successful identification, including a comprehensive key for identifying fungal growths in buildings. The author's knowledge of timber rot and insect infestation was helped considerably by attendance at a BWPDA course leading to the qualification 'CSRT' – the standard qualification for remedial treatment surveyors. But bear it in mind that it's probably wisest to spend your valuable time working out *why the building is damp enough for rot* – and devising improved detailing for a drier building – than exactly identifying a particular rot species and homing in on its obscure Latin name. In survey reports, however, you must not get the name of a rot or a wood damaging insect *wrong*! So, until such times as you have confirmed the insect or fungus responsible for damage, simply label the cause as a 'rot' or an 'insect attack'.

Dry rot conductor strands are often quite thick, white or greyish – often spreading behind wall linings – and are brittle when dry. Do not be confused by the thickish feathery conductor strands of the wet rot *fibroporia vaillanti* (mine fungus) which the author has also discovered creeping through gaps and cracks in masonry.

The remedy for wet rot is usually to cure the leak or damp, strip out and replace at least the structurally damaged timber, and making sure good detailing helps keep the new timber dry. Good detailing could utilise barriers to keep timber away from any potentially damp substrate, ventilation to help keep timber dry, and measures that helps drain any collecting water away from vulnerable timber. New timber is best pre-treated – if only to deter woodworm, which can damage timber with a moisture content even below 20%. Rideout[32] suggests application of fungicidal paste preservatives for timber during the drying-out phase after repairs have been executed to stop water ingress.

In old property, 'built-in timber' is a wet rot risk – when the masonry around the timber can be damp. New detailing might be designed to hold timber away from the damp masonry – for example on a metal support.

Most wet rot damage is by brown rots, such as *coniphora puteana* or *fibroporia vaillanti*, but can also be from white rots such as *phellinus contiguous* – more common on external joinery – where timber is degraded, bleached and stringy and the fruiting body brown and porous, a little like a hard, encrusted moss.

COMMON FURNITURE BEETLE

Introduction

We have all seen woodworm damage by the common furniture beetle (CFB), whether in chairs and tables or boards and joists.

Do not be influenced by those who say that CFB causes little structural damage to buildings in this country. To a certain extent it does depend on what we mean by 'structure'. For me and probably most other surveyors in Britain, the floorboard of a traditional floor *is* 'structural', as well as the rafters, purlins, roof battens, collars, ties, ceiling rafters, ceiling joists, floor joists, wallplates, partition studs, noggins. etc. so often discovered peppered with flight holes!

Many biocides and insecticides act to control and kill quite a range of organisms, so exact identification may not be as critical a factor as some experts would lead us to believe. Try and avoid the use of latin names! Latin is now rarely taught, and no longer spoken in the UK.

CFB LIFE CYCLE

Rather like the chicken and egg, which comes first – the egg, or the beetle that lays it?

Adult female beetles lay eggs in or on suitable timber – and prefer timber with a roughened surface, or with cracks and crevices, favouring too the end grain of timber, or even a pupal chamber.

Eggs hatch and larvae emerge. Larvae bore into the wood, and may continue boring for several years.

Eventually they munch and burrow towards the wood surface, pupate and by metamorphosis change into a beetle, that chews its way out from the wood leaving a roundish exit or flight hole. Emergence of the common furniture beetle is between May and September. During the time that the larvae are tunnelling away inside the timber, there would be no visible external evidence of their presence. The evidence is only visible once the beetle bites its way out to leave a hole, together with collectable and identifiable bore dust (frass).

For this reason it can be risky to pronounce in a report that woodworm in timber are not present – they could be working away as yet unseen. Even after timber has been chemically treated, woodworm can still be active, but might succumb eventually to the insecticide, which will often only have protected the outer margins of the timber.

If you wished to check whether an infestation was live by filling up flight holes or covering areas of timber with paper or card, remember that you would need to wait till the end of the flight season to find this out.

Timber of less than 12 per cent moisture content should be safe from woodworm. The optimum moisture level for growth of larvae would be much higher. Detailed discussion on optimum conditions for woodworm colonisation can be found in Chapter 5 of *Timber Decay in Buildings*[32].

Identification of insect responsible for damage

You will find useful advice for surveyors in *Surveying Buildings*[38]. The standard guide to identification, *Recognising Wood Rot and Insect Damage in Buildings*[37] explains in great detail how you might confirm the cause of wood damage in buildings. Basic identification advice follows below:

- **Bore dust – frass**: usually collects in cobwebs under attacked timber – light in colour, approximating to the colour of the freshly cut timber. Lemon-shaped pellets, gritty.
- **Beetle**: 3–5 mm long.
- **Larvae**: up to 6mm long.
- **Flight holes**: 1–2mm diameter. Recently cut holes would exhibit sharp edges and you would see the lighter inner sides of the hole. Eventually this light hole interior would darken from oxidisation. You will very easily insert a screwdriver into damaged timber. Timber will typically be quite crumbly where badly affected.
- **Damage** is restricted mainly to sapwood, except where rot is present.

You may find it worth investing in an illuminated car map reader or a 10x magnification lens to aid your inspection of flight holes, frass, insect damage and the insects themselves.

You may find other insect holes and damage on the same area of damaged timber – e.g. the smaller holes of parasitic wasps, or in damper wood, the damage from wood-boring weevil.

Where to find woodworm damage

The BRE tell us to expect woodworm where timber is damp – but follow the example of many surveying textbooks and single out timber near loft hatches or in stair cupboards! It always seems strange to me that woodworm appear to prefer timber most likely to be inspected by their arch enemy – the surveyor. It is surely under the stairs or just near a loft trap that surveyors *are most likely to look!*

There may often be evidence of woodworm and weevil in boards and joists near a WC pan, but this is not always due to WC pan leaks. Floor joists may be built into a wall and be very damp, or floorboards may be damp too – butted against damp masonry or plasters. Ground floors are becoming increasingly difficult to investigate due to the popularity of laminated flooring – so often fitted over original timber boardings. Woodworm may not be discovered until the infestation is quite advanced.

Figure 163: A classic case of misidentification? Yes, these are 'flight holes'! We hope you can pick these out on this pine door. But around a circular hole-free zone – about the size of a dart board …

Should we chemically treat a woodworm infestation?

If you follow through the decision-making flowcharts contained in BRE Good Repair Guide 13[39], you should be able to answer this question quite confidently. But you may also have sympathy for those who have a strong aversion to any type of chemical treatment. Those who have written most fervently about the risks of chemical timber treatments have almost certainly had an effect on how surveyors now remediate woodworm and rot. More and more surveyors are cautious concerning use of chemicals, and would more often recommend a very focused or 'targeted' treatment, developing improvements to building detailing to make conditions less favourable for any aspiring woodworm or fungal spore. Chemical suppliers have responded by marketing safer and more user/building-friendly chemicals.

For any woodworm or rot outbreak, we have to decide between chemical and non-chemical remediation. Consider each case on its merits and make sure that, if you do decide to use or specify chemicals, the treatment is carried out as safely as possible and in accordance with current good practice advice.

Sustainable remediation would in most cases involve careful upgrade of construction detailing in tandem with targeted chemical treatment. To ignore one side of this remedy equation is to court trouble. No matter how carefully treated, a joist end built into a wet wall will *eventually* rot. If it does, any guarantee will probably be invalidated as the property has not been properly maintained, i.e. kept free of undue dampness.

So for most scenarios consider:

- *targeted chemical treatment of retained timber or use of pre-treated new timber;*
- *isolate all timber from damp masonry; and*
- *ventilate it wherever possible.*

This is the remediation trilogy for rot or woodworm.

The BRE[37] classified CFB as a 'Damage Category A' insect – meaning that they would normally consider insecticidal treatment to be necessary.

It is clear from this advice that the BRE are supportive of chemical treatment against woodworm, i.e. CFB.

The BRE states in Part 1 of GRG 13[39] that:

'Infestations, [i.e. of common furniture beetle] even of long standing, are usually of little structural significance and therefore require little or no replacement of timber.'

In the author's opinion this is an underestimation of the amount of damage we see in the UK year after year from this particular woodworm. Much of the softwood in British homes is fast-grown pine, with a significant proportion of vulnerable sapwood. Please refer to figures 163–165.

Most textbooks cite CFB as the insect causing the greatest amount of timber damage in this country. As

Figure 164: Note how the woodworm damage is restricted to the outer sapwood at board edges. This is very common. Such a floorboard would crush at its edges when levered up by a surveyor's bolster or crowbar.

Figure 165: Even a well-built raised timber ground floor, with damp-proof courses under its wall plates, can suffer woodworm attack. This softwood joist has woodworm damage along its underside, i.e. to its outer sapwood. Old suspended floors are often built directly off damp lime sprinkled earth. The void can often be a little humid – making the softwood damp enough to suit wood-boring insects, say 16–18% MC. Timber close to or built into very damp masonry will commonly become much damper and suffer rot and wood-boring weevil damage. Suspended floors with a concrete 'oversite', can suffer a worse fate – when water ingress creates a pond on top of the slab and timber becomes covered in moulds.

mentioned above, the BRE appears to understate the sheer amount of damage woodworm can cause. This is neither the author's experience nor that of many remedial treatment surveyors consulted, who have usually been quite categorical concerning just how often CFB causes damage to structural timber.

The two-part Good Repair Guide 13[39] covers 'identifying and assessing damage', and 'treating damage'. The very title of Part 2 leads one to suspect the emphasis will be on 'treating' woodworm attack, and 'treating' means application of chemicals to kill off insects and kill or prevent damage by others that follow in the future. Part 1 covers basic information on the various wood borers; where to find the damage, information on the main culprits, etc. There is a sketch showing where one might find insect damage, and typically crosses are placed where the general house surveyor would normally look, e.g. near a loft trap, near a sanitary appliance, in the stairs cupboard! In Part 2 is a flow chart for decision making on whether or not to apply remedial treatments – i.e. chemicals.

In designing any remediation of woodworm damage we would very quickly move down the left hand column of the BRE flowchart from:

- 'Has insect damaged wood been found during inspection?' (YES) to
- 'Is damage of a type which could be active?' (YES) to
- 'Are there obvious fresh flight holes or fresh dust?' (YES) to
- 'Is damage widespread?' (YES) to
- **'Apply remedial preservative treatment to all timbers of affected floor or roof area.'**

But the BRE chart incorporates some quite complex threads of questioning too, and would veer away from chemical treatment in the following instances:

- there is evidence of previous treatment;
- infestation is inactive;
- less than 20% of timber is sapwood;
- timber affected is not structurally important;
- fresh bore dust (frass) or flight holes not present; or
- the damage is not widespread.

If the damage is not widespread there is the option of very localised and 'targeted' chemical treatment or timber replacement.

There are many surveying challenges here. It could be quite expensive to confirm a previous treatment. It would help if you knew the company that carried treatment out, as once the type of chemicals used were known, specific tests could be commissioned to verify this. If you have no knowledge on the type of treatments used, then quite a number of tests would need to be paid for.

Confirming whether or not an infestation is active could be difficult from a snapshot pre-purchase inspection. The definitive clue is the presence of freshly formed flight holes – so shine a torch across the woodwormed timber and look for light-coloured wood inside the hole, i.e. the colour of the freshly cut timber. Then seek out piles of freshly emitted bore dust (frass). Once timber is cut, oxidation darkens it.

As a general property surveyor you should be able yourself to know whether damaged timber is 'structural', but if in doubt, consult a structural engineer. The difficulty here is that damage may be quite serious but within the invisible thickness of a timber. There exist quite sophisticated instruments for assessing internal condition of timber, such as the 'resistograph', which drives a very narrow drill into timber, and creates a print out of the varying resistance through the member's thickness. Carpenters have in the past traditionally tested timbers using a hammer, or perhaps a wood bit driven in by hand drill – to get a feel for varying resistance as rotten wood or voids are encountered.

Establishing just how *widespread* a woodworm attack is could be a daunting task.

To fully check out just a timber ground floor could take hours! Many properties these days are covered by laminated boarding or glued vinyl, making inspection very difficult.

There may be a limited opportunity to actually inspect the timbers. Houses are likely to be fully accessible when they are empty between sale and purchase. This might be for a limited time only. Once carpet and furniture arrives, the floors become yet again difficult to access. So precautionary treatment is commonly carried out at this time. The preparatory work to treat, i.e. lifting every fifth floorboard, would be the same amount of access required for a full inspection – so there is a strong case to treat at this time.

Many properties have been given precautionary treatment against woodworm, probably often just because it can be so time-consuming and difficult to fully assess the scale and significance of an outbreak. This could be 'blanket treatment' when a fuller inspection might confirm a very localised treatment only to be necessary.

If you do plan to specify or carry out chemical treatment of timbers *as a precaution,* then the decision to treat should be taken following a COSHH (Control of Substances Hazardous to Health) assessment, in which amongst other things ease of future access should be considered.

You could learn more about past treatment by desk top research and site enquiries:

- Past maintenance records could shed light on past chemical applications.
- Guarantees may be available for specialist work and may even detail the exact chemicals used and the extent of treatment.
- You may find joinery repairs that indicate remediation of past insect or rot problems.

Monitoring woodworm

Church wardens have been known to keep records of numbers of death watch beetle collected. If you have the opportunity to check a building for common furniture beetle (CFB) over a period of time, you could affix paper or card to vulnerable timbers and check for flight holes periodically. You could, as Rideout mentions, clog up flight holes with furniture polish and observe whether new holes appear[32]. Such investigations take time, as the beetles only emerge in the summer. Monitoring might take a year.

In practice, most house surveyors will be making a one-off visit to a property, most often for a pre-purchase inspection. Such an inspection might only allow a few minutes for assessment of a woodworm outbreak – but in a limited inspection it would be often be quite possible to look closely at discovered woodworm affected areas to see if the holes appear fresh or old, and to verify the type of insect responsible for the damage.

Being the most common wood borer in UK properties, a house surveyor should have knowledge of the CFB. To pronounce an infestation active or inactive requires quite considerable experience. So many cases are passed on to specialist remedial contractors, where a chemical treatment and the accompanying guarantee might be the end result.

Timber treatment and the law

By Dr CJD George, with acknowledgment to the PCA for advice given.

Table 8: Legislation and the remedial treatment industry

Health and Safety at Work etc. Act 1974	Any company employing five or more people must have a Safety Policy Statement. The employer is responsible for the provision of a safe working environment, instruction, training and information on the safe use of plant, equipment, materials and safety equipment. The employee has a duty, whilst at work, to take *reasonable* care for the health and safety of himself and other persons who may be affected by his acts or omissions at work. He must comply with any duty or requirement imposed on his employer, or any other person by or under any of the relevant statutory provisions.
Control of Pollution Act 1974	Control of chemicals and their possible seepage into waterways.
Wildlife and Countryside Act 1981	Under this Act, bats are designated a protected species. It is an offence to kill or even to disturb any bats.
Classification, Packaging and Labelling of Dangerous Substances Regulations 1984	These regulations refer to dangerous substances, which fall into the following categories: Explosive, Oxidising, Extremely Flammable, Highly Flammable, Flammable, Very Toxic, Toxic, Harmful, Corrosive, or Irritant. The regulations define the type of packaging into which products may be put and the detail of the labelling requirements. Most products fall into the categories Flammable, Harmful, Corrosive and Irritant, but not the more dangerous categories. As far as is known there are no remedial treatment chemicals that are toxic or very toxic.
Food and the Environment Protection Act 1985 (FEPA)	This legislation allows the government to impose a variety of regulations. It extends the *Health and Safety at Work etc. Act* 1974 to include the 'environment' as well as the workplace.
Control of Pesticides Regulations 1986	Only products which have been registered are allowed to be offered for sale. Anyone using, transporting, storing or selling pesticides must be trained to carry out these duties in a safe manner. All registered products must have an HSE number.
Road Traffic (Carriage of Dangerous Substances in Packages etc.) Regulations 1986	These regulations lay down the rules for the marking of vehicles carrying dangerous substances. Unless the vehicle is carrying 500kg or more of dangerous substances in 200l containers, there is no need to carry identification on the outside of the vehicle. However, very dangerous substances on the vehicle must be labelled and sufficient information regarding the nature of the hazards carried in the cab. No such chemicals are known to be used in remedial treatment.

Table 8: Legislation and the remedial treatment industry – *continued*

Consumer Protection Act **1987**	This amends section 6 of the *Health and Safety at Work etc. Act* 1974 and places responsibility on companies to provide safety information relating to goods and services which they supply. *Hazards associated with work being carried out by the contractor must be drawn to the attention of the client.* This is a positive duty and not incidental, as under HSWA.
Control of Substances Hazardous to Health Regulations **(various dates) (as amended) (COSHH)**	These are the Health and Safety Commission's procedures for relatively recent and comprehensive egulations to control the risks arising from substances hazardous to health in the work place. These regulations were written to be sufficiently comprehensive to replace some 50 previously existing regulations and orders, which were becoming increasingly outdated. They require an assessment of health risks and controls that are neither less effective nor more complex or costly than is justified in the particular circumstances.
Environmental Protection Act **1990**	This appertains to the control of waste disposal.
Chemicals (Hazard Information Packaging) Regulations **1993 (CHIP)**	Since pesticides approved under the *Food and Environment Protection Act* 1985 are specifically excluded from the supply provision of CHIP, remedial suppliers are not obliged to provide formalised CHIP data sheets for wood preservatives and surface biocides.
Safety Signs Regulations **1996**	These regulations specify signs, sizes, colours and signals (visual and audible), etc. They are particularly concerned with permanent signs. However, it is considered that they also may be applicable to signs relating to work in progress on construction sites.
Party Wall etc. Act **1996**	This is the framework for undertaking work on party walls with the objective of preventing and resolving disputes in relation to party walls and boundaries.
Additional (health and safety) legislation that might be relevant to treatment:	<ul><li>*Management of Health and Safety at Work Regulations* 1999</li><li>*Health and Safety (Consultation with Employees) Regulations* 1996</li><li>*Personal Protective Equipment at Work Regulations* 1992</li><li>*Confined Spaces Regulations* 1997</li><li>*Provision and Use of Work Equipment Regulations* 1998</li><li>*Lifting Operations and Lifting Equipment Regulations* 1998</li><li>*Control of Noise at Work Regulations* 2005</li><li>*Construction (Design and Management) Regulations* 2007</li><li>*Work at Height Regulations* 2005</li><li>*Control of Asbestos at Work Regulations* 2006</li></ul>

Of all these, the key legislation of relevance to the contractor on site applying damp-proofing chemicals or pesticides is the *Control of Substances Hazardous to Health Regulations* (COSHH).

Control of substances hazardous to health

A substance is deemed to be hazardous to health when it is:

- specified as such by law;
- recognised from experience;
- recognised by common sense.

Substances 'specified at law' will often be required to be marked as 'very toxic', 'toxic', 'harmful', 'corrosive' or 'irritant'. The legal definition of 'hazardous substance' is very wide, but includes pesticides, cement, paints, solvents, oil, grease, dust, micro-organisms, fumes and many other substances used in construction. Hazardous substances may be inhaled, swallowed or absorbed through the skin. They can cause injury to health, disablement, disfigurement or death.

There are three key words used in the regulations which need to be defined clearly: substance, hazard, risk.

Substance

A substance can be anything. Micro-organisms such as the *Legionella* bacterium that causes Legionnaire's disease, and the virus that causes *Leptospirosis*, or Weil's disease, are specially covered by the regulations and thus are considered a 'substance'. A single substance can exist in more than one form and each form of the substance must be considered. Substances can harm in different ways: a substance splashed on the skin may be a nuisance, while the same substance swallowed could be fatal. Solvents used in dpc fluids, and pesticides used in wood preservers, are hazardous substances.

Hazard

The hazard presented by a substance is its **potential ability to cause harm, illness or to damage health.** The hazard can range from making the eyes smart or water, to coughing or choking, suffocation and death. It may also be much more subtle and unseen, like cancer caused by asbestos or damage to the liver by organic solvents.

Risk

The risk is the **likelihood of the substances actually causing harm** to the health of someone in the situation or circumstances in which it is used. The risk depends on the following factors.

With the proper assessment and controls, the risk presented to health by even the most toxic substances can be adequately controlled but, with poor controls and a lack of effective supervision, even substances with a low hazard potential can cause major risks.

The COSHH Regulations are quite specific as to what should be done by everyone concerned to reduce, where reasonably practicable, the actual hazard level at the workplace and minimise the risk. Thus, it is necessary to:

- identify substances used;
- assess risk in use;
- introduce control methods;
- inform, instruct, train and provide health surveillance where necessary; and
- monitor control methods and keep records.

The employer must:

- assess the health risks created by work involving substances hazardous to health and the measures necessary to control the exposure of employees, or others, to them;
- ensure that the exposure of employees is prevented or adequately controlled;
- ensure that any control methods provided are properly used and maintained;
- monitor the work environment as necessary;
- carry out health surveillance in specified circumstances; and
- provide information, instruction and training for employees on the risks to health and precautions to be taken regarding work with substances hazardous to health.

Under the regulations, an employer may not carry out any work which could expose employees to substances hazardous to health unless a 'suitable and sufficient' assessment of the risks created by that work has been carried out.

The assessments should be carried out by competent persons and should take account of such issues as:

- the nature of articles and substances;
- the use to which they are to be put;
- where they are to be used, stored and transported;
- the environment in which they are to be used, stored, transported; and
- their effects upon others when in use.

It is essential, therefore, that all employees are aware of these statutory obligations placed upon their employers, that they understand the need for them and that they comply with all safe systems and other control methods that are introduced as a result of them.

A common sense approach is to take note of, and if necessary enquire after, the nature of safe systems of work and any precautionary measures in respect of all materials to be used.

Manufacturers, importers, designers and suppliers of articles or substances are required by section 6 of the *Health and Safety at Work etc. Act* 1974 (as amended) to provide adequate information about the use for which the article is designed, or has been tested, and about any conditions necessary to ensure that it will be safe and without risks to health at all times.

Employers must, therefore, identify all substances in use. Having done this, they may require, from suppliers, adequate information concerning those substances. The information is normally in the form of hazard data sheets, showing the nature, associated hazards and risks, precautions to be observed and, where necessary, the personal protective equipment to be used.

While a great deal of responsibility rests with employers to set up assessments, control methods, safe systems of work and, generally, maintain the organisation necessary to ensure compliance with COSHH (as well as all other health and safety legislation), the regulations and the *Health and Safety at Work etc. Act* 1974 place quite specific duties upon all employees.

The responsibilities placed upon employees by COSHH and other health and safety laws are greater than many appreciate, and the penalties that can be incurred are heavy.

The employee must:

- cooperate with the employer so far as is necessary to enable the employer to meet its obligations;
- make full and proper use of any control measures, such as:
  - compliance with safe working procedures;
  - ensuring adequate ventilation when working in confined spaces;
  - safe storage, disposal and transport of substances; and
  - use of the correct personal protective equipment (masks or breathing apparatus, gloves, clothing, etc.);

and report defects in:

- all plant and machinery, etc.;
- any personal protective equipment any other control measures; and
- local exhaust ventilation systems, etc.

The HSE is a body to which consumers may report concerns in cases where they consider themselves at risk. The number of cases reported to the HSE and published in its annual report on such incidents where this involves remedial treatment fluids or the like is normally about five each year, and they are not normally caused by registered or affiliated contractors but a DIY or other (unqualified to use remedial chemicals) contractor.

CASE STUDY 1: DRY ROT – ARMCHAIR SURVEYING IN ACTION!

Figure 166: The Gothic splendour of a late Victorian mansion. Unfortunately the red brickwork has been obliterated by roughcast, which will trap dampness.

Property details

Detached, probably late Victorian.
Solid brick walls, raised timber ground floor.
Timber joisted upper floors.

Background

The author visited the property prior to major repair work to the rear bay, which was thought to have suffered damage from dry rot.

The author was commissioned only to give a second opinion on the cause of the rot outbreak, as to whether chemical treatment would be required, and on the suitability of the proposed structural support being tendered for by the contractor.

The client, wheelchair-bound, was finding it increasingly difficult to live in the property. An elderly client *sometimes* has a shorter-term view on building upgrades.

Initial temporary builder's work

As is so often the case, defects only came to the occupier's attention when water dripped from the bay ceiling after rain. By then the underlying defects had matured. A builder discovered the existing bay roof to be quite badly cracked, with cracks along its length – some wide enough to admit a finger.

The original bay roof was neither slated, leaded, tiled, asphalted, nor zinced, but *concreted!* The material is often not easy to recognise, frequently being heavily disguised by liberal applications of black tar. Lapped coverings such as lead flashings and slating can accommodate movement and still remain *weatherproof*.

The general contractor described the roof as being 'made of a very hard concrete, dark coloured'. This kind of concrete could have been a Victorian concrete incorporating 'slag', a by-product of the steel industry blast furnaces. Slag contained mixed oxides, sulphur, phosphorus and aluminium, ash and limestone.

The builder considered water penetration to have been caused by the bay roof defects, and applied strips of torch-on roofing felt as temporary weathering. He

Figure 167: The ailing Ealing rear bay – rainwater goods need a rethink at high level. Yes, you are looking at temporary torch-on felt to weatherproof the bay.

Figure 168: A similar bay roof, as original, observed on the next door property. Note beautiful original brickwork with decorative red coursing. Note also the cementitious cornice mouldings, with probably a slag/clinker concrete roof substrate. Such a roof can soak in moisture – but there is no designed ventilation system. They are lobster traps for moisture. All of these properties are bressummer time bombs!

also hacked off plasters internally, mainly below the two first floor window cills, and discovered the right end of the timber bressummer to be rotted. Built-up timber skirtings along the rear wall of the first floor bedroom were removed, and carted away. Advice was sought from a structural engineer and steel beams duly calculated and specified to replace the original failed timber beams. The builder recommended chemical treatment for what was thought to be dry rot.

Dampness investigation

Beams to support openings for bays, or shop front openings often fronted by a narrow flat roof, are often called 'bressummers' – as are beams over fireplace openings or main beams in historic timber framed houses.

A screwdriver pushed in very easily to the right end of the exposed bressummer, and chunks of soft honey-coloured and decayed cubes of timber were easily levered out. (See figure 172.) All this damage could be lurking *behind* plasters and skirtings to catch you out! The damage seemed typical of *serpula lacrymans* – dry rot. Incidentally, 'dry rot' should really be called *damp rot* – as moisture is needed for spores to germinate and the fungus develop.

Prodding the right-hand beam end, the author estimated that the beam was of around 75mm in thickness, but it was not possible to confirm the presence of a likely second beam behind. It must be in there somewhere – the regularly spaced bolts were

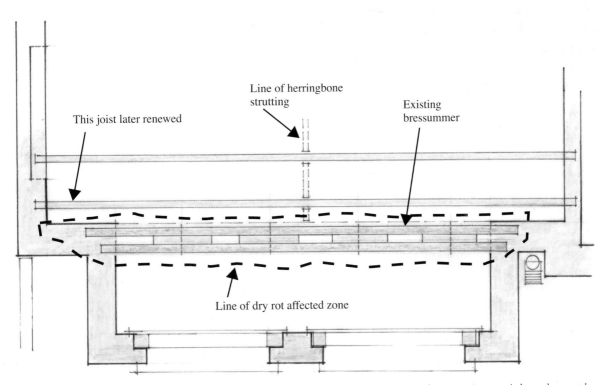

Figure 169: The rear bay on plan. Note the close proximity of bressummer beam ends to potentially wet external masonry. Any new timber replacement beam would need to be installed to save ends from rot damage.

Figure 170: Note lack of the usual bonding timber under the window sub-cill, and the rather crude cutting of floorboards on the line of second floor joist. Wedging of herringbone strutting must be reinstated. The right end of the bressummer has rotted. Note how first floor joists span parallel to the bressummer beam.

almost certainly there to secure beams aligned in parallel. This inner beam measured a depth of 225mm.

Looking at old building textbooks can help you determine how such a period building was originally put together before you embark upon any stripping out. In chapter VIII of *Brickwork and Masonry* by E. Molloy[40] entitled 'Lintels, Bressummers and Arches', you would find descriptions of a number of alternative lintels, relieving arches, built-up lintels and flitched bressumers.

Figure 3 of that chapter, *Built-up lintel with distancing blocks* (reproduced below), looked the likely beam configuration. Molloy showed here two 6″ × 2″ fir joists, with '4″ × 2″ distance pieces bolted at intervals'. Such timber sizings are considered suitable for 'ordinary door and window openings' and are the smaller cousin of what I expected to finally see exposed at Ealing.

It is incredibly exciting peeling back the finishes of a building to see exactly how it was built. You may find newspapers of the day, to give date clues, discarded cigarette packets – even the occasional dropped and lost tool.

Back to the rot . . . whatever mycelium might have been present on exposed masonry, it had been cleaned off. Some isolated strands were discovered, thought to be dry rot rhizomes.

But curiosity prompted a look into builder's rubble bags leaning against the flank wall This was to provide

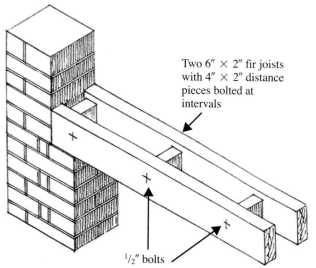

Two 6″ × 2″ fir joists with 4″ × 2″ distance pieces bolted at intervals

¹/₂″ bolts

Figure 171: Built-up lintel with distance blocks. Molloy's bressummer drawing[40].

the final piece of the identification jigsaw: the unmistakeable plates of dry rot mycelium clinging to the ends of stripped out floorboards, and a mushroomy smell to boot.

At Ealing we firstly noted the large cuboidal cracking of the timber, the typical honey brown colour of the degraded wood, the deep cracking and the lack of a veneer of sound timber. The fungal strands seemed to suggest dry rot. And the mycelium nailed it.

Although much is often made of the importance of correctly identifying fungus that has wrecked our homes, the remedies needed for either a dry or wet rot outbreak are not that different. It is just that dry rot has the expensive habit of reaching out further from its epicentre.

The first floor joisting was parallel to the bressummer, with the rot having only encroached a few inches into the first floor structure over the undersides of floorboards. Being quite a restricted attack, it would not be necessary to use significantly large volumes of chemical to treat it.

Figure 172: A screwdriver allows you to feel just how friable the rot-affected timber really is, and how deeply the rot extends. You are only damaging what is already destroyed.

Figure 187: And lifting the floor vinyl near the bath – mould! The hardboard under the vinyl was wet, expanded and puffed out.

Figure 189: Although this fungus may well have 'galloped', it is certainly not dry rot. We are looking at a fruiting body, clinging to the underside of a softwood floorboard. It has a porous texture and is most probably the wet rot Phellinus Contiguus, a white rot. The timber is degraded into a stringy fibrous consistency (refer to BRE, 2003[37]). This is clearly not the cuboidal cracking associated with the brown rots (dry rot, cellar or mine fungus). Several joists have been severely degraded by the fungus too and it's truly surprising that the heavy cast-iron bath was not discovered down in the kitchen below.

Figure 188: The screwed-in bath panel, without any smaller access door, would make it virtually impossible to look under such a bath in a standard house survey. You might succeed in taking the panel off – but you would struggle to refit it. You need an endoscope in the car boot for such eventualities – look what you could have missed!

unknown for surveyors to diagnose dry rot in such a case. The expanding yellow filler you see near the external masonry in figure 185 – used by so many of the cowboy builder fraternity – is sometimes mistaken for dry rot fungus.

Summarising the key bathroom problems in this property, we find:

- floorboarding subject to wet rot damage under the bath;
- several joists subject to rot at ends;
- a gas water heater sited in the bathroom;
- a window sited inconveniently;

Figure 190: You are looking at the end of a joist, dark from wet rot attack. And all along the flank wall, is a wallplate – possibly rotted too – and very difficult to access for replacement. Such a wallplate helped the builders set out a neat line of joists during the building of this rear addition, nearly 125 years ago. But it now returns to haunt us.

Take a second, closer look – can you see that a horizontal bed joint in the brickwork is opening up?

Note too there are stop valves that could drip and leak unseen. Tiny drips provide water enough for rots.

Figure 191: The landlord with one of the rotted joists from the bathroom. Perhaps he is already speaking to his bank manager, making overdraft arrangements to fund the imminent structural repair.

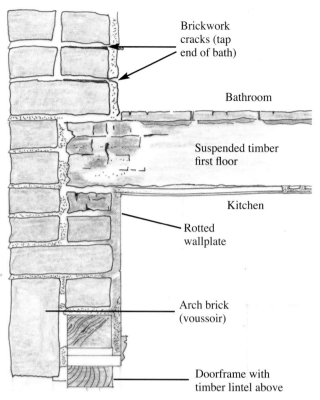

Figure 192: Damaged joist end under bath. On removal of the bath panel, horizontal cracks were noted in the brickwork bed joints due to the subsidence of rotting joist ends under masonry courses.

- floor hardboarding water damaged/mouldy;
- wall tiling untidy;
- bath edge sealing unsatisfactory; and
- a shower curtain which does not contain water spray.

Remedy decisions

A complete bathroom refurbishment would be needed The author advised bricking up the rear window opening, and forming a new window opening to the flank wall. The new bath would be fitted with a removable inspection door, large enough for maintaining plumbing at the tap end of the bath.

Structural repair

What now follows is an illustration of perhaps one of the commonest repairs for Victorian properties – the splicing in of a damaged joist end. It means a joist can be saved, rather than completely renewed, resulting in less disturbance to the building (complete joist replacement will nearly always mean complete ceiling replacement).

The second major work for the bathroom involves taking out the rear window, bricking up the opening, and forming a new flank window opening. Traditional brickwork skills apply here, involving the use of a 'turning piece' to shape and build the brick arch. The inner half of the new arch will comprise a $100 \times 75mm$, prestressed concrete lintel, tied into the brick voissoirs using several stainless steel ties.

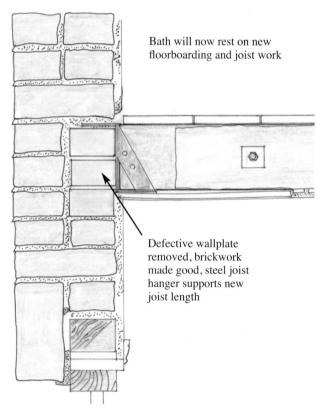

Figure 193: Joist end repair technique. For the time being, part of the ceiling will be made good.

Figure 194: Rear elevation.

Figure 195: Flank elevation.

Figure 196: The underside exposed! Perhaps an endoscope is worth considering, so that you can see just a glimpse of what lies behind panels and coverings. Note that when the electrics were rewired, the electrician had run some cables over the tops of joists in notches – extremely bad practice, and a health and safety risk, not to mention not complying with IEE Regulations.

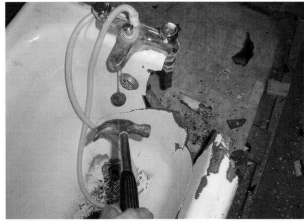

Figure 197: In this contract the bath needed to be hammered to pieces. There was nowhere to store it during the works, it was stained and the enamelling was chipped and damaged around overflow and waste positions.

Figure 198: A simple dead shore sufficed to support the ceiling – no real burden, as just one joist at a time was cut away and spliced in. The wedge can be easily tapped out and the support withdrawn once the brickwork around the steel hanger support strengthens up.

Work on site

Splicing in new joist sections (in this case three) just requires standard builder skills. Here we illustrate some key stages of the work.

The bath ledges each side of the taps often create problem leak zones. Instead of water travelling downwards from tiles to the bath edge and into bath, water *settles* on the horizontal surface, and can then seep through any tiny flaws in edge seals. Special care in sealing at this position is needed to make sure this can't happen.

If at all possible, water must be kept on the move downwards – whether we are considering shower/ bath seals or how we ensure good weatherproofing of a roof.

At least at Danby, splashing shower water at the top end of the bath was easily remedied by fitting a narrow glazed screen, which contained any shower spray that found a way past the left end of the shower curtain.

135

Figure 199: A new support joist was drilled for bolts using a right-angle chuck drill. The new joist was 10mm shallower than the existing, but a little wider, so it could be manipulated into position a fraction above the existing ceiling boarding, which was still supported by the existing joist in position (it only had its end trimmed back a few inches). Without any contact with damp masonry the existing joist will quickly dry down to an acceptable moisture equilibrium.

The timber damage could be considered as two separate issues. True, we were in a bathroom. The floorboard rot was most certainly caused by water leaks from the bath, creating an ideal environment for white rot. But the joist end damage, although adjacent to the floorboard rot, had to be considered differently. There may have been no link at all between the bath over-spillage and the joist end rot. The ends of joists built into masonry can rot whether or not there is a bathroom, as a result of water penetration from driving rain. There are only a few centimetres of brick protection between external wall faces and timber joist ends. This environment is not ventilated. Rot can occur, so thinking holistically, consider whether further examination of joist ends and wallplates is needed along the remainder of the elevation beyond the bathroom zone The second most vulnerable location will be the front end of the flank – at this position a main rainwater downpipe from the roof fed into the end of the flank gutter, was blocked and had caused the flank to become saturated, and could have wetted up built-in joist end and wallplates.

Figure 200: And the finished result! Here you see the bathroom as completed, rear and flank walls completely replastered and tiled, new bath, pine panelling with an access door at the bath end, a new pedestal basin and a window with a convenient opening fan light for ventilation. An existing extractor fan operated by pull cord (just out of view) was retained. But water was to find a way onto the floor at the tap end of the bath: the shower curtain could only be drawn up against the tiling, leaving an inviting gap at the end of the bath for shower spray. This was easily remedied by fitting a narrow glazed screen, shown right, to contain splashing water and spray.

Typical damp damage under a bath on a solid floor

In retrospect, in a case such as at Danby where tenants use the shower probably several times a day, the flooring needed an improved specification to contain any water after showering. Any water dripping onto the vinyl floor must not be allowed to trickle or track under the bath via the vinyl edge. Consider slightly lipping up the vinyl edge, perhaps to an edge bead, to prevent this.

Figure 201: We can learn from hotel bathrooms. Floor coverings are taken up at edges, and careful detailing at the base of tiling means any sprayed water will just run down onto the floor. The WC pan is sealed too, so any drips running down the pan will not find their way under floor coverings that have been trimmed around the pan. This bath could also be hiding some damp damge – so if you can't see under a bath by removing an access panel, make sure you state the potential for unseen problems in any survey report.

Figure 203: This is a typical symptom of long running leaks past missing bath edge seals, where water has tracked down the plasterwork under the bath and has eroded the skim plaster away to form vertical grooves – like a glacier carving out valleys.

Figure 202: The bath shown in figure 201 has now been taken out. You can see that much water was running past poor bath seals near the tap end of the bath where a shower fitting had been used. The floor screed is saturated and the softwood bath framing had been sitting in a virtual water puddle and had rotted beyond repair.

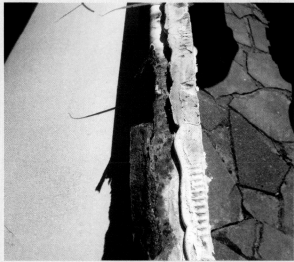

Figure 204: You rarely see so much corrosion to the edge of a steel bath, but in this case the rusting is very advanced and obviously a new bath is required. All looked intact until we began removing the bath panel for a closer look.

Figure 205: Careful colourless silicone sealing at junction of a bathroom floor to entrance door frame and metal carpet edge trim.

7 Mould and ventilation

INTRODUCTION

The English House Condition Survey of 1996 estimated that 15 per cent of all households suffer mould growth on walls, ceilings, carpets or furniture. Two-thirds of mould cases are classified as slight, with the remainder moderate or severe. This *could* be an underestimation, as more mould than we realise may be hidden from view in ducts and voids or behind furniture.

Mould is most common in the rented sector. Problems are more widespread amongst older flats, terraced houses, larger households and homes without adequate central heating. However, more positively, the incidence of mould growth had fallen from a level of 17 per cent in the 1991 House Condition Survey. The EHCS does not link ventilation in homes to incidence of mould, and it is extremely likely that the amount and type of ventilation in a home will have a bearing on incidence of mould.

Mould is often linked to 'fuel poverty'. Those households that spend more than 10 per cent of their annual income on fuel, or whose actual fuel spend falls below the required fuel cost, are usually considered to be suffering 'fuel poverty'.

If householders simply cannot afford to heat their home satisfactorily, thermostats might be turned down, radiators turned off, windows kept shut, and mould may often develop on the cold surfaces of an unheated room (typically a bedroom) or in cupboards and behind furniture. In the worst cases, occupiers may use portable gas bottle heaters in a vain attempt to save heating bills. Gas heaters *produce water vapour* from the fuel combustion, and are a fire hazard.

There are thousands of mould species. Once a suitable substrate becomes wetted/damp, moulds can colonise within less than a day. We all see how quickly moulds proliferate on foodstuffs in the home.

Mould has been with us in buildings for centuries, but over the past few decades changes in how we heat, ventilate and insulate buildings have, according to most commentators, produced conditions more and more favourable for them.

Mould is a symptom of a damp problem, but unusually this symptom itself can be a threat to health.

Surveyors have been referred to as '*property* doctors', but surely we cannot be expected to be *medical* doctors too? But if we survey occupied property, where we see occupiers suffering symptoms commonly associated with bad air, and more specifically mould contamination, then could we be held accountable for failing to see the link between human health and building condition? So listen more carefully for that tell-tale cough, or a child using an asthma pump.

Surveyors read about mould and discuss the issues more than ever before. We are probably still a little behind the USA and Scandinavia, where the public are more 'mould aware'.

Research into mould and the implications for chartered surveyors

An RICS report on mould was published in 2005 entitled *Research into Mould and the Implications for Chartered Surveyors*[45,46]. The word 'toxic mould' was deemed in this report to be a misnomer, although the report did not clearly explain why. It may be because research has not yet been produced to conclusively link particular moulds to certain illnesses or health symptoms. I have come across a number of mould experts (mycologists) who recoil from the term 'toxic mould'.

In preparation of that research paper, 1200 properties were surveyed. Mould was most commonly found in bedrooms, then bathrooms and kitchens. Forty per cent of mould contamination was discovered in bedrooms. This backs up the author's experience. It is usual for moisture to be heavily generated in bathrooms and kitchens, by cooking or washing, then condense there, or on cold surfaces in another room – even far removed – perhaps a poorly heated spare bedroom.Living rooms exhibited the least mould development (only 3 per cent of identified mould).

No information was published on the types of residential unit surveyed, ages of buildings, tenure, etc. but it was clear that mould can derive from penetrating damp very commonly (28 per cent of cases) as well as condensation (58 per cent). Damp penetration can promote condensation, as wet building fabric becomes a cold bridge.

The surveys carried out included the taking of mould samples for laboratory analysis.

But how useful it is to actually identify the mould species? Some experts consider that it is not always easy in any case to identify *species* – although the genus can be more positively verified. It is also said by some mycologists that the identification of species might sometimes be of limited practical use, as we know so little concerning the risk to health of the many thousands of mould species. We do, however, have knowledge of certain species, and if species proven to be a health risk are identified, we will know just how carefully the mould colonisation will need to be dealt with. Some experts suggest that the species is not the key factor concerning the risk to health, but the *amount* of mould. We have also developed a fear of moulds that have hit the headlines, such as *stachybotrys chartarum*.

In the USA, some extremely high-profile court settlements concerning mould, which have run into millions of dollars, make all those involved in designing or surveying buildings on this side of the pond rather edgy concerning potential future claims.

Melinda Ballard v Farmers Insurance Group

(For more details, see www.usaweekend.com/99_issues/ 991205/991205mold.html.)

This landmark US legal case all started with a series of plumbing leaks to a dream home. The house's copper pipework sprang leaks in 1998 which caused hardwood floors to warp. By 1999 the family had developed headaches, dizziness, fatigue, respiratory and sinus problems.

The link between a very mouldy house and the symptoms was made following a chance meeting with an indoor air quality consultant, who saw Melinda coughing up blood, which led to a question about water damage. Visiting her home to investigate, samples of mould tested positive – with a level 4 *Stachybotrys* colonisation diagnosed.

Stachybotrys altra (also *chartarum*) is considered by experts to be a particularly harmful mould, which produces airborne toxins that can cause serious illness – e.g. breathing difficulties, memory and hearing loss, dizziness, flu-like symptoms and bleeding in the lungs.

The resulting legal award amounted to $32 million dollars damages (June 2001).

Key lessons learned from such cases include:

- Take early professional advice when musty smells are noticed.
- Consider advising tests of plumbing in survey reports.
- Be alert to typical illness symptoms associated with exposure to moulds.
- Remember that mould can develop extensively out of view, so consider opening up when surface symptoms of mould or damp appear.
- If you suspect hidden mould may be present, advise *further investigation*.

THE CAUSE OF MOULD IN BUILDINGS

Mould will always mean there has been (or is) significant dampness present – but there are many possible reasons for dampness. Many companies market products to eliminate condensation – but mould can develop from other causes:

- condensation;
- a plumbing leak;
- penetrating damp;
- rising damp;
- following a natural flood;
- fabrics/clothes etc. become damp from damp air; and
- other sources, e.g. trapped moisture, construction moisture, fire fighting water, cleaning, spillage.

Mould from condensation

Often condensation is caused by unsatisfactory heating, ventilation, insulation, or possibly 'lifestyle'. The remedy here would normally involve improving heating and ventilation of the property, sometimes applying internal or external insulation, perhaps in tandem with some acceptable lifestyle changes. Where property is rented, there is a fine line between lifestyle that is deemed acceptable and unacceptable. Should fish be boiled on a stove? Should the building be designed to cope with the steam? Ventilate without occupier intervention to close doors, turn on fans, open windows, etc? Are we being judgmental on culture or lifestyle?

Mould stemming from a plumbing leak

This can be quite extensive if the leak has continued unknown for some time. Pipe leaks are usually easy to repair once pipework is isolated.

Mould from penetrating damp

Areas of mould usually spreads outwards from the point of water entry. It may be combined with condensation damp. It is often possible to find the cause of penetration from internal and external visual inspection.

Mould from rising damp

Do not be influenced by those that suggest that condensation and rising damp cannot co-exist! There may well be salts present at and near the surface of plasters subject to rising damp, but the dampness could dampen timber skirtings to create a damp micro-climate behind, conducive to mould.

Mould following a natural flood

Mould only takes 24 hours to develop, so it is important to bring air conditions under control quickly after a flood – e.g. reduce air humidity and heat up the building interior – to prevent 'secondary mould'.

Mouldy clothes/fabric from damp air

You will often find cases where there is not much or any actual condensation occurring on cold walls or floors, but piled up fabrics and clothes in wardrobes suffer mould because the materials are absorbent and take in water vapour from humid air. Mould takes hold with a vengeance.

Mould from other sources

These include entrapped moisture, construction moisture, fire fighting water, cleaning, spillage. Building timber is stored on site to be rained on! Wet timber can be built into the building structure, moisture sealed in by plastic membranes – ideal conditions for mould. Even well stored timber could be superficially damaged by 'blue stain in service' – a mouldy discoloration of blue-black streaks. See BRE guidance: *Recognising Wood Rot and Insect Damage in Buildings*[37].

THE SCIENCE

Moulds fall within two phyla – *Ascomycota* or *Zygomycota*. Fungi are set apart from other plants by virtue of the fact that they do not have chlorophyll, and survive by breaking down plant and other organic matter for food. They are thus non-photosynthetic. Moulds, which are fungi, are commonly saprophytic – i.e. live on dead organic matter. Moulds are found growing indoors and outdoors.

Moulds *do not need light* and can therefore flourish in dark places.

Mould fungi are mainly aerobic – they obtain oxygen for growth from the air. When germination occurs, thin tubes called hyphae grow from a spore, as a root might grow from a seed. Collections of hyphae are called mycelium. The hyphae spread over and *through* the substrate.

Mould spores may land on damp material, and then begin growing, digesting what they need to survive and spread. Moulds absorb nutrients outside their bodies.

Organic matter can be found in building materials or finishes, or in build up of waste material, dust and grime. Mould cannot colonise clean glass, for example, but you can quite often find it growing on *dirty* glass. Mould could not obtain energy from Rockwool insulation, which is inorganic, but such inorganic insulation could be damp and covered by organic dust, containing the nutrient fungi need to grow.

Plasters containing salts might not support growth of moulds, but when wallpapered, moulds can thrive, enjoying nutrition from the paper and paste.

Organic material such as wood, chipboard, paper, cotton, wool, and some paints, provide suitable nutrients for mould. Carpets often support mould, especially in damp environments. Many moulds can feed off materials containing cellulose. Avoid using plasterboards in wet rooms, as such materials can support mould and can physically break down from repeated wetting.

We see the same life cycle in mould as in other fungi such as dry or wet rot. Spores can loosely be described as the seeds of fungus, and there are always mould spores in the air, both inside and outside buildings. However, inside a building suffering from mould contamination you would be likely to find higher concentrations of spores than outside. Mould spores are present in dust, that can accumulate on both vertical and horizontal surfaces.

Moulds can often cope with changing moisture availability, and the spores can remain dormant in dry conditions. They can then germinate, either where free water is present (although some moulds hate free water), on damp surfaces, or even in moist air – but for all moulds, as indeed for all life forms on this planet, water is a key requirement, in whatever form.

Experts consider that for spores to germinate, certain critical conditions are needed:

- moisture;
- food source;
- oxygen;
- temperature 5–40°C;
- humidity 55%+; or most commonly a threshold of 65%.

How long does mould take to form?

- In the drying industry the first 24 hours after a flood is considered a sufficient period for mould to take hold.
- Spores can germinate within 12 hours of wetting.
- Enzymes are released into the substrate to absorb nutrients.
- Mould spores can form within 5–16 days.

It has often been suggested that the key factor in assessing condensation risk in homes is how often relative humidity is above a critical percentage – often said to be 70–75%. So in order to combat mould colonisation we often target RH quite directly – when either reducing moisture in the air or raising air temperature will reduce RH.

Coupled with measures to reduce RH may be those that raise surface temperatures – and we might find for example insulating sheet polystyrene glued to walls will achieve this.

A high RH may not necessarily mean there actually is any surface condensation – just that surface condensation will be more likely then. This is where monitoring can help us understand exactly what is happening in a property over a given time period – when RH and air temperature are logged, with surface temperature logged too at key room positions.

Moulds proliferate in quite a range of conditions. The problem is that *humans and mould can coexist in the same humidity and temperature conditions*. Jagjit Singh reminds us in *Building Mycology*[47] that although mould fungi may have wide temperature and humidity tolerances, relative humidities exceeding 70% and temperatures in the range of 15–20°C are generally required.

Some fungi can grow in much higher temperatures – up to 30°C and even below freezing. How often have you found mouldy food in your fridge?

HEALTH ISSUES

It's a shame there's no such thing as a *freshairometer*! People vary in how aware they are of stale air – some living in persistently bad air just get used to it. They may not relate any health problems to indoor air quality. A *freshairometer* would tell us all if our house air needed improving. But we can detect quite a few pollutants using sophisticated equipment, and can quite easily measure the relative dampness of air using humidity and temperature sensors.

There is a huge range of indoor contaminants, and when bad building air impairs health, the term 'sick building syndrome' is often used. Causes of sick building syndrome can be bad ventilation, ventilation ducting contaminated by bacteria and fungi (including moulds), and ineffective air filters allowing the passage of dust and other pollutants.

Measures to remedy condensation not only reduce mould colonisation, but can also diminish other pollutants. For example, filters used in conjunction with ventilation equipment may filter out a range of pollutants such as tobacco smoke, pollen, etc.

We are almost certainly at the beginning of a long journey to fully understanding moulds. Some scientists estimate there to be more than 100,000 mould species, with probably only 200 studied with respect to health implications. So no wonder there is caution concerning mould risk. We do not know how many moulds are toxic moulds, although certain species, such as *stachybotrys chartarum* or various *aspergillus* moulds, are considered potentially harmful to humans. The US Environmental Protection Agency warns that any mould 'in profusion' can cause health problems.

Health issues relating to mould can be summarised as follows:

Allergic reactions from inhaling or touching mould or mould spores can be immediate or delayed, and can include hay fever-type symptoms, sneezing, runny nose, red eyes and skin rash. Repeated exposure increases sensitivity to mould. Once an allergy develops, it can be a permanent lifetime condition.

Asthma attacks can be triggered in persons allergic to mould.

Hypersensitivity pneumonitis can follow short- or long-term exposure to mould. The disease resembles bacterial pneumonia but is uncommon.

Irritant effects can include irritation of eyes, skin, nose, throat and lungs – sometimes experienced as a burning sensation in these areas.

Opportunistic infections may affect those with weakened immune systems – notably lung infections by *Aspergillus fumigatus*. *Trichoderma* has affected immune-compromised children. Healthy individuals are not likely to be affected.

Mould toxins – moulds can produce toxic substances called mycotoxins. These can be from within a spore or on the outside of a spore. Mycotoxins can affect individuals who inhale, ingest or touch them.

Aspergillus versicor and *stachybotrys atra* (also known as *stachybotrys chartarum*) produce potent toxins – there is a possible link between *stachybotrys chartarum* and pulmonary haemorrhage in infants.

Children, the elderly and those in poor health seem most vulnerable to mould toxins.

Microbial volatile organic compounds (mVOCs) are compounds produced by moulds that are volatile and released directly into the air. Often strong odours are produced. Exposure to mVOCs has been linked to symptoms such as headaches, nasal irritation, dizziness, fatigue, and nausea.

Spores may measure 2–10 microns, i.e. 0.002–0.01 millimetre. The size of spore dictates how far into the human body the spore will infiltrate. The smaller the spore, the further it can travel into the respiratory tract. Apparently spores greater than 10 microns are trapped in the nasal passages, whereas spores smaller than 4 microns can travel into the lungs. But interestingly breathing through the mouth can allow *larger* spores to travel as far as the lungs. As well as breathing them in, we can be affected by spores through skin contact or ingestion, i.e. by eating mould-affected foodstuffs.

HOUSE SURVEY PROCEDURES – GENERAL APPROACH

The key principle here is that in a pre-purchase survey in the UK, the inspection is essentially visual, with the aid of some basic tools and equipment, such as an electronic moisture meter.

In a pre-purchase survey, a surveyor would be expected to note *visible mould* (it can also be *smelt*), and depending on the circumstances may recommend further investigation. The health risk of mould may need in some cases to be assessed and commented on. A surveyor who does not feel confident to make conclusions regarding the mould threat should recommend further investigations to identify risk and possibly how to deal with the mould.

Hidden mould presents problems that may not yet have been clarified or decided by legal case law. Surveyors should be familiar with building types, and know whether a particular building type or building with certain constructional detailing might be likely to contain mould or be susceptible to mould development. For example, a surveyor should note where a void is not ventilated and may be likely to harbour mould and other fungi. Non-surveyors are familiar with the smell of household mould. In *Hacker v Thomas Deal & Co* (see Murdoch, 2002[48]) the judge made the point that even a surveyor with limited experience should be familiar with the distinctive smell of dry rot.

A surveyor's professional indemnity insurance cover needs to be scrutinised to see whether there is any exclusion of insurance cover for mould-related building problems. If there is no insurance cover, then a surveyor would need to incorporate a suitable clause in the survey report to protect his or her (and the client's) interests. But no number of limitation clauses will rid a property of mould or alleviate an occupier's health problems suffered because of mould.

Key pointers to reporting mould in pre-purchase surveys:

Surveyors may need to report on:

- mould actually seen, describing its extent and severity;
- mould smells noted;
- any information on mould offered by occupiers, building users or any other party;
- any occupiers' or building users' obvious health symptoms likely to have developed from exposure to mould;
- any industry or local knowledge regarding particular sites, buildings, construction techniques, or scenarios where mould is likely or known to be present or a past threat;
- any dampness noted where mould could be a problem;
- the potential or actual health risk of mould noted or suspected; and
- further investigation of mould involving additional surveying equipment (e.g. to open up or inspect by borescope) or requiring additional expertise (e.g. mycologist or medical expert) should be advised depending on the nature of the mould development as found, suspected or referred to by any party or report, etc.

Where a surveyor might look for or find mould

Surface mould may be found:

- on surfaces at cold bridges;
- on ceilings subject to roof leaks;
- on surfaces of unused or unheated rooms;
- at a high or low level in a room corner – crescent shaped;
- as dots of mould in a bathroom – e.g. along the line of the sealant;
- around window panes near the frame and, on dirty glass, on the pane itself;
- on roof timbers in the loft;

- on clothing and bedding; and/or
- on leather.

Hidden mould could be:

- behind wall coverings;
- behind cupboards;
- under floors or carpets;
- within ducts or hollow partitions; and/or
- behind bathroom panels
- behind skirtings

Four-level inspection of mould

Level 1:

- visual inspection;
- linkage of damp to mould.

Level 2:

- visual inspection;
- use of moisture meters.

Level 3:

- visual inspection;
- use of moisture meters;
- moisture meter with accessories (surface thermometer, air temp, relative humidity of air or void, dew point calculation);
- borescope;
- surface sampling;
- opening up, e.g. covers, ducts, boards;
- use of basic leak detection equipment, e.g. listening stick;
- thermal imaging.

Level 4 (usually a team inspection):

- visual inspection;
- use of moisture meters;
- borescope;
- surface sampling;
- air sampling;
- air monitoring;
- surface data logging;
- water sampling;
- collation/study of health records.

The team could include:

- remediation coordinator/project manager;
- professional damage management contractor;
- tenant/occupier liaison;
- services engineer;
- architect/building surveyor;
- mycologist/indoor air consultant;
- building contractor/subcontractors;
- leak detection (contractor/supplier).

In pre-purchase property inspection, inspection of mould would at least go as far as level 2. Some of the techniques listed under level 3, such as borescope inspection, would more often be used in a 'building survey'. However, survey methods under level 4, such as mould sampling, would normally be a specialist activity which could be part of 'further investigation' – advised in the pre-purchase report.

Mould surveying: a surveyor's checklist

Property surveys vary in their aims and scope, but the assumption here is that the survey should identify risks to the building, and the occupants/users/client, and make comment on further investigation or required remediation.

1 Site survey

- Measure area of mould.
- Check mould colour, consistency, characteristics, concentration.
- Check for air smells.
- Check substrate condition.
- Check air temperature, humidity, dew point.
- Check surface temperature pattern.
- Check condition of voids and/or concealed places if scope of survey allows.
- Check out likely mould zones following perusal of building plans.

2 Mould testing

- Carry out sampling if required to confirm mould presence, concentration, species, etc.
- Advise testing of surfaces, building substrates, finishes, components, personal effects, beddings.
- Monitoring of building air condition may be required to determine spaces or parts of building with unhealthy air and to assess the risk to the building and human health (and in the context of any relevant health and safety law, law relating to private or public places of work, living, leisure and commerce, or any other legal requirement to provide or maintain a building and its air to a given standard).

3 Mould reporting

- Note findings from survey and testing above.
- Note that some mould may be as yet unseen – covered up or in voids and/or concealed spaces.
- Note that moulds may be associated with ill-health of occupants.
- Note that mould may be cleaned or removed, and that remediation may include change to lifestyle, use of heating/ventilation, and/or upgrade/redesign of heating/ventilation/insulation.
- Advise further investigation of dampness, mould, heating/ventilation/insulation, health risk.

4 Mould remediation

- Unless the cause of mould is identified and addressed/ remediated, or building conditions change to discourage colonisation, mould may persist, worsen, or recolonise following cleaning, removal of damaged substrate or finishes, etc., or other short-term measures.
- Remediation may include sterilisation, cleaning, removal of mould or mould-affected items. Measures to improve ventilation, heating, insulation or other aspects of building performance would usually be implemented to eliminate future mould colonisation.

5 Points to note

- You may not be able to see or even feel condensation on porous wall or ceiling finishes.
- Surfaces such as glazing or tiling may be warmer than other 'apparently warmer' surfaces such as ceiling plasterboards.
- The amount of mould may not need to be large in area for it to create an unhealthy environment when, for example, a space is small or badly ventilated.
- The home bathroom is an ideal place for any surveyor to study psychrometrics or practise using data loggers. Radical changes in air condition to produce condensate can happen over minutes.
- Even if a bathroom suffers significant mould colonisation, a snapshot survey in a time frame outside the time of bathroom use or the time of greatest condensation, may provide little evidence of a significant damp problem, if you just rely on surface damp readings.

WHEN IS THERE A REAL MOULD PROBLEM?

We define *significant mould* as: mould sufficient to damage, degrade or adversely affect appearance or undermine the performance of building material, fabric, component or finish to adversely affect use and enjoyment of the building or health and well-being of users and occupants, or is symptomatic of an underlying/evident damp problem that needs to be remediated to reduce further or ongoing risk to the building, building occupants, users or other interested party.

The BRE offer three photographs of mould on the front cover of Digest 297[49]: the mould ranges from 'mould growth causing inconvenience' – what looks to be nominal mould in a room corner at high level, to 'persistent patches of mould causing discomfort' – a wall with 2–3 square metres of quite blackish mould,to finally a photo showing a black mould over almost an entire room wall – described as 'extensive mould growth causing acute distress'. These photographs reflect quite closely levels of mould severity we will go on to describe below as 'trivial mould', 'larger areas' and 'extensive outbreaks'.

As with any other defect we survey, we may visit a property on date X, and over time the subject defect could be:

- diminishing, as the cause has already been resolved;
- more or less stable/static; or
- worsening.

It's probably true that the very minor cases of 'trivial mould' will be quite easy to identify and assess, and the serious extensive mould colonisations obvious to any surveyor, but in between the extremes there will lie cases of mould development that are more difficult to categorise.

There will also be cases where mould has been cleaned or hidden by occupiers or building users. We may directly ask if this has taken place, or look for evidence of cleaning/remediation/cleaning materials on site, etc. Some experts advise that 70 per cent of mould is hidden – so immediately we could have a problem if only a small amount of mould is visible without any stripping out.

Some countries, such as the USA, have a more formalised approach to mould remediation in this country than the UK. For example, in *Guidelines on Assessment and Remediation of Fungi in Indoor Environments*[50], we find a very belt and braces approach to mould remediation, on the basis of the amount of mould discovered. Protection for operatives working in mouldy environments is stressed and the risks associated with mould are listed. An escalating regime of recommended operational and safety measures for dealing with mould is specified, corresponding to five 'levels' relating to the area of mould:

- Level I: small isolated areas (10 sq. ft or less);
- Level II: mid-sized isolated areas (10–30 sq. ft);
- Level III: large isolated areas (30–100 sq. ft);
- Level IV: extensive contamination (greater than 100 contiguous sq. ft);
- Level V: remediation of ventilation systems:

  a) small isolated area of contamination (less than 10 sq. ft);

  b) more than 10 sq. ft.

Levels III, IV and V require you to seek help from a qualified safety and health professional. Looking at the 'level III' classification, it is clear that there does not need to be that much mould for the remediation to require a specialist contractor. Thirty square feet (under $3m^2$) is only in effect a wall area of $3m \times 1m$ in size.

There is also a huge difference between scattered mould spotting and the kind of heavy black mould we

see in the more serious contaminations. So *area* is one way of assessing extent of mould colonisation, but *intensity* must surely be another.

The Danish Building Research Institute (SBI) has also published guidelines in SBI Direction 204[51]. In it, risk is categorised as follows:

Visible mould growth in room

- under $0.25m^2$ – small – risk acceptable level for most people;
- from 0.25 to $3m^2$ – moderate risk;
- above $3m^2$ – large risk.

Hidden mould growth

- under $0.5m^2$ – no risk;
- 0.5 to $3m^2$ – small risk;
- 3 to $10m^2$ – moderate risk;
- above $10m^2$ – large risk.

Again, we see a key change in perceived mould risk when the area of mould goes beyond $3m^2$ (corresponding to the 10 sq. ft US criterion).

Many factors other than area of contamination need to be taken into account, such as:

- the history of the building;
- the type of building;
- the type of material;
- whether the material is wet or dry (wet materials hold onto spores);
- health of building inhabitants (e.g. infants and women tend to react before men);
- the activity levels in building – spore movement;
- the use of building; and
- the location within building, e.g. cellar or bedroom.

KEY ELEMENTS OF MOULD REMEDIATION

Sources of advice

The UK has not really woken up to mould remediation as a necessary professional activity. The main reference standard was published in the USA, but did include some expert input from practitioners over here. The industry standard damage management qualifications are also ratified by a USA body, the Institute of Inspection, Cleaning and Restoration (IICRC – www.iicrc.org). It is easy to access US Environmental Protection Agency documents regarding mould from their websites (www.epa.gov). RICS members can also download the RICS research report on mould[45] via the RICS website (www. rics.org/builtenvironment/ buildingpathology/infestationfungal/research_into_ mould. html).

Secondary damage mould can often be avoided if action is taken to prevent the almost inevitable mould growth from 24 to 48 hours after a water damage event. For example, in *Mold Remediation in Schools and Commercial Buildings*[52] there is a comprehensive list of prevention measures, including the disposal of wet, porous materials, removal of vulnerable items such as books and papers, drying of upholstered furniture, etc.

Mould results from a moisture imbalance in air or materials, therefore to reduce recontamination the moisture problem needs to be solved; i.e. to properly remediate the mould, you will need to solve the damp problem. There is little point spending resources on a thorough clean-up operation if the mould will soon return.

Range of available remediation techniques

Bearing in mind advice from New York City and Scandinavia, mould remediation could divide itself into three or even four categories. Listed below are the author's three key mould classifications that could help us to devise a suitable remediation approach. You will note that no specific areas of mould are specified. This is deliberate, as quoting square metres of mould can be misleading, for reasons already described. It is likely that yet more advice will be available to surveyors in the future, so it is perhaps more useful for me to offer the general principles on mould surveying at this stage.

- **Level 1: trivial mould** – DIY cleaning – *very small* areas of mould – e.g. around a bath or sink – householder;
- **Level 2: larger areas** – trained staff, PPE, vacate adjacent areas;
- **Level 3: extensive outbreak** – expert team including health and safety professional.

Level 1: trivial mould

Some would make the comment that there is no such thing as trivial mould because:

a) some of us are hyper-sensitive to mould:
b) we have not carried out sufficient research to know which moulds are the greatest health threat: and
c) as a symptom of 'damp', we cannot be sure whether the dampness represents a serious but as yet underlying property threat.

However, BRE also alludes to less serious mould and in Digest 297[49] refers to a category of mould that is really nothing more than an inconvenience. By inconvenience, BRE refers most probably to the marring of decorations, mainly affecting appearance of finishes.

Trivial mould could be mould spotting to perimeter bath, wash basin or sink sealant. It could be small traces of mould forming on a window cill, perhaps even on dirty glazing. It could be a light dusting of mould on a bathroom ceiling, or perhaps mould spotting to the hard wall at the side of the washing machine. It is unlikely to cause much damage to the building finishes or fabric, and it is unlikely to be a health threat to occupiers. We have all seen 'trivial mould' and know what this means. The property might be generally quite well heated and ventilated, but perhaps subject to some 'occasional' rather than 'persistent' dampening/wetting of surfaces, e.g. limited condensation during washing or cooking times. The accommodation is otherwise generally quite comfortable to live in.

Key procedures would include:

- use of very basic protective clothing – overalls, gloves, goggles;
- use of cleaning/sterilisation agents – e.g. diluted bleach, fungicides;
- very localised wiping off of mould;
- some small areas of wallpaper/lining stripping;
- After cleaning, if 'ghosting' mars décor, redecoration locally might be necessary.

In the UK, advice can be obtained from local authorities by way of advice sheets for social housing tenants. If water droplets from condensation are not allowed to linger for too long or soak into a substrate, mould can be avoided. So a council advised house-holders – in *What to do about Condensation*[53] – to wipe off any condensation that formed on windows. The advice leaflet went on to advise that mould could be cleaned off walls, floors, etc. using a 1:4 bleach solution.

In a more recent advice leaflet – *Condensation in the Home – putting your health on the line?*[54] – the tone seems to have changed. It does not include any self-help mould cleaning advice; instead there is an emphasis on health issues triggered by mould, and explanations of how condensation can be designed out by improving heating, insulating cold surfaces and improving ventilation. This leaflet encourages occupiers to claim benefit money for heating and contact the council to sort out damp problems.

The change of emphasis may reflect growing concerns of the health risk of mould. While a surveyor might be able to distinguish whether mould is 'trivial' or more serious, tenants attempting to sort out a more serious mould colonisation using the kind of DIY methods promoted in the earlier leaflet may often do no more than address symptoms of an underlying damp problem.

When single-glazed windows are changed to new double-glazed units, it is not uncommon for mould problems to suddenly arise or be exacerbated. Double-glazed units may be very tightly sealed when shut and may or may not have the facility for a small ventilation gap to be created by locking a sash slightly ajar. Condensation may become more difficult to manage. The old windows acted as crude dehumidifiers, and condensation was simply wiped off as it arose, but the new warmer window glazing does not produce condensation. This now forms elsewhere on colder wall surfaces where it cannot be simply wiped off – and the wall finishes can be an ideal food source for the mould.

It is common for landlords to respond to condensation and mould by giving the occupier a dehumidifier. This can stall effective measures to cure a damp problem – occupiers may be lulled into a false sense of security by the volume of water collected, as any UK air will contain water vapour that the dehumidifier can extract ad infinitum.

Recent BRE advice on cleaning mould

The BRE, in *Understanding Dampness*[11] advises firstly not to remove mould growth by dry brushing or rubbing – this could release spores into the air (and also fungal fragments), which could induce an allergic reaction. BRE recommends using:

'a vacuum cleaner then dampen the infected area with a 1:4 solution of domestic bleach in water containing a small amount of washing up liquid. Wipe down the surfaces with a damp cloth rinsed out regularly. Wooden windows may need several applications. Keep windows open to promote dispersion of spores and moisture and wear appropriate protection.'

The BRE also makes the point that if any fungicide products that are used should have an HSE number.

BRE Digest 297[49], advises that as a first step to alleviating condensation and mould:

'many minor problems can be alleviated by careful attention to the heating and ventilation of the house …[and]

A number of chemical treatments are available to kill mould fungi growing on walls.'

It is underlined in the digest that such measures 'have little lasting effect where mould has been severe', but that they can be useful in tandem with other remedial measures. Anti-condensation and fungicidal paints are considered potentially longer-lasting. But BRE are very practical and honest here, and suggest that 'simple redecoration with ordinary paint may satisfy tenants at relatively little cost'. Manufacturers of specialist fungicidal paints may be a little disappointed by that advice.

In *A Brief Guide to Mold, Moisture, and Your Home*[55] the following advice is worth noting under the 'Mold Cleanup Guidelines':

- fix plumbing leaks and other water problems as soon as possible;
- dry all items completely;
- scrub mould off hard surfaces with detergent and water and dry completely;

It also advises that a respirator be worn when cleaning mouldy areas. Gloves need to be long – standard washing-up gloves may or may not be good enough. Goggles with ventilation slots are not recommended!

There is also a huge difference between cleaning mould in your own home as an owner-occupier, and attempting to clean mould in rented accommodation – when there may be a legal duty on the part of a building owner/manager to rectify even quite a minor defect. So check the terms of the lease before carrying out even the most minor of works.

The product you see being used for cleaning mouldy vinyl is a ready-to-use fungicidal cleaner for amateur use against mould, mildew or algae on internal surfaces such as masonry, tiles, wood and painted surfaces. Incorporating a brush, there is a combination of biocidal and mechanical cleaning.

Figure 206: Pulling back the vinyl floor covering, which has not been glued at its edges, we see much more mould on the underside of vinyl and on the hardboard under-sheeting.

Figure 207: Attempts are made to clean and sterilise the mould using a dedicated mould-cleaning product. The operative should be wearing protective gloves. Cleaning equipment courtesy ACS Limited, www.wood-protection.co.uk

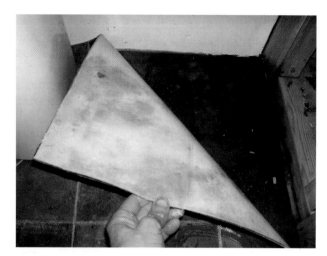

Figure 208: But after cleaning, the vinyl underside cannot be returned to its original pristine whiteness – the greyish stain that we cannot remove is called 'ghosting'. The hardboard has swelled from wetting and will need to be replaced.

The active ingredient of the cleaner is benzalkonium chloride. This is less volatile than common household bleach, which would have a shorter-lasting effect on the substrate applied to. Bleach may be used diluted, but it gives off chlorine gas which may be quite unpleasant and potentially harmful. Bleach also as we all know discolours fabrics and materials. Any product must have an HSE number, the instructions regarding any mixing or application must be rigorously followed, and the correct protective clothing must be worn. You can of course just clean surfaces of 'trivial mould' with standard household cleaning products as part of the normal housework routine. In many cases this will be perfectly suitable. But as a surveying professional, it might sometimes be wiser to recommend a specific and dedicated mould-cleaning product known to be safe and effective.

Level 1: checklist for cleaning trivial mould

Make sure it *is* trivial mould. Seek advice from an expert if the extent of mould colonisation cannot be verified or the source of dampness cannot be explained.

If any occupants are suffering health complaints that could be attributed to mould contact, take medical advice. If susceptible individuals are in the proximity of even a relatively restricted colonisation, a more intensive clean-up operation may need to be considered.

- Inform the building owner/manager, or those responsible for the building as appropriate, before cleaning off mould. Record mould by dated photograph and written description.
- Remediate moisture responsible for mould if possible.
- Assess whether the mouldy material can be surface cleaned.
- Wear appropriate gloves, goggles, face mask/ respirator as appropriate.

- Discard personal effects, furnishings or building finishes that cannot be cleaned or salvaged.
- Ventilate space containing mould.
- Consider misting surfaces prior to remediation.
- Wet wipe off mould using solution of water and bleach, or water and detergent as necessary.
- Thoroughly dry off the cleaned area.
- Leave clean-up area dry and visibly free from contamination and debris.
- Discard disposable PPE.
- Monitor and evaluate success of the cleaning, if permitted.
- Inform the building owner/manager, or those responsible for building maintenance, if your attempts to clean the mould prove ineffective, or an unknown cause of dampness persists.

Much of the published advice on cleaning various categories of mould is sourced from the USA. In some cases the methods are rather more rigorous than probably needed. It would be hard to imagine the occupier of a local authority flat donning full PPE to clean off a small amount of trivial mould in the bathroom!

Level 2: larger areas – trained staff, PPE, vacate adjacent areas

At level 2, we would be dealing with probably quite large areas of mould in several rooms of a house, flat or other occupied premises, requiring an organised and coordinated approach to mould remediation.

Mould remediation would be carried out in most cases by operatives with some basic training, or at least an in-house house team carefully briefed, and ideally having attended dedicated training courses.

The prime concern is to protect occupants, remediation operatives, and any third parties. The careful protection of those persons liable to be affected by the subject mould needs to be considered before, during and after the mould remediation.

Pre-site remediation

There should, of course, be plenty of notice of a clean-up. There may be a need to rehouse occupants or sensitive individuals. The clean-up area should be *unoccupied*. This may be all or part of an accommodation unit, depending on the size and configuration of the unit, the rooms affected, etc.

Before the actual mould clean-up, there may be some opening up to assess the extent of the mould colonisation and to firm-up the package of remediation measures. Such exploratory work could present a risk to health where friable material could be disturbed (e.g. asbestos) or mould spores and fungal fragments released. Care must therefore be taken to ensure that no health and safety risk results from it.

Consider organising inspection by independent consultant before mould is removed.

Site work

While operatives are on site, they are in effect occupiers – probably during the time of greatest release of potentially harmful mould spores and associated fungal fragments.

Remediation operatives must wear suitable PPE.

It is terribly important that workers do not become blasé concerning self-protection. Even though you can't see spores in the air, they are there and are potentially harmful.

The spread of contamination must be controlled during the clean-up. This is done using 'engineering controls and work practices'[56].

Engineering controls include:

- controlled demolition, which minimises dust creation;
- vacuum-assisted power tools and air filtration devices close to the work area.

Air conditioning can spread contamination from area to area, so if possible this should be switched off.

As noted in by Malcolm Richardson in his discussion paper *Moulds and Health* (unpublished personal paper), care must be taken to avoid redistribution of newly exposed contaminants via ventilation systems – such systems will require decontamination themselves.

Air pressure control is the creation of negative pressure in the clean-up area, to reduce/prevent air movement outwards from it, preventing the spread of contamination to clean areas. The Institute of Inspection, Cleaning and Restoration (IICRC) recommends the use of HEPA air filtration devices (AFDs), which can be set up to produce positive or negative air systems, or as 'air scrubbers'. Compartmentalisation can be achieved by tightly fitted plastic sheeting.

Source containment is where a mouldy wall area is covered by plastic film until such time as it can be gradually peeled back during the mould cleaning process. Individual items can also be 'source contained' by encapsulation in plastic and later removed from site. Careful encapsulation reduces the amount of spores becoming suspended in air.

Source removal is where the source of contamination (e.g. mouldy insulation quilting) is removed. It is sealed in plastic bags and removed for disposal.

Local containment, which could be a room or part of a room. The space is sheeted in the same way as one might 'tent' an area to promote effective localised drying. The plastic sheeting enclosure can be simply fixed by duct tape, or sometimes a frame is erected using poles, telescopic structs, timber uprights, etc. Within the tenting, HEPA filtered AFDs can be installed to create a negative pressure differential, to reduce outward spread of contaminated air from the work area.

Compartmentalisation (also termed full-scale containment) is where the part of the building subject to the mould is isolated from adjacent areas. Failure to properly compartmentalise could result in the mould spreading elsewhere in the building. This method can be used where it is found difficult to isolate the contamination at source, or to locally contain it.

Drying

At the same time as mould remediation is in progress, there will often also be dehumidification as part of a drying operation – probably most often when mould has arisen as 'secondary damage' after a flood. The key risk here is the movement of contaminated air from a contaminated to a clean area and this must of course not be allowed to happen.

Mould cleaning

The key item of equipment is the HEPA vacuum unit. A HEPA filter effectively filters 99.97 per cent of particles, down to 0.3 microns. If mould is hoovered up using such equipment, there should be successful containment of spores and fungal fragments.

Mouldy porous materials such as gypsum plasterboards, carpets and insulation are carefully removed from site bagged up in polythene sheeting, to reduce release of spores.

IICRC discourages spraying, wetting or misting mouldy material, as spores could be dispersed by the spray. Where heavy mould is being remediated in conjunction with asbestos removal, then mist spraying may be allowable, with engineering controls. These could include extraction of run-off water and dehumidification.

Level 2: checklist for cleaning large mould areas

- Ensure that sensitive individuals are isolated from the mould remediation zone.
- The mould remediation must be carried out by operatives with basic training; they need not necessarily be specialist mould remediation contractors.
- There must be an organised approach to remediation, agreed with client or relevant authority.
- Operatives should wear suitable PPE.
- Erect necessary compartmentation screening between contaminated and uncontaminated zones.
- Erect source and local area containment.
- Create a negative pressure chamber to limit the release of spores/fungal fragments outside the treatment zone.
- Clean the mould using HEPA filter vacuum equipment, or other equipment as needed.
- Remove contaminated materials encapsulated in plastic sheeting or in plastic bags.
- Undertake necessary post-remediation restoration works.

- Ensure that the treated area is mould-free and ready for reoccupation.
- Check that the treated building zone is mould-free on completion of mould remediation and conduct post-remediation monitoring of building air and fabric.

Level 3: extensive outbreak

This level would apply to an extensive outbreak or to any case when there is deemed to exist a serious enough property threat to warrant the best remediation affordable/obtainable.

This category of remediation would always involve a team approach. The team would include:

- remediation coordinator/project manager;
- professional damage management contractor;
- tenant/occupier liaison;
- services engineer;
- architect/building surveyor;
- mycologist/indoor air consultant;
- building contractor/subcontractors;
- leak detection specialist.

A legal consultant may also be required for very large, complex or sensitive projects.

There are only a handful of agencies in the UK that could offer this level of mould remediation, which would include all of the elements of remediation contained in the first two remediation levels, but in addition a holistic approach to mould remediation.

A much greater emphasis would be placed on:

- scientific appraisal of the colonisation;
- monitoring of building condition leading up to the site remediation and during the remediation; and
- post-site works to appraise the remedies and systems applied to maintain good air quality and satisfactory building condition.

Decontamination chambers are probably only used in the most severe and extensive mould colonisation or where there is a considerable threat to health from it. We are now moving into the kind of extremely rigorous approach we might associate with asbestos removal contracts (when even three-chamber decontamination chambers are used). It is well worth consulting the mould standard IICRC S520 here, should you wish to know in detail the kind of careful approach that may be necessary to remediate the most serious mould colonisations. Even the air scrubbers and air movers are encapsulated in plastic wrapping, prior to their removal from site at the end of the cleaning operation.

We may rarely become involved in the kind of remediation described in the mould standard, but still need to be aware of the general principles of remediation contained within it, which could still apply to the less serious mould clean-ups.

Level 3: checklist for cleaning extensive mould

Depending on the circumstances, a team leader or project manager may or may not be required.

Measures in addition to level 1 trivial mould advice are:

- Organise decanting of tenants or occupiers to either a separate building or a mould-free zone.
- Organise a mould remediation team.
- Fully investigate cause of moisture imbalance, including full survey investigation using leak detection specialists, dampness investigation consultant or building ventilation and heating specialist.
- Remediate obvious cause of water damage.
- Design improved indoor air environment by devising and installing lifestyle or other environmental change and improvement.
- Pre-mould remediation survey (usually destructive) to include opening up, material testing and/or air sampling.
- Operatives should wear suitable PPE.
- Erect necessary compartmentation screening between contaminated and uncontaminated zones.
- Erect source and local area containment.
- Prepare two- or three-chamber decontamination facility, if necessary.
- Create negative pressure chamber to limit release of spores/fungal fragments outside the treatment zone.
- Clean the mould using HEPA filter vacuum equipment, or other equipment as needed.
- Remove contaminated materials encapsulated in plastic sheeting or in plastic bags.
- Undertake necessary post-remediation restoration works.
- Ensure treated area is mould-free and ready for reoccupation.
- Check treated building zone is mould-free on completion of mould remediation, conduct post-remediation monitoring of building air and fabric.
- Monitor health of building occupants post remediation.
- Evaluate mould remediation exercise and further develop techniques for future contracts.

IMPROVING HOUSE VENTILATION TO REDUCE CONDENSATION MOULD

Is improved house ventilation needed to reduce condensation and combat mould?

I have come across quite a few surveyors who quite automatically pass on problems such as condensation and the associated mould development to specialist manufacturers and installers of ventilation equipment.

A house surveyor ought to be aware of the basic ventilation systems available on the market, and in broad terms, the advantages and disadvantages of each. He or she should also be able to recognise when quite simple and acceptable adjustments to lifestyle could be agreed and put into practice to minimise condensation in the home to an acceptable level and help reduce mould.

In recent discussions with a technical representative for a ventilation company, the rep admitted that there would be a percentage of cases where the ventilation systems installed were not really needed, and the condensation could have been simply reduced by adjustments to lifestyle. Please refer to *Diagnosing Damp*[1], Chapter 4. Mechanical ventilation systems act often simply to override much-needed lifestyle changes – that occupiers are not able or indeed willing to make.

On finding mould development in a house, surveyors should consider very carefully why this is happening, in order for the correct remediation to be designed and implemented. Mould typically arises because of an event or because of longer-term moisture imbalance.

Events

Causes attributed to a particular event may create conditions suitable for mould development, but once remediated, the property returns to its normal (i.e. pre-event) moisture equilibrium.

Mould caused by damp penetration could more often be the result of poor external maintenance of the building fabric or associated external plumbing. Mould from rising damp is rarer, and could be due to defective damp-proofing, poorly executed works, or damp-proofing compromised by poor associated detailing. In such instances I have often found mould behind skirting boards, where there has been close contact with a damp wall. In cases of penetrating or rising damp, a remedy would be required to address the poor property condition or design deficiency.

It is extremely common to find that internal redecoration to make good mouldy decorations is marred by a return of the mould, in exactly the same place. Clearly the cause was not addressed – only the symptoms.

Longer-term moisture imbalance

Mould is often caused by condensation resulting from imbalances and deficiencies in the way a property is heated, insulated and ventilated. More than just a basic repair is needed to remediate condensation damp and mould.

There are two distinct routes that can be taken to remedy a longer-term condensation problem:

- **Adjustments to 'lifestyle'** may eliminate or sufficiently limit condensation and mould. An occupier can often reduce condensation and mould by making changes in the way they make use of existing heating systems, ventilation installations and how moisture generation can be reduced or controlled. For more detail on this, see

Diagnosing Damp[1] Appendix B and Chapter 4, pp 34–35, under 'Occupier's lifestyle'.

In some cases it will be practical and possible to solve a condensation problem without investing in heating or ventilation systems or improving home insulation. – and specialist ventilation companies (understandably perhaps) may be more likely to suggest options for dealing with the condensation arising from lifestyle than directing a client towards the more emotive option of a lifestyle change.

- **Install improved heating, insulation or ventilation** – if condensation problems are deemed to be significant and cannot be simply addressed by a change in lifestyle, it will be necessary to consider improvements to heating, insulation and ventilation. It is worth carrying out feasibility research to clarify the best value solution. Such research could be carried out at various different decision-making stages:

  - **Feasibility Study A** – compare options: lifestyle adjustment versus design change, assess the heating/insulation/ventilation issues.
  - **Feasibility Study B** – compare options: improved heating versus improved insulation versus improved ventilation.
  - **Feasibility Study C** (having decided, for example, on improved ventilation) – compare options: e.g. local mechanical extractor fans versus background ventilation versus ventilation incorporated in a window replacement work package versus positive input ventilation versus whole house mechanical extraction.

Feasibility research should ideally include discussion and input from all interested parties – e.g. funding authorities, clients, occupiers, managing surveyors, legal advisors, relevant third parties, etc.

The prime aim of the feasibility research will usually be to establish value for money in terms of the costs of options versus how fully certain key criteria are met.

Even a one-off house condensation problem needs very organised thinking behind any remediation strategies, ideally set out in the form of a written appraisal. When a surveyor prepares a feasibility report to evaluate options for damp remedy, for example to address a condensation problem, the surveyor's report may perhaps best conclude by identifying a preferred strategy, but should explain how the various remedy options meet key criteria. It may often be the client that has the greatest influence on remedy decision, as after all, it will be the client who pays.

The surveyor need only include remedies with a good chance of success in the feasibility report.

Other reasons to install/improve house ventilation

The most common reason for installing additional ventilation may be to combat condensation-led mould, but there are other reasons too. Improvements to house ventilation can:

- provide fresher air;
- reduce air humidity to an acceptable level;
- control condensation;
- reduce mould colonisation on surfaces;
- reduce airborne mould spores and fragments;
- remove pollutants generally, for example:
  - allergens (e.g. house dust mites);
  - volatile organic compounds (VOCs) such as formaldehyde;
  - carbon dioxide;
  - carbon monoxide;
  - oxides of nitrogen;
  - tobacco smoke;
  - odours;
  - ensure safe operation of some combustion appliances.

A useful table of indoor air pollutants (Table 3.3) can be found in *Environment and Services* by Peter Burberry[57].

So if our original aim were purely to reduce mould colonisation, in improving ventilation *we could also achieve other important benefits.*

If all we do is install an extractor fan in a kitchen or bathroom, we may not significantly reduce air pollutants in the property as a whole. To significantly reduce the range of indoor air pollutants, a whole-house mechanical ventilation system would be required incorporating the appropriate filters.

There are other reasons why we should consider improving ventilation to reduce condensation and mould (rather than upgrading heating or installing additional insulation):

- upgrading ventilation is likely to be the most cost effective remedy;
- installing local or whole house ventilation systems would in most cases cause less disruption;
- extractor fans and even whole-house ventilation systems are surprisingly cheap to run, using very little electricity and requiring minimal maintenance.

Ventilation and building airtightness

We need to draw a distinction here between 'leaky buildings' and 'breathing buildings'. Some buildings self-ventilate effectively due to gaps around window sashes or in floors, roof coverings, etc. that allow movement of air from inside to outside and vice-versa. Such a building may be *leaky from air movement, but may not necessarily 'breathe'.* Buildings do not 'breathe' primarily by virtue of gaps in building elements or components, but because the basic building fabric is porous and can take in and evaporate out moisture.

Are buildings becoming 'tighter'?

Successive revisions to Building Regulations have increased thermal insulation requirements, but often at the expense of ventilation.

Many experts in the industry agree that over the past few decades, buildings have become more sealed up. In recent discussions with a house ventilation consultant it became clear that ventilation specialists follow the double glazers! It is common for the installation of double glazing to have a very negative impact on house ventilation. The new windows usually incorporate extremely efficient seals, and rarely include a small 'night ventilator'. Occupants might keep windows shut to maintain security or to keep out noise. Sashes are so often large sized, and cannot always be slightly opened in a locked position to allow modest background ventilation. Any property improvement should therefore consider the knock-on effects on ventilation. Locking devices may not be trusted, and a window ajar offers temptation to would-be burglars, so the sash is locked shut.

In estate improvement works, overcladding and indeed over-roofing are also usually installed with the aim of improving thermal insulation, weathertightness and building appearance. The down side may be less ventilation.

Table 3.2 of *Environment and Services*[57] lists factors which have reduced ventilation rates in buildings:

- abandonment between 1965 and 1990 of the requirement for flues or vents in habitable rooms;
- more tightly sealed windows;
- lack of night ventilators in windows;
- dense airtight construction in some cases;
- weather stripping;
- security dictating that windows must be kept closed; and
- flueless heating systems or balanced flues not drawing air from interior.

I could also add to that list laminate flooring. Many older houses, perhaps with uneven boarded floors, are being covered by new wood or wood effect flooring systems, which are closely fitting and reduce the opportunity for any fortuitous ventilation through gaps in adjacent floorboards. You will also often find a run of sealant between new floor covering and the base of the perimeter skirting board, reducing ventilation by air leakage at that position. (They also make access to the floor void very difficult for surveyor or builder.)

No building yet built has been perfectly airtight. Movement of air can occur into and out of the building through cracks, gaps and holes. The sum total of the routes through the building envelope is usually expressed in terms of air changes per hour (ach) when the building is subject to a pressure test of 50 Pascals (Pa), achieved by a fan normally sited in a removable door panel.

The effect of airtightness on ventilation efficiency

It is usually considered that for whole-house ventilation to be effective, a rate of 0.5 to 1 air change per hour (ach) should be achieved. The key issue is how much of this is achieved by controlled mechanical ventilation and how much by air leakage. Air leakage is not always predictable, as it depends on atmospheric conditions. Experts predict that by reducing air leakage to an acceptable level, ventilation becomes more predictable and energy efficient[58].

The Building Research Establishment informs us that houses typically have a natural infiltration rate of 0.7ach[59]. Some tightly sealed homes have a natural infiltration rate of as low as 0.2ach, meaning that there are insufficient air changes to achieve good indoor air quality.

In Digest 398 the BRE state that 'the dwelling should be as airtight as practicable for economic operation of an MEV or MVHR system'[59].

Types of ventilation system available

A basic requirement of the Building Regulations is that 'There shall be adequate means of ventilation provided for people in the building.' The implication is that the primary purpose of ventilation is to create satisfactory living conditions for occupiers, people, rather than to promote good conditions for the well-being of the building fabric, finishes and components. But in most cases the level of humidity achieved by good ventilation to suit humans (i.e. around 50 per cent) would be a suitable condition for many building materials and very often suits the contents as well. High humidity causes materials to expand and distort, and moulds to develop. Excessive dryness causes some materials to damagingly shrink and warp.

Approved Document F has been prepared in the light of changing perceptions of what ventilation needs to provide – for occupiers and the wider national interests:

- good air circulation as buildings are becoming increasingly airtight;
- reduction in internal relative humidity to inhibit mould development;
- reduction in relative humidity to reduce colonisation by dust mites;
- improved air circulation and filtering to reduce build-up of VOCs (volatile organic compounds), pollens, smoke and other pollutants and to generally improve indoor air quality (IAQ);
- reduction in background ventilators to reduce noise ingress;
- increased energy efficiency of fan motors;
- reduction in wasted heat from air extraction without heat recovery;
- increased efficiency rates of heat exchangers.

Clause 0.4 'performance' clearly underlines how seriously Building Regulations are now addressing energy issues in ventilation – with heat recovery featuring prominently.

The beauty of a mechanical ventilation system with heat recovery, according to industry experts, is that an effective ventilation solution can meet both the new AD F and AD L (Energy Efficiency) requirements. Another bonus of using this kind of system is that no window trickle ventilation is required, so noise ingress can be limited.

Under new Approved Document F, one of four systems is to be selected for consideration:

- System 1 – background ventilators and intermittent extractor fans;
- System 2 – passive stack ventilation (PSV);
- System 3 – continuous mechanical extraction (CME);
- System 4 – continuous mechanical supply and extraction with heat recovery (MVHR).

The chosen product or installation should comply with the relevant Building Regulations. (Systems or products carrying a BBA certificate may be considered more reliable.)

System 1 Background ventilators and intermittent extractor fans

This system is usually used in kitchens, bathrooms and WCs for removal of wet air and odours.

The new Approved Document F stipulates fan flow rates for various room types, e.g. 60 or 30 litres/second for kitchens and 15 litres/second for bathrooms (very much as per the existing Approved Document). The fans need to be used in conjunction with trickle (i.e. background) ventilation to achieve the required flow rates as set out in tables in AD F.

In the new AD F, a dedicated section on installation has been included in Appendix E *Good Practice Guide to the Installation of Fans for Dwellings*, which contains good design guidance on the alternative types of fan (axial, centrifugal, in-line) and the terminals to be fitted. Much guidance is included on how to design and fit ducts from fans, which are so often badly routed, kinked or just too lengthy to allow efficient air extraction.

BRE advice

The BRE Good Repair Guide 21, *Improving Ventilation in Housing*[60] highlights the popularity of mechanical extractor fans for removing moisture from wet rooms and points out that fans can be operated manually or mechanically. The Guide also cites the Building Regulations fan rate requirements.

In the Guide, BRE warns us that long ducts from ceiling fans reduce air flow rate. There are standard formulae for calculating the loss in efficiency. It is important to ensure that the power of a ceiling-mounted fan matches the length and configuration of the associated duct. This is where manufacturer's advice is key. Noise from ceiling mounted fans is a common problem, as the ceiling can act as a sounding box and vibrations can cause noise. BRE advises us to mount fans, if possible, on more solid construction, and away from bedrooms and living rooms. We are also advised that circular ducts cause less noise that square or rectangular sections. Further advice is contained in BRE Good Repair Guide 21 *Improving Ventilation in Housing*[60].

Always consult a suitably qualified plumbing engineer when an extractor fan is used that could affect an open-flued combustion appliance. Dangerous 'spillage' can occur, i.e. where the extractor fan pulls flue gases back into the room.

It is also important to bear in mind that the AD F sizing of fans for various house rooms is a minimum, not a maximum sizing. So it might be worth considering a more powerful fan to reduce motor wear and save running the fan on maximum speed.

Electrical works, particularly in a bathroom, shower room or kitchen, must be carried out by a suitably qualified electrician and all work tested on completion.

Even though a fan is correctly installed, a house or flat may still suffer condensation and mould due to moisture generation from a bathroom or kitchen because occupiers have not obeyed key rules. For example, the fan may be operating during bathing, and still running after bathing, but the occupier dresses in the bedroom leaving the bathroom door ajar or quite open. Alternatively, trickle vents could cause draughts – and be closed. This defeats the efforts to remove moisture at source as it can now readily migrate to other parts of the accommodation. Bathroom and kitchen doors should remain closed until such time as moist air has been expelled to the outside.

Fans are also best fitted with a filter to help keep the motors clean and free from dirt and grease. Filters need to be removed and washed or replaced as necessary. For maintenance by consumers, fans should be designed for easy removal of filters, etc., ideally without the need to use screwdrivers to remove face covers. A reputable fan manufacturer will offer all the best advice on running maintenance.

How a humidistat-controlled fan can be fooled

We know from basic psychrometrics that as air cools, and is not subject to any change in the moisture it contains, relative humidity will increase. This is a very basic law of physics. So air at say 20°C and 50% RH when cooled at nightfall in an unheated bathroom, could drop to say 16.5°C. This drop in air temperature would activate the fan, as RH will have risen to 65% (the common threshold RH for the fan to activate).

The running of an extractor fan could be a source of annoyance for an occupier, who might resent any noise or vibration from it, especially at night, and might think that electricity was being wasted (no matter how efficient the motor). So a frustrated occupier may disconnect the offending extractor fan!

Key points – System 1: background ventilators and intermittent extractor fans

- Extractor fans remove moist air at source, so help combat condensation.
- Mechanical extractor fans sited in wet areas can produce ventilation that meets Building Regulation performance requirements.
- Trickle vents are required for replacement air.
- Intermittent fans are required to wet areas.
- There is the potential for noise ingress.
- Fans themselves can be noisy.
- Background ventilators such as trickle vents may allow noise ingress or draughts and be simply closed by occupiers.
- There is no recovery of heat from the air extracted.
- Because they are seen to cost money to run, they are often just switched off or disconnected.
- Fans may be activated by a humidistat even when air is relatively dry, because when air cools, RH rises.
- Extractor fans are only as good as the replacement air.
- Extractor fans are sometimes fitted by general contractors without specialist ventilation knowledge or training or trade skills.
- Extractor fans would not be expected to produce good whole house air quality.
- Safety extra low voltage (SELV) fans can be used in risk areas such as bathrooms. (See Case Study 1 of this chapter.)

System 2: Passive stack ventilation

Passive stack ventilation systems (PSV) can be designed and installed for both new and existing buildings. The system might comprise little more than 100mm PVCU soil stack pipework routed from a kitchen or bathroom to the ridge or slope of the roof. There may be a humidistat or infrared sensor fitted at the ceiling vent, opening the system when the room is entered. (And of course, old houses often already incorporate a type of PSV system – otherwise known as a chimney flue!)

You need a separate stack for each wet area, so the installation is likely to be expensive. Also, as air is pulled out of the dwelling, there needs to be an opportunity for replacement air to come in, usually by trickle vents – which can be a noise problem and may simply be closed or shut off.

A PSV can be used as a substitute for, or in addition to, mechanical extractors in rooms such as kitchens, utility rooms and bathrooms.

The system is incredibly simple and described as follows by the BRE[60]:

'During the heating season, and under normal UK weather conditions, warm moist air from the room travels up the duct to the outside. When the indoor air temperature goes up, because of cooking, washing or bathing, the airflow rate in the duct increases. So the PSV system is more effective at the time it is most needed.'

BRE consider PSV systems to be adequate in removing moisture from dwellings, 'keeping condensation and mould growth under control', providing of course that they are properly designed and installed.

The BRE Information Paper IP 13/94[61], published several years before GBG 21, explains that a PSV system depends for operation on:

- firstly a difference between inside and outside temperature; and
- secondly the effect of wind passing over the roof of the dwelling.

This means that the system might not work effectively in certain weather conditions, such as outside the cold season or when there is insufficient wind.

The cost of a PSV installation would include not only the cost of ductwork, routing the ducts through the property, but also hiding ducts in casing. PSV could be difficult to install in a property of multiple tenure, work being needed in several accommodation units. Costs can double or treble where several rooms need to be ventilated, as each room must be fitted with its own independent stack. BRE recommend a duct size of 125mm internal diameter for a kitchen, 100mm for a utility room or bathroom, and 80mm for a WC. BRE mention problems from external noise, and suggest that PSV cannot be installed close to a tall building.

Key points – System 2: Passive stack ventilation

- Passive stack ventilation can be designed and installed to meet Building Regulations performance requirements.
- Background ventilation, such as trickle vents, is required for replacement air.
- Trickle vents may allow noise ingress or draughts and be simply closed by occupiers.
- There is no recovery of heat from air exiting to atmosphere.
- Separate ducts are required from each wet area, usually meaning several ducts projecting through the roof covering.
- Stacks may be activated by humidistats or infrared sensors triggered by entry of occupier into wet area.
- PSV can remove moist air at source and so can help combat condensation.
- PSV will usually be installed by skilled fitters in new-build applications.

- PSV efficiency varies with external climatic conditions and the system cannot therefore always be dependably controlled.
- PSV can help improve indoor air quality, but incoming air would not usually be filtered or processed in any way.
- PSV is difficult to install into existing property, particularly existing flatted accommodation.

System 3: Continuous mechanical extraction

There are quite a few advantages with continuous mechanical extraction (CME) systems.

CME systems basically use a single energy-efficient fan with multi-speed control, located in a loft or airing cupboard, and with ducts to wet areas or WCs. Pollutants are removed at source from bathrooms, WCs and utility rooms. The fan runs continuously; being sited away from living areas, there will be little noise disturbance from its operation.

But as with other systems, there is a down side. There will be a need for replacement air via background ventilators, and therefore draughts and possible noise ingress. There is no heat recovery.

Such systems may or may not have the ability to 'purge ventilate'. You can imagine that when a kitchen fills with smoke from cooking, there will be a need to get rid of the polluted air very quickly. It may often be possible to just open a window, but some kitchens, bathrooms or WCs are sited towards the inner zones of the building plan, with no openable window available for rapid air dilution. So a means of quickly and efficiently ejecting foul air would be needed. Mechanical ventilation systems are designed to lowish extraction rates, being designed to run continuously rather than as a swift response to an urgent air ventilation requirement. In a kitchen, of course, a cooker extraction hood could be installed to provide additional extract ventilation at source.

Key points – System 3: continuous mechanical extraction

- CME ventilation can be designed and installed to meet Building Regulations performance requirements.
- Background ventilators such as trickle vents are required for replacement air.
- Trickle vents may allow noise ingress or draughts and be simply closed by occupiers.
- The fan can be sited away from the habitable spaces and therefore not cause a noise nuisance.
- There is no recovery of heat from extracted air.
- CME can remove moist air at source and so can help combat condensation.
- CME can help improve indoor air quality, but incoming air would not usually be filtered or processed in any way.

- CME would be difficult to install into existing property, particularly existing flatted accommodation.

System 4: Continuous mechanical supply and extraction with heat recovery systems (MVHR)

With MVHR systems, fresh air is drawn into a heat recovery unit which also pushes stale air out of the building. The incoming fresh air is warmed from the heat of outgoing air. A typical heat recovery room fan is shown in figure 210.

Heat recovery fan units can be used to ventilate a whole house, or an individual room or space.

Background ventilation is not needed for this type of ventilation system, unless the units are used for individual rooms and are then deemed to need background ventilation as per standard extractor fans. Some current equipment claims to have a 95 per cent heat recovery efficiency. There is little noise ingress with such systems.

Manufacturers make quite optimistic claims concerning the efficiency of the heat exchanger; energy efficiency is highest when external temperatures are lower.

DETR Good Practice Guide 268[58] refers to typical heat recovery of 60 per cent of heat from outgoing air. (Remember that standard extractor fans lose *all* the heat from outgoing air!)

A continually running fan will also change house air, so ridding it of pollutants and unwanted humidity developed inside the building envelope.

Figure 210: A heat recovery room ventilator. Photo © courtesy Kair Ventilation Ltd, www.kair.co.uk

Under the DETR *Best Practice Programme*, it was shown that heat recovery mechanical ventilation systems can successfully reduce indoor relative humidity.

Systems usually incorporate low speed and high speed or 'booster' settings for periods of high moisture generation. The fans can provide background as well as rapid extract ventilation under manual or humidistat controls.

Ducting will be required from extractor diffuser positions and the heat recovery/fan units, often sited on an external wall in an entrance hallway at high level.

Key points – System 4: continuous mechanical supply and extraction with heat recovery (MVHR)

- MVHR can be designed and installed to meet Building Regulations performance requirements.

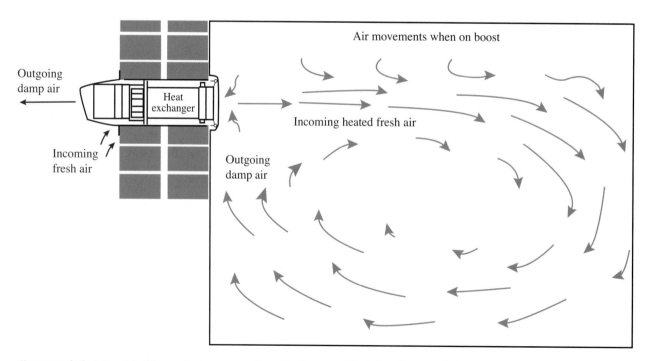

Figure 209: The basic principle of the room heat recovery ventilator. Note how a good circulation of incoming fresh air replaces the outgoing stale and moist air. © Courtesy Kair Ventilation Ltd, www.kair.co.uk

Figure 225: Standard tap water is poured into the machine to produce a reservoir of steam. The operative wears protective gloves, overalls and respirator. Skirting boards have already been removed.

Figure 228: Working towards the room corner using a lance to power steam onto the mouldy surface.

Figure 226: The machine heats up the water to 6 bar pressure (typical house water pressure may be 3 bars).

Figure 229: A cotton or microfibre cloth swabs mould off the surface.

Figure 227: Steam jets to the surface, to kill mould, which the operative scrubs and loosens.

Figure 230: Dead mould on the disposable cloth.

Figure 231: A lancette in this case cleans mould along the top of a retained skirting board (specialist cleaners usually request that skirting boards be removed).

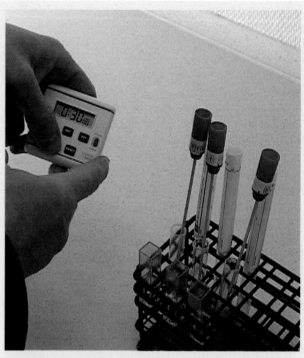

Figure 234: Swabs of mould are tested for their biomass. Biomass includes fungal fragments, spores and hyphae. The amount of biomass present on the sampled area will be reflected in a mycometer reading. Post-cleaning, a very low reading should be logged.

Figure 232: Brush head loosens mould and cleans the surface.

Figure 235: Testing completed, results will form part of the final clean-up report.

Figure 233: The mould has gone and the air is now fresh and safe, so the surveyor taking a post-clean-up mould sample has no need for personal protective equipment (PPE).

Photos © courtesy Micro Clean Ltd, www.microclean.dk

The ceiling lining would be stripped and replaced. Ceiling plasterboard appeared sound and may not need to be replaced. If replaced, it should incorporate a vapour check (Any membrane that is punctured, e.g. by fixings, cannot be described as a vapour 'barrier'!) A vapour 'barrier' could be achieved using an appropriate ceiling finish or a vapour check installed during the plasterboard fitting.

Ventilation

It was proposed to install extractor ventilation with humidistat and manual control, to meet current Building Regulations.

The occupiers were reluctant to open the fanlight in the winter, and were more preoccupied with changing clothes after a bath than opening fanlights to help eject moisture-laden air. The fan would take care of this.

The existing 225 × 150mm airbrick opening would be used to house the extractor fan. The airbrick would be taken out, and the opening adjusted to suit the new fan.

It was recommended by the fan manufacturer that a fan sited in the bath zone should be SELV (safety extra low voltage). The fan would be triggered by a 12V humidistat located outside the splash zone, and would also incorporate a manual override. The fan itself had a safety isolation transformer to BS EN 60742. The fan met the Building Regulation requirement of 15 litres/second for a bathroom (see Table 1.1a in Approved Document F, available at www. planningportal.gov.uk/england/professionals/en/4000000000339.html). The

selected fan had a telescopic sleeve which could adjust to wall thicknesses between 255–360mm.

Replacement air was available via a 10mm gap under the bathroom door – which met recommendations as per Appendix E: *Good Practice Guide to the Installation of Fans for Dwellings* of the new Approved Document F.

Site work notes: installing the low voltage bathroom mechanical extractor fan

The position was dictated by that of the existing airbrick. This position should not present any problems. Where extractor fans are sited too low, their effectiveness can be compromised. Make sure that only the fan is within the splash zone.

The kit included:

- The low voltage fan with manual override and adjustable humidity control:

  – to be sited 50mm min. below ceiling level.

- The transformer:

  – must be sited away from the splash zone;
  – could be sited in the loft, but would not advise this as any electrical malfunction would not be immediately detectable. It could be sited in the hallway, probably the best location;
  – three pole isolator switch fused spur required.

- The humidistat:

  – ideally would be sited on an inner wall, 100mm below ceiling level;

Guide to siting equipment in a location containing a bath

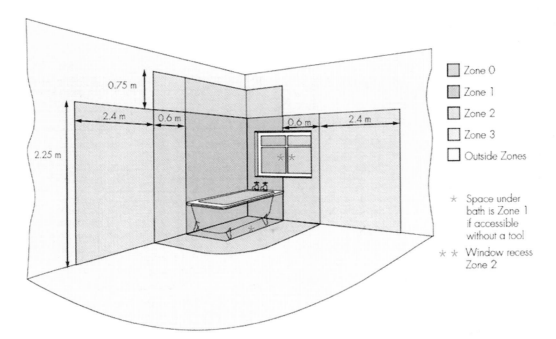

Figure 248: The purple zone above and near the bath is the 'splash zone'. It extends to 2.25 metres above floor level. It is not recommended to site mains voltage fans in this area, nor transformers or humidistats. Sketch © courtesy Vent-Axia.

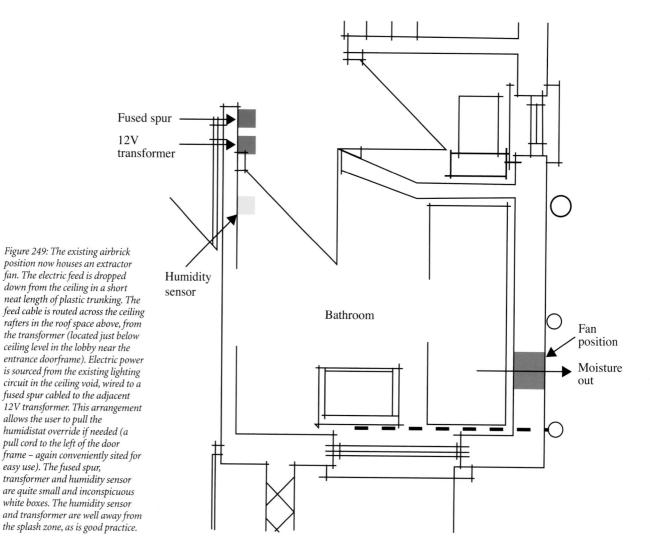

Figure 249: The existing airbrick position now houses an extractor fan. The electric feed is dropped down from the ceiling in a short neat length of plastic trunking. The feed cable is routed across the ceiling rafters in the roof space above, from the transformer (located just below ceiling level in the lobby near the entrance doorframe). Electric power is sourced from the existing lighting circuit in the ceiling void, wired to a fused spur cabled to the adjacent 12V transformer. This arrangement allows the user to pull the humidistat override if needed (a pull cord to the left of the door frame – again conveniently sited for easy use). The fused spur, transformer and humidity sensor are quite small and inconspicuous white boxes. The humidity sensor and transformer are well away from the splash zone, as is good practice.

Fused spur

12V transformer

Humidity sensor

Bathroom

Fan position

Moisture out

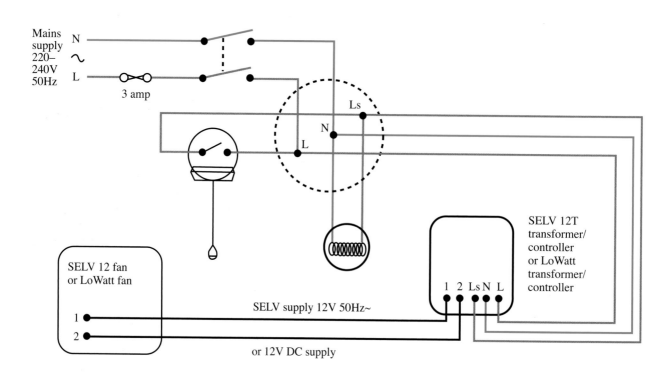

Figure 250: You may note the isolation of the fan from the mains supply, where the fan is connected to a transformer. Diagram © courtesy Vent-Axia.

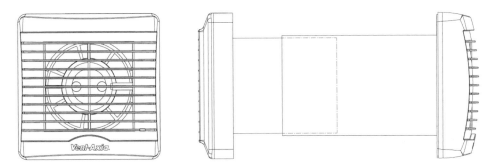

Figure 251: Front view and cross-section of a low voltage extractor fan, which has a telescopic circular duct to suit various wall thicknesses. Image © courtesy Vent-Axia.

Figure 252: Low voltage axial fan selected. Image © courtesy Vent-Axia.

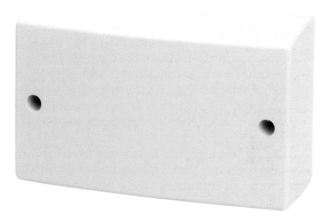

Figure 253: Transformer, which may be fitted into a standard surface-mounted plastic double socket mounting box. Image © courtesy Vent-Axia.

- the humidistat selected had an adjustable %RH trigger and could be manually adjusted (by the turn of a screw) between 65–90RH, in case the fan was running for too long or vice versa.

● Cabling: mains supply to transformer to humidistat sensor to fan:

- a fused spur was needed from the mains. (Of course all electrical work in a bathroom must be carried out by a qualified electrician to satisfy Part P of the Building Regulations, which came into force on 1 January 2005. For work in a bathroom, notify the local authority Building Control department, or employ an electrician who is a member of a competent person self-certification scheme, who will be able to certify that the work complies with Building Regulations.)

The advantages of the localised mechanical extract ventilation specified were:

● safe – fed by low voltage electricity;
● good control – manual over-ride and adjustable humidity control;
● met current Building Regulations of 15 litres/second;
● moisture-laden air removed at source;
● would markedly help eliminate or control mould colonisation.

Worked example of a mould risk assessment, by Stuart Athol, Environmental Health Officer (EHO)

An EHO was called by a tenant of a private landlord to inspect her top floor flat due to the presence of mould growth and the fact that her landlord did not want to bother himself with the problem. The premises were approximately 25 years old, with cavity walls, two bedrooms, lounge, bathroom, kitchen, store cupboard, pitched roof and were double glazed throughout. The flat was located in an urban location within Essex and only the tenant and her sister lived there. Heavy mould growth was present along the junctions of the external wall and ceiling in the lounge and bedrooms and above the skirting boards on the internal partition walls behind sofas and beds. The tenants had only lived there for seven months and the flat had been decorated just prior to them moving in.

HHSRS

1 What is the likelihood of a 14-year-old or less person's health being affected by the presence of the mould? National average for a post-1979 built single occupancy dwelling is 1 in 725. Because the mould is present in all rooms, there is no realistic way that a 14-year-old person could ever escape from its effects. Therefore, based on that justification, the EHO decided that the likelihood in this case would be more like 1 in 3.

2 The outcome incorporating classes of harm for this particular hazard are 0% for Class 1 (highly unlikely that the 14-year-old would die from the mould presence), 1% for Class 2, 10% for Class 3 and 89% for Class 4 (regular coughs and colds).

3 Calculate the HHSRS Score: the calculation produced a score of 1630, which meant that it was in band C and therefore classed as a Category 1 hazard.

4 The EHO must now consider the most appropriate form of enforcement action based on who actually lives there. Consideration of the vulnerable age group is only relevant to arriving at the HHSRS score.

5 The EHO decided that serving the landlord with an Improvement Notice forcing him to install heat recovery air extraction vents in the habitable rooms was the best course of action.

CASE STUDY 2: BRIXTON – 'SOMETHING IN THE AIR'

Figure 255: Visible mould, 'ghosting' on the bathroom ceiling, where tenants had attempted to clean off mould.

The extractor fan pushes damp bathroom air straight into a redundant chimney flue, which is also the dumping ground for the gas boiler's products of combustion.

Figure 256: This rather tasteless corner bath hides a dark secret.

Figure 254: You are about to see inside the lower ground floor flat. You will nearly always find yourself heading downstairs to inspect damp.

Figure 257: Once the front bath panel was removed we found animal remains, probably a dead rat. The animal seemed to have been collecting mineral insulation wool from the adjacent partition to make a nest.

Figure 258: A dark shiny beetle makes its run for freedom along the length of a steel tape. It measured a little over 5mm.

The small beetle was picked up on a sheet of paper, popped into a matchbox and later identified as a *Dermestid* beetle (common names: larder, bacon or hide beetle). This beetle (see BRE, *Recognising Wood Rot and Insect Damage in Buildings*[37]) is likely to be found on dry materials of animal origin, such as leather, fur, feathers – and dead rodents. The beetle was only a few feet away from the rat's final resting place.

Do not be put off from easing back a bath panel – it's always a likely place to find damp damage – damage needing a remedy.

Pulling up a corner of the heavy dark brown carpet revealed heavy tacky black mould underneath.

The flat's layout is typical of so many 1970s flat conversions, with a very deep floor plan – difficult to ventilate naturally. See figure 259. Such a long corridor can be oppressive, even more so when sealed off with bland fire doors. The bedrooms both had an outside window or door, but not the bathroom.

This house was on a noisy thoroughfare. Tenants were reluctant to open sashes to ventilate their flat, being concerned also regarding security, and avoiding cold draughts in the winter. With the flat often virtually sealed up in the winter, RH would often be sufficiently high to cause condensation and mould.

Moisture generation in the bathroom relied on a poorly installed and almost certainly inefficient extractor fan operating off the light pull switch.

100mm diameter axial fans meet good practice for ventilating a bathroom when the ceiling mounted fan is linked to flexible duct up to 1.5 metres in length, with no more than two 90° bends. A longer duct or more bends might cause a performance drop. A wall/ceiling mounted centrifugal fan may be suitable for a bathroom if rated at 15 litres per second, and with flexible or rectangular ducting of up to 6 metres – and again with no more than two 90° bends. So it may be possible to achieve good local mechanical extract ventilation, providing the fan and associated ductwork is carefully selected and installed.

It is very common for today's surveyors to recommend humidistat-controlled extractor fans – such a fan would probably be more effective than one

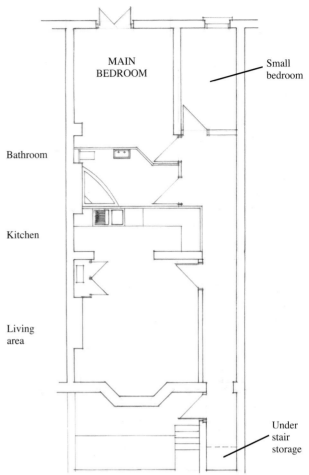

Figure 259: Brixton plan. Sketch X – Lower Ground Floor – Brixton Flat Conversion. It is likely that the small rear bedroom is located on the line of an original single storey rear addition, with the larger main bedroom where an outside yard used to be located.

operated on a light switch. It is often said, however, that humidistat-controlled fans kick in at too high a humidity level (often being factory set at 60–65%, when the optimum condition for living is closer to 50% RH). And not forgetting that high RH is only one parameter of bad air – just think of the range of odours and contaminants that could build up.

The other problem of localised extractor fans is the very fact that they are localised. If damp air is pulled out of a room by such a fan, the air will then simply be replaced by other air from another adjacent space – and this replacement air might also be damp, stale or polluted.

And of course once the bathroom door is opened after a bath or shower, damp air migrates into the far reaches of the flat. The common scenario is for the bather to leave the bathroom, to dress in a bedroom, leaving the bathroom door wide open. Even if shut, the door may have gaps, providing exit routes for wet air.

Migrating damp air could find its way to the small rear bedroom – intermittently or even unheated – perhaps used only as a store room or occasional study. So condensation forms on the cold room surfaces and mould colonies develop.

It is also common to find radiators in such a corridor draped with drying clothes. This obviously stifles heat from the radiator and creates a cold space with a high humidity. Again, these conditions favour condensation.

Remedy options

An efficient mechanical ventilation system will help maintain a healthy internal environment, free of unpleasant odours, volatile organic compounds (VOCs), allergens, oxides of nitrogen, carbon monoxide, carbon dioxide and tobacco smoke.

The beauty of mechanical ventilation *with heat recovery*, is that an effective ventilation solution can meet both the new AD F *and* AD L (Energy Efficiency) standards. There are other bonuses with using this kind of system, in that no window trickle ventilation is required, so noise ingress can be limited.

But just how healthy internal air from efficient mechanical ventilation might be is of course dependent very much on how good the quality of air around the building is. You cannot introduce fresh Scottish Highland air into a Brixton flat – all you can do is *pull in the best local air you can lay your fans on!*

Remedy option 1: Three heat recovery units – one for each bedroom and one in the front living room/kitchen area

Fans such as we show in figure 210 (see page 156) can be installed through-the-wall and exchange warmed incoming fresh air for outgoing damper and stale air.

With such a fan, room air is pulled into the side of the front grille, is taken down the sides of the unit to the heat exchanger, and pulled out of the front of the unit by the front fan. Incoming air is pulled through a grille, through intake filters, through the heat exchanger, then through the front fan and thence through the front of the unit. There is no actual contact between outgoing and incoming air, but the cellular structure of the heat exchanger box enables heat to be transferred between each air stream.

It is possible to fit heat exchangers with various types of filters. For example a HEPA filter will filter out very fine particles. Other filters could also be used as needed, but using more filters means more powerful fans, which in turn means more electricity to run them.

The unit can be fitted and serviced from inside the dwelling – saving expensive access costs for high buildings. Maintenance would include replacing or cleaning filters regularly. Some filters can be cleaned using a domestic vacuum cleaner, or washed using suitable detergents. Twelve volt motors are guaranteed typically for five years.

In this option, heat recovery through-the-wall room ventilator units are fitted to the two bedrooms and the front kitchen/living room. The moisture-laden air from the bathroom would migrate via the corridor into bedrooms, where it would be extracted by the heat recovery units. We have to be careful here, as moist air migrating out from the bathroom must not remain for long within the long corridor, which, if underheated, could create a condensation trap.

The heat recovery units operate 24 hours a day on trickle mode. Linked to each unit is a wall-mounted humidity sensor control that may be adjusted by a thumb wheel to the humidity level, that will activate fans from trickle to boost mode. There is also the option of a pull cord override. The fans can also be linked to timers, thermostats or to remote sensors in other areas. Some fans incorporate night sensors, so the unit does not kick in to boost mode at night (so keeping noise to an absolute minimum during sleep time).

The heat recovery fan is a safe 12 volt unit, operating on an electrical supply from the dual purpose transformer/humidity sensor unit.

Each heat recovery ventilation unit is able to produce an airflow of 12.6m³ per hour on trickle mode, or 35.6m³ per hour on boost. So the three units could achieve a whole-house air change in less than 90 minutes on boost mode.

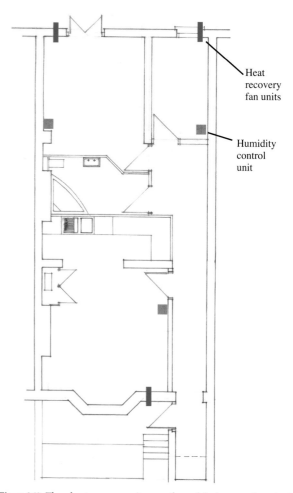

Heat recovery fan units

Humidity control unit

Figure 260: Three heat recovery units – one for each bedroom and one in the front living room/kitchen area.

Figure 261: A heat recovery ventilation fan in a typical installation – note the humidistat sensor unit to the left of the fan unit. Surface trunking is run for convenience, but the electricity supply could of course be chased in and plastered over.

If you need to monitor use of the fans, digital hour meters may be fitted. Such a facility is extremely useful if you need to know for certain whether or not the units are being used and for how long. Even though such a unit requires very little energy to run, occupiers may be tempted to turn them off, to save a few pennies.

The unit shown is rated at a meagre 4.2 watts on trickle mode, and 17.3 watts on boost – this is less than a standard electric light bulb. Such a heat recovery unit is said to recover up to 73% of exhaust heat. Other heat recovery fan units boast higher rates of heat recovery efficiency, even 90–95%. However, the efficiency quoted by competing manufacturers may depend on conditions of use and method of calculating efficiency.

You need to check there are not too many air leak opportunities in the flat or house, as this type of ventilation system operates best when the building is quite airtight.

Remedy option 2: Flat ventilator unit in hallway together with a heat recovery ventilator in each bedroom

In each living space the units you see extract stale and damp air. The main flat ventilation system pulls stale air out of the kitchen and bathroom, operating continually on trickle mode. A heat recovery ventilator in each of the rear bedrooms will eliminate

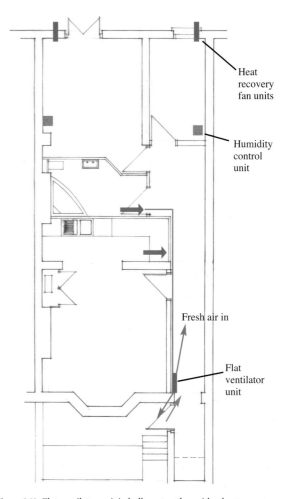

Figure 262: Flat ventilator unit in hallway together with a heat recovery ventilator in each bedroom

completely any chance of dumping of moisture on the colder surfaces of rooms that may not be sufficiently heated. This is probably the best of the three systems technically, but the client wished to save funds by just installing the flat ventilator unit (option 3). Should this not prove sufficient it would of course be easy to install two further room heat recovery fan units as per option 2.

Remedy option 3: Mechanical ventilation with heat recovery – flat ventilator to service extracts in bathroom and kitchen

This was the selected system. A flat input ventilator would be sited at high level in the hallway near the front door. The ventilation unit looks fairly inconspicuous – a white box, sized 380 × 290 × 156mm. Holes are bored through the main front wall through which incoming and outgoing pipe ducts are fitted.

A fairly efficient duct layout allows air to be extracted from both the kitchen and the bathroom. This moisture-laden warm air passes through a heat exchanger in the input ventilator, which warms the colder incoming air. Incoming colder air, pulled through

181

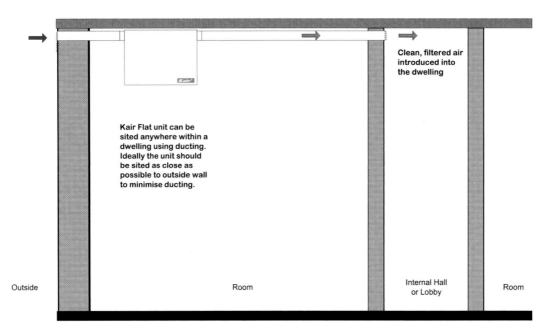

Clean, filtered air introduced into the dwelling

Kair Flat unit can be sited anywhere within a dwelling using ducting. Ideally the unit should be sited as close as possible to outside wall to minimise ducting.

Outside

Room

Internal Hall or Lobby

Room

Figure 263: The selected option. © Kiltox Damp Free Solutions.

from outside the building is warmed by outgoing air by the heat exchanger. This warmed fresh air is pushed out by a fan into the hallway area. The system not only removes *moist* air produced from bathing, but also removes odours from use of the WC in the bathroom.

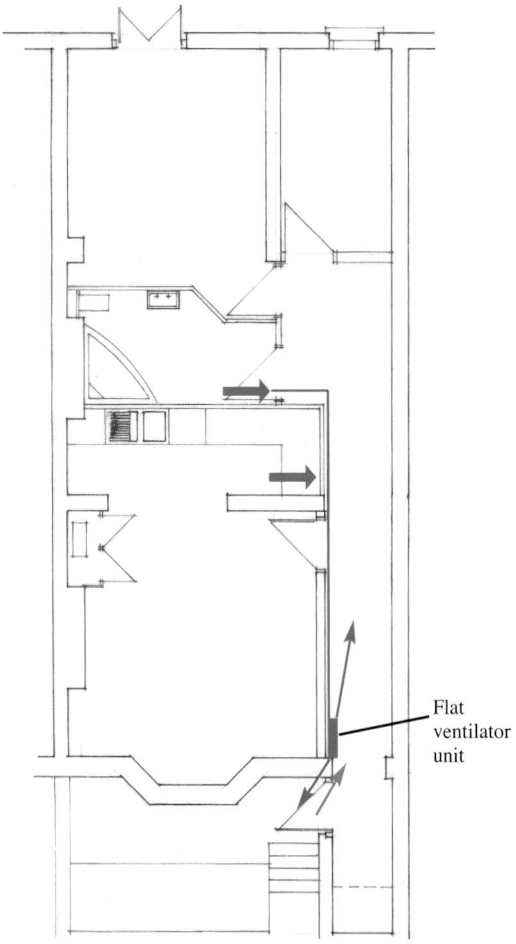

The flat ventilation unit is fitted snugly at high level near the flat entrance door, with the inlets and outlets routed through core drilled 102mm diameter holes.

Such a ventilation unit is able to produce an airflow on trickle mode of 33m^3 per hour, and works at a heat exchange efficiency of 65% (according to product literature). This flat has a volume of around 150m^3, so with the unit on trickle mode, an air change for the whole property would take around five hours, and on

Flat ventilator unit

Figure 264: Siting the ventilator unit.

Figure 265: Inlet and outlet grilles are above the flat entrance doorway.

boost (i.e. airflow 100m³/hour), 90 minutes. On boost this therefore equates to 0.66 air changes per hour.

You can see why changes in internal environmental conditions can be improved so quickly, with condensation risk virtually eliminated in an hour or two from first switching on the equipment.

Such equipment should keep relative humidity in the property down to 50% or less, reducing not only the condensation risk but improving air quality from the continual replenishment of fresh and warmed air within the dwelling.

The 'boost' setting might be required during the heating season when moisture generation is high. The system is designed to run continuously on trickle mode to maintain a satisfactory indoor air quality. In the summer months an occupier may be inclined to augment ventilation using openable windows.

In the system shown in option 3, the ventilator unit and the associated ductwork is in the hallway, and any noise from the fan operation or air movement through ducting should cause no nuisance whatsoever. Modern fans are said by manufacturers to be quite silent runners and in any case can operate on trickle-only at night by override and automatic switching from a light sensor.

The system can also be used to 'purge' foul smells, e.g. paint odours, smells from the kitchen, etc. when switched to boost mode.

General notes on installation

Looking at option 3, you will appreciate that the air intake is very close to the air extract – the two are side-by-side above the entrance door. Ideally, the air pulled into the property should not be the stale air that is being ejected. This is termed 'short circuiting'.

The air intake at Brixton is sited at the front of the building, approximately four metres away from the combination boiler flue terminal. This should be a sufficient separation. However, in the front yard is a line of refuse bins, which could in some circumstances create unpleasant odours one would not wish to be sucked into the property. The same risk applies with natural ventilation – the opening top lights of the bay windows are also rather close to the wheelie bins.

Monitoring

Bear in mind that there may have been other remedial works carried out in tandem – for example heating upgrade, some insulation work, external repairs etc. It is unlikely that installing a new ventilation system will remedy *all* the property's damp woes.

The proof of the pudding is always in the eating, so when you visit to check out the new ventilation system, some key questions would be:

1. Have the occupiers experienced improved health?
2. Have the occupiers noticed improvement in air quality?
3. Has there been less condensation?
4. Is there less or indeed any fresh mould colonisation?
5. Is relative humidity now at an acceptable level? (Take a reading.)
6. Are room temperatures achieved satisfactory? (Take some readings.)
7. Does the air smell fresher?

Internal temperature and humidity conditions can of course be monitored using data logging equipment such as we describe in Chapter 8.

Ideally, you would check the effectiveness of the new ventilation system when it's most needed – at times of the day when there is heavy moisture generation and at a time of the year with the greatest condensation risk.

8 Monitoring moisture condition

INTRODUCTION

House surveyors have advised 'monitoring' in survey reports for many years, for cracks – to help us determine if a building is still on the move – and we can do the same for dampness. Monitoring includes observation and recording of all manner of events inside and outside a building, not just measuring moisture condition. Monitoring can help in a diagnosis or help evaluate a remedy.

Do not be under the false impression that monitoring necessitates complex set-ups of sensors, wires and probes linked to unfathomable computer software. True, there are experts in the industry who are able to monitor building performance using all manner of sophisticated techniques – but the aim of this book is to advise the working house surveyor, on techniques that are practical and useful.

This chapter introduces a way of categorising monitoring into five levels. It then shows a series of moisture measuring tests undertaken by the author using various types of moisture measuring equipment, and takes you through some examples of monitoring to demonstrate how monitoring data might be interpreted.

Many property inspections are single-visit inspections, snapshots of the building – so there is no opportunity to observe moisture conditions over time, to find out if dampness is regressive, unchanged or progressive. For house surveyors, monitoring could be useful for a number of reasons:

- To assess the influence of lifestyle.
- To help evaluate the influence of weather on dampness or wetness.
- To assess the impact of damp-proofing or waterproofing on the internal environment.
- To appraise the effect of a new ventilation scheme.

You may sometimes need to think outside the box, when an occupier might innocently water plants or clean a floor, wetting areas of the building being monitored during the drying process after a flood.

Two sectors of the property industry have been taking monitoring very seriously for some years, the **flooring industry** and the **damage management industry.**

The procedure for checking the dryness of screeds is laid down in BS 8203[65]. Later in the chapter we will

Figure 266: This newly fitted stripped hardwood floor – tongue and grooved oak – is the pride and joy of the home owner.

Figure 267: Joy turns to shocked horror as the floor covering buckles upwards like a roller coaster from dampness underneath in the screed. If only the floor contractor – or a local surveyor – had checked the screed for dampness, before rushing to complete the house makeover.

show you how surveying instruments can help you check this yourself.

Damage management contractors dry buildings after all manner of flood events. Low surface moisture meter readings from an electronic moisture meter alone would not usually be sufficient evidence of dryness to convince them to switch off dehumidifiers and leave the site. If they have failed to monitor drying carefully enough and the walls and floors are still in fact damp *at depth*, then decorations and finishes will be ruined a second time around by the still lingering underlying dampness.

In the context of a dampness investigation, checks are made of the moisture condition of air, solid porous materials, and air within solid porous materials or trapped over a substrate.

Using standard survey equipment, measurements are taken of the following to help us understand change in moisture condition:

- air temperature;
- humidity;
- conductance;
- capacitance.

THE KEY MONITORING LEVELS

- Level 1 – mainly visual but also using other senses – building/human interactive.
- Level 2 – using electronic moisture meters (EMM), in resistance and capacitance modes.
- Level 3 – using EMM accessories:
  - non-invasive, and/or
  - invasive.
- Level 4 – using carbide meters (sometimes oven drying).
- Level 5 – using sophisticated data logging and wireless equipment.

House surveyors mainly use level 1–2 techniques, flooring contractors and drying contractors chiefly use level 1–3 techniques. Level 4 and 5 techniques are used by some house surveyors to diagnose condensation problems, particularly in social housing when disputes need to be resolved between property manager and occupier. Level 5 methods are used by specialist environmental consultants to solve complex dampness problems.

When we visit a site to check building condition, we use *all our senses* to assess change. We also interact with occupiers and find out key information regarding not only the building itself, but how occupiers and users are experiencing it and reacting to it.

THE KEY MONITORING PROCEDURES

- Establishing key aims of monitoring.
- Initial assessment of moisture condition in the building materials, indoor and outdoor air.
- Key decisions on methodology – *what*, *where* and *how* to monitor (NB there may physical access issues to take into consideration here).
- Installing monitoring stations or development of monitoring positions.
- Taking moisture condition readings at intervals (as a basic rule, results from three monitoring visit would be needed to establish any kind of definable trend – i.e. that any part of the building is becoming wetter or drier. Two site visits producing declining damp readings might not be conclusive enough. Occupiers' permissions may limit the number of times you can return to a property).

- Analysis of readings and information collecting.
- Fine tuning of remediation in the light of readings collected.
- Evaluation.

Many of the monitoring examples featured in this chapter are in a drying scenario, following flood damage.

Any survey you carry out on any building could potentially become part of a monitoring exercise – as you may later return to the property and compare what you saw and noted on day X to what you see and note on the subsequent visit, day Y.

MONITORING LEVELS EXPLAINED IN DETAIL

Level 1 monitoring – mainly visual but also using other senses – building/human interactive

There really is no substitute for regular visual inspection, no matter how sophisticated remote monitoring systems become. A remote monitoring system cannot interface with an occupier, who may divulge useful information concerning how the property is performing or being used, or how the environment is controlled. Sights, sounds and smells inform the visiting surveyor.

As materials dry out or wet up, they often exhibit visual change. Masonry lightens in colour as it dries, or darkens as it wets. Stains remain after a material dries. Water levels rise and drop, leaving tide lines or collected detritus. Fungi and moulds may show signs of extension or regression. You may notice formation of salts on an exposed brick substrate. Perhaps equipment (e.g. dehumidifiers) has been moved or switched off. Outside you note rain penetration problems where faults in rainwater goods allow water to soak through onto an internal wall or floor, or flooding of certain areas occurs at times of high rainfall. The rooflight carelessly left open to allow in drips of water that wets the floor you are trying to dry. The scratching and scuttling sounds from the loft above – and didn't we learn from the caretaker that some creature has chewed through a plastic pipe from the storage cistern? The musty smell you noticed in the entrance porch with the flat roof. You need to *be there* to hear it, smell it, and ask the questions.

Level 2 monitoring – using electronic moisture meters (EMM), in resistance and capacitance modes

All surveyors will have standard moisture meters with just the pin probe facility. Many will have the facility for use in capacitance or pin probe mode, which can be extremely useful in monitoring dampness, especially if the readings captured on a screen are *numbers*. Better still if the screen has a backlight.

The key thing is to be **very methodical,** but also to interpret the readings correctly. Log the exact position of all readings, so later visits to take a reading will be to *the same place*.

Prepare a monitoring table on which to log your readings.

You may find it useful to monitor dampness by setting out a grid of readings on a sketch. It can be a slow and laborious activity, but you can reap rich rewards.

You need to know the limitations of electronic moisture meter readings. For more detail see *Diagnosing Damp*[1], Chapter 7.

The conductance moisture meter can potentially tell you:

- whether position A is damper or drier near the surface than position B at time X;
- whether A is damper or drier at time X or time Y.

Note of caution

An electronic moisture meter offers quite a good indication of the percentage moisture content of timber, but near the surface only using standard pin probes for conductance readings.

Some resistance meters (the other name for a *conductance* meter) offer a percentage moisture content in other material – such as concrete or screed. Meters that are calibrated for concrete will be of less use in a cement/sand screed, as concrete is a material with different physical properties. Concrete itself varies considerably, from the very porous 'no-fines' mixes to the denser more structurally efficient grades. Concrete might potentially contain say 5 per cent of its dry weight as water, but a cementitious screed perhaps 15 per cent.

A moisture meter can only give you a percentage moisture content in:

- a material for which it has been specifically calibrated by the manufacturer;
- another material that by coincidence has similar properties of electrical resistance;
- material for which you have prepared a calibration graph (see Appendix F);

and always providing that:

- the subject material does not contain unexpected carbon, salt or metal to magnify readings;
- the readings are not taken in the proximity of metals, e.g. a capacitance reading to wall plaster near a cast-iron fireplace surround or electrical cable;
- the batteries are of suitable type and charged; and
- the moisture meter is in good working order and used correctly.

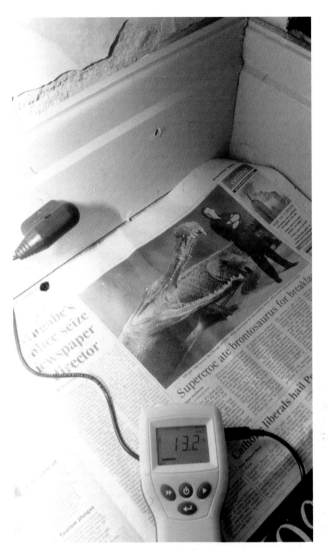

Figure 269: A moisture meter reading of 13.2% is recorded in quite a thick skirting board.

Figure 268: A capacitance reading of 1000 means it is extremely likely this floor screed is significantly damp. You could check the timber edge gripper using the pin probes – a reading of 17% or more will probably mean you are at the scene of a damp problem. Make sure you have noted exactly where you checked the floor – e.g. 'rear room floor screed, rear wall, 150mm from skirting, 1450mm from NE corner'. Mark this position too on a floor plan sketch. If checking under a floor underlay, sniff the underlay for mould.

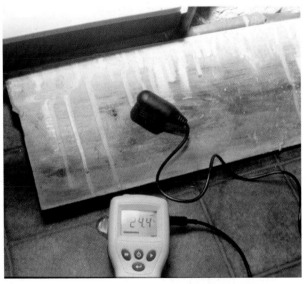

Figure 270: The same skirting section is removed, and you can at once see its dark discoloration – and mould. The pins are pronged, and a much higher reading behind the skirting of 24.4% fills our screen. A clear lesson that moisture meter readings taken on the room face of thick skirting boards can be misleading.

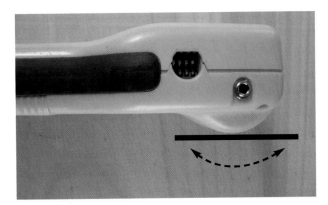

Figure 271: The contact position for this capacitance meter is curved, so you must rotate the instrument till the highest reading is on screen, then log it. This instrument is multi-functional as it can also be used with pins for obtaining a resistance reading, and a thermo-hygrometer and surface thermometer supplied with the instrument allow the user to check for live condensation.

Figure 272: The two rubber pads of this capacitance meter enable a good contact with the substrate to be achieved, and a thermo-hygrometer can also be connected to the unit. Top photo © courtesy Tramex Ltd.

Figure 273: This capacitance meter has been developed for checking concrete and screeds, and its calibration can be checked using a dedicated calibration plate. Note the intriguing but well thought out spring-loaded feet which could achieve a good contact on a rough or uneven surface. Top photo © courtesy Tramex Ltd.

The moisture meter will not be able to offer even a relative reading over the materials moisture content range if the calibration graph has a flat or near-flat section – i.e. an L-shaped calibration test graph.

Your readings of dampness, and all the notes you take on building condition at date A, *could be* referred back to on a later visit – date B – when you might have been asked to check the building to assess whether there has been a condition change. In other words, *any* survey could be a first monitoring visit.

Level 3 monitoring – using EMM accessories

Standard surveyor's moisture meters with accessories

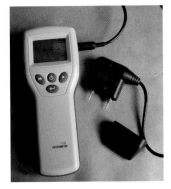

Figure 274: Standard pin probes.

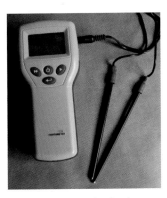

Figure 275: Deep insulated probes.

Figure 276: Thermo-hygrometer.

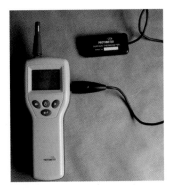

Figure 277: Thermo-hygrometer and surface temperature sensor.

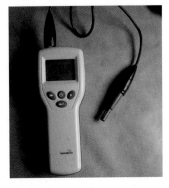

Figure 278: Thermo-hygrometer on a lead.

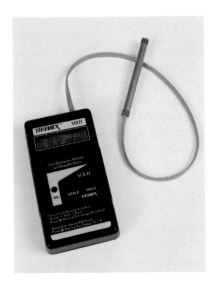

Figure 279: Dual-pad type capacitance meter with thermo-hygrometer. Photo © courtesy Tramex Ltd.

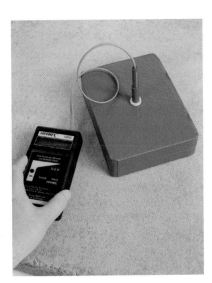

Figure 280: Capacitance meter used in conjunction with humidity box. Photo © courtesy Tramex Ltd.

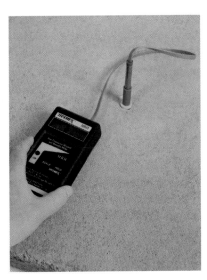

Figure 281: Meter used to check RH/temperature of a drilled hole. Photo © courtesy Tramex Ltd.

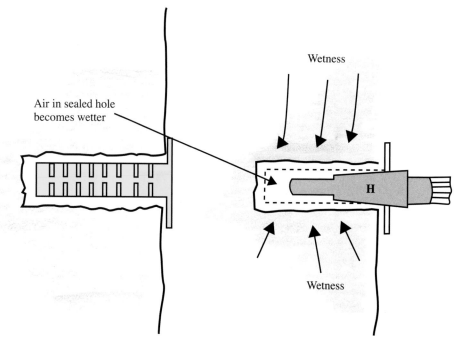

Figure 282: Sensor in wall.

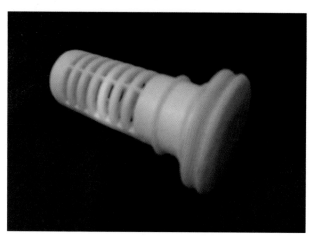

Figure 283: Sensor sleeve, for insertion into a drilled hole.

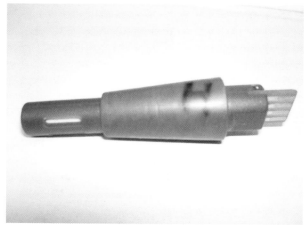

Figure 284: Thermo-hygrometer sensor (THS); note it has an identification letter H.

Using an inserted electronic humidity/temperature sensor

In figure 282, on the left, a plastic sleeve has been tapped tightly into a 16mm hole drilled into the brickwork substrate. On the right, an electronic thermo-hygro-meter is pushed tightly inside the plastic sleeve, a good seal obtained from its tapered rubbery shape. But would you consider it wise to use sensor 'H'? (See later advice on checking your sensors.) Wetness in the masonry will create a humid hole in which you have inserted your sensor. The wetter the surrounding masonry, the more humid the air within your drilled hole – the relative humidity (RH) is of course influenced also by temperature. Measurement of the RH and temperature offer the surveyor a useful indication of how damp the surrounding masonry is, and return visits to take the humidity measurement can help you determine whether the masonry is becoming damper or drier.

Measuring conductance of masonry offers quite an indirect way of measuring moisture, but measuring air in a sealed hole gives you a *direct measurement of moisture condition inside the drilled hole air* – which is *directly influenced by dampness in the surrounding substrate.* The measurement is *within the substrate* rather than at its surface, and is not directly influenced by metals or salts.

But you need to know how to interpret the readings – the tests and case studies that follow demonstrate this.

At level 3 we may have begun to be invasive. Drilling holes in walls and floors is certainly invasive, and is a major feature of level 3 monitoring. Leading equipment suppliers have sold 'insulated deep probes' for the EMM for many years – but how many surveyors have used them?

Key principles for siting monitoring stations

A monitoring station is a fixed position where you are checking moisture condition over time. It is labelled and usually noted on a table, probably loaded later into a spreadsheet and then easily translated automatically into a graph.

a) Create monitoring stations where you would *learn most*, bearing in mind points b) and c).
b) Drill holes where it is *safest* to do so.
c) Drill holes where it would create the *least damage or disturbance*.
d) *Create a monitoring position at the* epicentre *of dampness, in wall and (if safe to do so) in solid floor.*
e) Consider a monitoring position away from the damp zone – *as a control*.
f) Consider a monitoring position *at the margins* of the damp area.
g) If you consider there are insufficient monitoring positions for the size of damp area under study, invest in additional sensors or allow more time for site visits.

Hole drilling – the practice and perils

Hole drilling will nearly always be required, if probes are to be inserted into sleeved holes. Hole drilling requires practical skills and a knowledge of how buildings are wired and plumbed, so cables and pipes can be avoided. This can be further checked using *professional* metal detectors. If you do not wish to drill, then consider commissioning an independent dampness investigator with the required skills. If you take the plunge, you will get your hands a little dirty! Do you check with a metal detector each time you drill for shelves at home? The same risks apply.

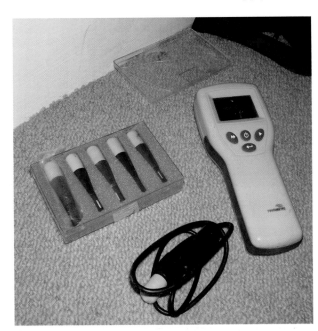

Figure 285: A pack of five sensors. You could drill five holes, or 10 holes, or 15 or 20 holes. With just one pack of sensors each group of five holes would take 30–60 minutes to take a reading from. This means our selection of monitoring 'stations' needs to be very carefully thought out.

Kitchens are a huge problem, as cables are often routed from socket to socket at all manner of angles. And damaging plasters that are guaranteed in association with basement waterproofing or above-ground damp coursing would be another professional embarrassment. You can sometimes access the substrate at a socket or light switch back box position.

But the dangers are greatest in floor screeds – they could even contain grids of heating pipes, and being thicker than wall plasters, your metal detector could let you down and not pick up the deeper pipes or cables. For this reason I tend not to drill floor holes too often – even armed with a £600 metal detector that is said to detect cables at 100mm depth! And floors can incorporate damp-proof membranes...

Using inserted thermo-hygrometers

You will have switched your electric drill to 'hammer' mode. As you drill, collect the outpouring dust, for later carbide meter analysis. Ideally, vacuum out dust, and tap in a plastic sleeve, followed by a thermo-hygrometer. You will need to wait a minimum of 30 minutes for any worthwhile humidity reading, and further checks after 45 minutes and 60 minutes should help you know that readings have stabilised. You would take the relative humidity and the temperature. Take the readings using a stopwatch.

I would advise you to label all your sensors, e.g. A, B, C, etc., and use the same sensor each time you check a particular hole. If a sensor malfunctions, it will create less of a problem if at least you know which monitoring hole it was used in.

Nine easy steps to fitting an inserted monitoring sensor

1) **Obtain permission for hole drilling.**
2) Select wall or floor position for installing sensor
3) Assess the risk of drilling. If a wall is plastered, take care to drill away from cable or pipe runs. Use a professional and reliable metal detector to confirm hidden dangers, or alternatively hack off plaster in area to be drilled – bolstering off plaster is a little less risky than directly drilling.
4) Log sensor position on a plan or in a table in your site notes.
5) Drill the required diameter hole (check manufacturer of sleeve).
6) Collect drillings in a sealed container for possible analysis.
7) Insert patent sleeve.
8) Seal between sleeve flange and substrate (if necessary).
9) Fit your thermo-hygrometer, start your stopwatch.

Using humidity boxes

If you are checking a floor screed in a one-off survey, the humidity box must remain sealed to the floor for at least four hours for anything like a useful indication of the amount of dampness in a screed to be obtained.

Figure 286: A standard humidity box is sealed onto a solid floor. For convenience you can seal the box to the floor using duct tape. An electronic thermo-hygrometer is fitted into the side, and measures the relative humidity and temperature of a pocket of air under the box. After a time, the humidity of the trapped air equates with the humidity condition within the floor. See figure 287.

Level 4 monitoring – using carbide meters (sometimes oven drying)

This amount of time would not usually be available in a standard house survey – so the technique will tend to be used in 'further investigations' of damp problems and when monitoring is required. In most cases An ERH of 75% means your floor will be acceptably dry. Always take damp meter readings as well.

Once the humidity box is sealed to the floor, the longer you leave it, the more reflective the humidity reading will be of moisture within the screed it sits upon. After one hour, you record a reading of 72%, but readings are very gradually rising. After about two hours the humidity is stabilising, and just increasing very gradually, until after four hours we note an ERH of 76.1%.

Figure 288: What you might need to drill out a sample and carbide test it. The metal detector to bottom right really is a key piece of equipment, and helps steer you away from risky drill sites. But assess also where the pipes and cables may run.

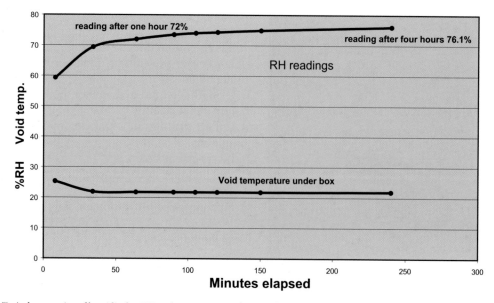

Figure 287: Typical progression of humidity box RH and temperature readings. In this case, after 2 hours a reliable ERH was achieved for the floor under test.

CASE STUDY 2 (LEVEL 2): SLATE ROOF TIMBERS – USING PIN PROBES OF THE CONDUCTANCE METER

The author inspected a roof in East Dulwich where quite serious roof leaks through the slating had caused very noticeable wetting to structural timbers, but rot had not yet set in. Chinks of light gave away the position of quite a large hole near the ridge (see figure 301), not to mention the puddles of rainwater collecting on an old camping groundsheet spread out over ceiling joists underneath. Rainwater had been trickling down rafters, to soak battens and purlins. It took just a few minutes to mark several monitoring positions on batten, rafter and purlin (as shown in figure 303). Electronic moisture meter (EMM) readings using the pin probes were taken at A, B, C, D and E. After the roof slating had been overhauled, further visits to check the roof timbers confirmed satisfactory drying out. Visually, the puddle on the groundsheet had dried up. The table of readings below confirmed drying out. It had even rained quite persistently after the repair work.

Figure 301: Damaged roof – before overhaul.

Figure 299: Measurements show what is now certainly a rain seepage via a crack across the yard at the bottom of the steps.

Figure 300: The crack is made good, the damp remedied.

Figure 302: The client shows how water from the roof leaks collects in a camping groundsheet draped over the ceiling rafters.

Figure 303: Monitoring position A.

Table 11: Monitoring after roof repair – EMM pin probe readings					
Date	A Batten	B Batten	C Purlin	D Rafter	E Batten
Pre-repair 7/3/03	17.3%	19.1%	16.1%	38.5%	57.2%
Post-repair 12/3/03	16%	15.3%	14.4%	17.2%	34.2%
18/3/03	11.4%	13.4%	11.3%	12.7%	10.1%

The very high % readings for D and E on 7/3/03 reflect *very wet or saturated timber* rather than offering an accurate moisture content.

The client was pleased with the extra service provided – and yet again the usefulness of electronic moisture meters was proven. It was not possible to be sure the roof timbers were drying out from visual observation alone.

Monitoring by drying contractors

Many drying contractors undertake monitoring of drying out using level 3 techniques – often invasive techniques, using inserted electronic thermo-hygrometers. This method of checking progress of drying down has proved to be extremely useful and most often very reliable.

Once the contractor has addressed health and safety issues, preliminary clearing out of the property, removal of standing water, sterilisation, etc., an assessment is made of how much moisture needs to be removed from the walls, floors, etc. and the extent of the water damage. It is at this stage that moisture meters have a leading role. The contractor takes readings over surfaces within the flood affected zone of the property and records them (and should also take a few readings away from the wet zone for comparison). The moisture meter readings may be used to create a 'moisture map' – showing on plan, by sketches of elevations of rooms or by isometric sketch, the patterns of moisture meter readings as found. Some contractors note down exactly where some specific moisture meter readings are taken, and some even attack stickers or labels to walls to

identify positions of readings. Once drying equipment is installed, the contractor will very often set up fixed monitoring stations (typically half a dozen drilled sleeve positions for a typically sized flood zone – see figure 219), and on each visit to the property humidity and temperature readings for each monitoring position will be recorded and tabulated.

As well as monitoring moisture in materials, the contractor will also log inside and outside air humidity and temperature on every visit. It is important the contractor knows that a suitable drying chamber is maintained during the drying, and it is critical that air humidity is reduced very early on in the drying contract to prevent secondary mould development (likely when internal RH is say 65% or above).

Monitoring is a way of life for drying contractors.

CASE STUDY 3 (LEVEL 3): MONITORING BUILDING DRYING AFTER A FLOOD CAUSED BY A PIPE LEAK – CONTOUR MAPPING OF CAPACITANCE READINGS

The drying contractor monitored the drying of a property in Tenterden by continually checking moisture meter readings on walls, in woodwork and on the floor – making best use of the pin probes and capacitance function. The dehumidifier was watched closely and the water collected was recorded. Air was monitored too, both room air and the trapped air within holes drilled in the walls.

It was interesting to use a capacitance meter over the ground floor screed to see what readings might be during the first site survey, when the kitchen area was clearly very wet from a plumbing leak. Usefully much of the remainder of the house floor had not been affected – a control 'dry zone'. Readings using 'search mode' were made very methodically on this first inspection day, and later, when the floor was considered by the contractor to be close to being dry, again search mode readings were taken over the whole floor zone. (Note: A *'search mode'* reading is terminology of one manufacturer and refers to a moisture meter reading with the instrument switched to capacitance mode.)

Figure 304: It's a daunting task taking search mode readings all over a floor – but the chance to find out what this could tell us about floor screed drying was too good to miss. Readings were taken on a metre square grid. See figures 305 and 306.

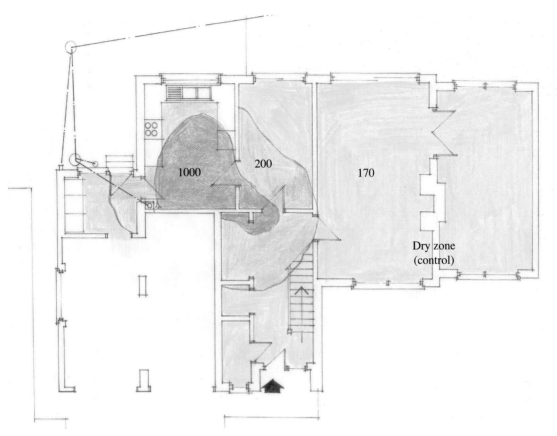

Figure 305: 19 July 2003, search mode readings – floor. Very high (maximum) search mode readings were obtained in the kitchen area – the seat of a leak. Dry zone readings were 170. Readings all over the floor would be expected to gravitate to 170 as it dries.

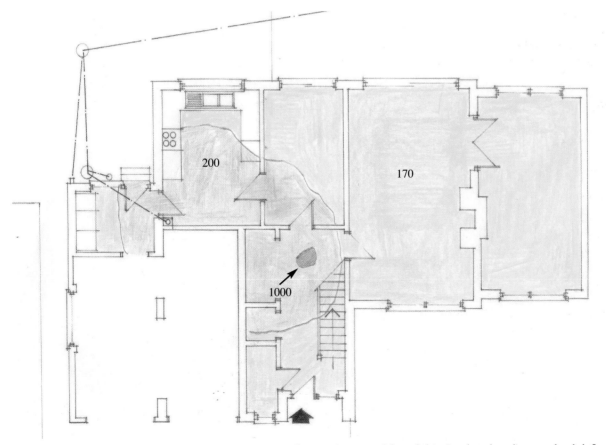

Figure 306: 3 October 2003, search mode readings – floor. The very wet floor zone is now certainly much drier. Search mode readings over the whole floor area would be likely to equate to dry zone readings of 170 eventually – so a little more drying is needed here. Checks by humidity box or by taking drilled samples for carbide test would clarify the floor moisture condition beyond doubt.

You can appreciate that between July and October there was a significant change in capacitance readings taken over the floor screed – as if a plug had been pulled out in the centre of the property! The place where high capacitance readings persisted would probably be the lowest point on the concrete slab.

You cannot be convinced by capacitance meter readings alone that a screed has dried enough for drying equipment to be switched off and wheeled or carried out, but it is a very useful piece of evidence. It certainly shows you where the screed may still be a little damp. You would feel happier if the whole floor produced readings around 170 – the level of reading in the dry zone. A reading of 200 means the screed may still be a significantly damp and this is a 1970s chalet bungalow with almost certainly a plastic floor membrane. In an old property without a proper concrete slab you will find that even after rigorous drying the screed is still 'damp' and will never become 'dry'.

CASE STUDY 4 (LEVEL 4): BLOCKWORK DRYING OR NOT? THE 'TWIN PEAKS' OF TENTERDEN, KENT

The author made two site visits to Tenterden. The first was on 19 July 2003, a 'dampness investigation' as drying seemed to be far more protracted than expected

for a localised kitchen water damage. A further inspection by the author on 2 October was to help confirm whether the property was by then dry, and if drying equipment could be switched off and removed from site. The author was not involved in the daily monitoring of the drying process.

We looked at how the screed was checked using a capacitance meter in this property in Case Study 3. But what about the walls? How were they monitored to check drying progress?

In Case Study 3 we explained how a drying contractor set up equipment to dry out a property suffering badly from a plumbing leak. During drying the contractor found it very difficult to know for certain if a blockwork wall between the kitchen and the garage was actually drying.

The contractor was unsure whether moisture meter readings on either side of the wall could be relied upon – after all, this type of lightweight blockwork contains carbon, doesn't it? Checks on the garage side could be influenced by this integral carbon – and be magnified due to the inherent conductance of the PFA (pulverised fuel ash) block material.

It was necessary to make sure. Moisture meter readings might not reflect the actual moisture content – so on 19 July we firstly set up three humidity sensors in the wall (one on the garage side and two on the kitchen side). This would at least offer a humidity

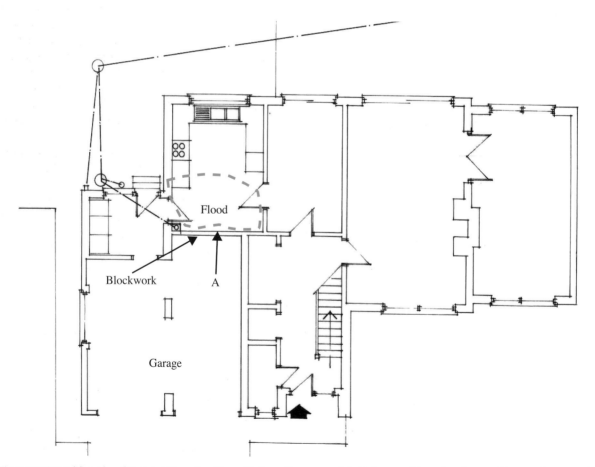

Figure 307: Ground floor plan of Kent chalet bungalow. The wall between the garage and the kitchen was right at the epicentre of the water damage. Is this blockwork partition wet or dry, drying or not?

Appendices

Appendix A: Approximate water content of typical construction materials

Table 14: Water content of construction materials

	Thickness	Max. absorption	Bone dry weight kg/m²	Acceptably dry litres/m²	Saturated litres/m²
Brickwork (fletton)	225mm	25%	375	3.5	95
	100mm	25%	165	1.5	40
Brickwork	225mm (engineering)	5%	500	1.5	25
Lightweight blockwork	200mm	55%	120	2.5	65
	100mm	55%	60	1.5	33
Plaster finish	Traditional lime 20mm	25%	10	0.05	2.5
	Cement render 20mm	15%	12	0.075	2
Concrete slab	100mm	5%	225	0.25	10
Cement/sand screed	65mm	15%	39	0.1	6
Softwood	100 x 50	30%	2.6 kg per metre run	0.2 litre per metre run	0.75 litre per metre run

Appendix D: Alternative techniques for monitoring changes in moisture content of a substrate

Any of the electronic sensors or probes featured in the main text may be remotely monitored. This allows information to be collected when the surveyor is not on site, although the monitoring equipment is expensive and is at risk of tampering, vandalism or malfunction when left unattended. There have also been cases when whole monitoring exercises have failed from simple battery problems or computer failures.

Remote monitoring is an essential tool when data is required over the course of the 24-hour day over perhaps a week – when, for example, internal condition is monitored in conjunction with a housing condensation investigation. Equipment now on the market usually includes data loggers, processing unit and a computer software CD.

In order to monitor most effectively there must be a careful selection of the best instruments and techniques to use in the light of site conditions, resources available (in terms of time and money), and the client's needs and requirements.

If possible, track changes in moisture condition using more than one technique. When results are analysed, look out for irregularities in trends of readings – and try to establish the reason for this.

Select very carefully positions to monitor to obtain the best information. And each time readings are taken, include site notes of visual observations.

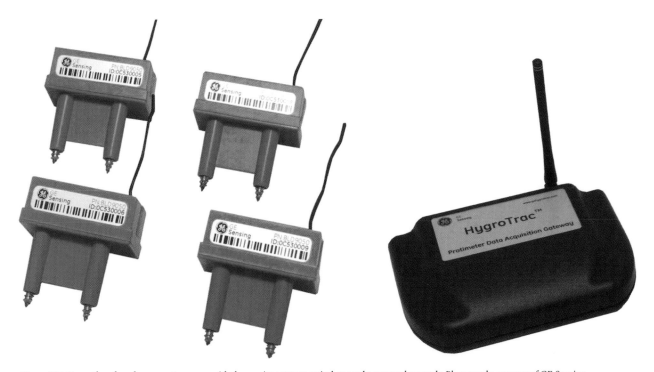

Figure 314: Examples of modern remote sensors with the on-site gateway unit that can be accessed remotely. Photographs courtesy of GE Sensing, www.gesensing.com

Table 15: Alternative techniques for monitoring changes in moisture content of a substrate

	Calibration	Influence of metals/salts/carbonaceous material*	Risk of invasive testing	Likelihood of equipment damage during/between tests	Effectiveness in tracking change in moisture content	Practicality of multiple test positions
Pin probes	Manufacturer supplies calibration testing device.	YES – they may influence readings.	NIL – although pins can cause nominal damage to sensitive surfaces.	NIL – equipment does not remain in situ.	Tracks moisture change positively/reliably at material surface only But: *	Multiple readings easily and quickly taken, but positions of readings must be carefully noted.
Deep probes	Manufacturer supplies testing unit.	YES – they may influence readings.	YES drilling invasive and a risk to cables/pipes.	NIL – Holes should be plugged between tests and probes withdrawn after use.	Tracks moisture change positively/reliably at depth used But: *	Multiple test positions take time due to drilling procedure, checking for metal and of course each hole (6mm) causes destructive damage to substrate.
Search mode	Not easy to check; battery charge affects readings. Author uses a square of marble as a calibration check.	YES – they may influence readings	NIL	NIL	Tracks moisture change reliable although the general trend can include occasional readings out of step But: *	Multiple readings easily and quickly taken, but positions of readings must be carefully noted.
Drilled hole ERH using electronic thermo hygrometer	Sensors may have calibration certificate, and can be checked against others or in a humidity chamber.	NIL	YES – drilling invasive and a risk to cables/pipes	NIL holes capped between tests, sensors usually withdrawn after use	Probably the most user-friendly, reliable and positive method for tracking mc change within substrate.	Multiple test positions take time due to drilling procedure, checking for metal and of course each hole (16mm) causes destructive damage to substrate.
Humidity box ERH using electronic thermo hygrometer	Sensors may have calibration certificate, and can be checked against others.	NIL	NIL	Humidity box may be left in situ or removed between tests (if to remain in situ must be protected from damage).	Changes in mc of substrate can be reliably tracked using this method, although trend in ERH change can be affected by temperature. Box must be sealed to substrate.	Equipment not prohibitively expensive so multiple test positions feasible, and one thermo-hygrometer can be used for several boxes.
Mechanical hygrometer ERH natural or synthetic hair	Calibration tricky and time consuming, and requires reliable 75% RH chamber using salt solution.	NIL	NIL	Hygrometer may be left in situ or removed between tests (if to remain in situ must be protected from damage).	Changes in mc of substrate can be reliably tracked using this method, although trend in ERH change can be affected by temperature. Hygrometer must be insulated and sealed to substrate.	Reliable equipment relatively expensive, so use of numerous hygrometers not often feasible. Problems of obtaining comparable results from different hygrometers.
Carbide meter to test drilled sample	Recalibration of instrument required periodically. Carbide result can be checked using oven-drying method.	NIL	YES – drilling invasive and a risk to cables/pipes and damp-proofing membranes.	NIL – hole from drilling can also be tested by electronic thermo-hygrometer and capped for subsequent testing.	Very accurate method for obtaining a reliable total moisture content, can be used in conjunction with other test methods – certainly useful at beginning and end of monitoring phase.	Multiple test positions take time due to drilling procedure, checking for metal and of course each hole (10–16mm) causes destructive damage to substrate.

Appendix E: Black ash mortar

Because the main constituent of black ash mortar is coal ash, its high metallic content could cause a damp meter to register an apparently high moisture reading.

COMMENTARY AND ANALYSIS

A surveyor provided a sample of black ash mortar for checking, as it was thought that high moisture meter readings recorded in this type of mortar gave a falsely high impression of moisture condition.

The sample was found capable of holding up to 14.37% of its dry weight as moisture. As the sample dried down, it was repeatedly weighed and checked by capacitance and pin probe moisture meter.

As for almost all masonry or plasters, the reading on screen will be a relative indication only of moisture content – a relative reading (R/R).

When the black ash sample was saturated at 14.37%, a reading on screen of nearly 40 was recorded. Unless you had experience in checking such a material using a resistance meter you would not be able to make sense of such a reading. Note that a reading of 8 using the pin probes was recorded even when the sample was oven dry, due to the carbon present in this mortar.

The moisture meter recorded a reading of 20 with the word 'WET' on screen when the material was very damp (nearly 6%). This means if we wish to make use of the EMM risk bands, we should tread carefully, as such a mortar would already be very damp with a lower moisture content.

The moisture meter calibration actually suits this material, as from bone dry to saturated we have a continually rising graph of EMM reading against actual moisture content. If this test is typical for such a mortar, we would at least have some idea of how wet or dry the material is from the EMM reading. But this test was just on one sample of black ash mortar from one building.

If you compare the EMM readings for black ash mortar as compared to say lime plaster (see page 198), for both materials the EMM readings do not reflect

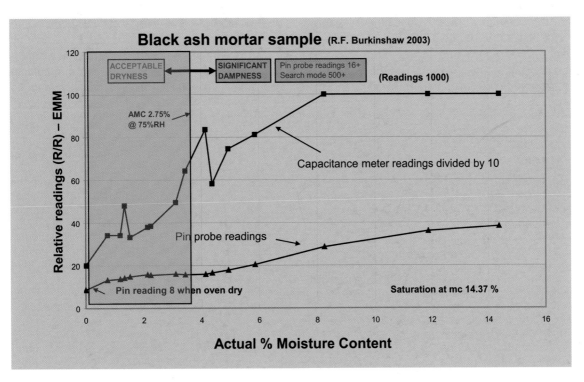

Figure 315: Calibration graph – black ash mortar sample.

Figure 316: Sample provided.

actual moisture content, and if thought by a surveyor to be a percentage, would give a falsely high indication of actual moisture content.

For the black ash mortar sample tested, the mortar would probably be significantly damp at an actual moisture content of approx. 1.75% and above, reflected in a pin probe reading of 16+ and search mode reading of 350+.

Note that search mode (capacitance) readings reached a plateau of 1000 when the sample was very damp at 8.25% AMC, and as the sample became wetter it continued to record a maximum reading.

The surveyor was correct to think that moisture meter readings gave a falsely high impression of dampness in that material. But interestingly, the RISK BANDS actually kicked in too late in pin probe mode – meaning risk bands actually *underestimated* the amount of dampness present at critical phases of moisture content!

Where you are unsure of the actual moisture content of a material on site, consider extracting a sample for on- or off-site testing for total moisture content by carbide meter. But you would need to know at what moisture content the particular material would be significantly damp (from experience of similar materials or from bench tests).

Appendix F: Moisture condition of lightweight blockwork

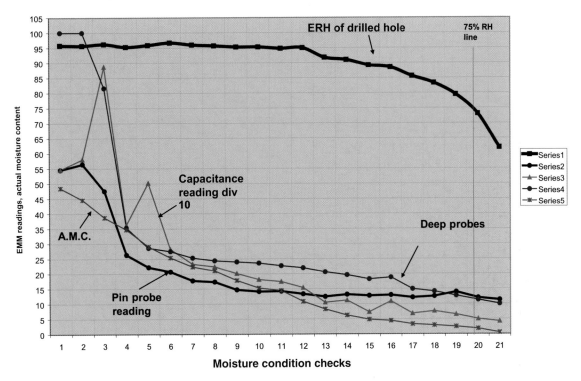

Figure 317: Drying of lightweight (PFA) blockwork.

The above graph (figure 317) gives a realistic indication of the moisture meter readings you would obtain as lightweight blockwork is becoming progressively either drier or wetter.

The graph was derived from bench testing of quite a large block sample (¼ sized standard block). Every time the block was checked by moisture meter from saturation to dry, it was accurately weighed using laboratory scales.

As it dried, moisture meter readings gradually dropped, whether the moisture meter was used in standard pin probe, insulated deep probe or capacitance mode (although readings by capacitance meter during initial stages of drying were more unpredictable).

The ERH readings remained very high at around 95% for the first stage of the drying (as the blockwork dried down from 48% to about 14% AMC and then declined noticeably.

The temperature of the blockwork was also logged – it remained around 15°C during the test period.

By the time ERH of the drilled hole dropped to 75%, standard pin probe and deep probe damp meter readings had converged to around 12–13 R/R.

Table 16: Damp meter and ERH readings when blockwork is 'dry'

ERH (of drilled hole)	75%
AMC by carbide test:	2%
Standard pin probe reading	13 R/R
Capacitance reading	60
Deep probe reading	12 R/R

The ERH 75% threshold is a useful indication of acceptable dryness.

Appendix G: Housing Health and Safety Rating Scheme – a new approach

By Stuart Athol

In April 2006 Part 1 of the *Housing Act* 2004 came into force and introduced a rating scheme based on 29 different types of hazard, ranging from damp and mould growth to structural collapse and falling elements. The underlying principle of the Housing Health and Safety Rating System (HHSRS) is that any residential premises should provide a safe and healthy environment for any potential occupier or visitor. When inspecting a property the local authority Environmental Health Officer (EHO) must make a justified assessment for each of the 29 hazards as to the likelihood of them affecting the health and safety of the designated vulnerable age groups – e.g. the chance of a damp and mould growth hazard impinging on the health and safety of someone of 14 years or under would be 1 in 10, 1 in 100, or 1 in 1000, etc. The national average for the hazard is also given in the scheme. For damp and mould growth in say, a pre-1920 single household dwelling, this is set at 1 in 446. This means that it is statistically expected that out of 446 houses, one of them would have a problem with damp and mould. The age groups for each hazard are specified in the scheme, and account must be taken of them even if nobody of that age is actually living there.

Having decided on the likelihood, the percentage degree of harm outcome for the hazard in question must now be looked at. There are four classes of harm, ranging from Class 1 (extreme harm, such as severe pneumonia) to Class 4 (regular coughs and colds). The outcome percentages are based on research and are already stipulated for each hazard. The EHO can alter them for subsequent calculations but he/she must be able to justify such alterations. The calculation will ultimately show a numerical figure for the hazard which will fall within one of a number of bands stretching from A to J. Those hazards scoring 1000 or more will fall within one of the bands A to C and are therefore classed as Category 1 Hazards. Any hazards scoring less will come under a band in D to J and be classed as Category 2 Hazards. The difference between the two categories is that for Category 1 the EHO **must** consider enforcement action, ranging from emergency remedial work being commissioned down to the occupier and owner just being informed that a hazard is present in the property. With Category 2 Hazards the EHO **may** take action.

Appendix H: Copper pipe failure

Three types of pitting corrosion are described in *Copper Tube in Domestic Water Services*[65]

- Type A1 – Carbon film: attack occurs when a thin film of carbon (that should have been removed as part of the cleaning process) remains in the tube after manufacturing.
- Type A2 – Hot, soft water: rare in the UK. It may occur in soft water areas when operating temperatures are above 60°C.
- Type A3 – Flux: excessive use of flux results in flux runs within the tube.

Embedded pipework – copper is actually quite resistant to cement, concrete or plaster. But problems may arise if pipework is embedded in acidic plasters, cements or coke breeze. Pipes can suffer too from some concrete additives or even some cleaning fluids that could permeate through the screed to the tubing. For example, ammonia contained in cleaning or disinfectant bleach. Copper pipe needs to be readily exposed or located in ducts with removable covers.

The Water Regulations (3.18) merely stipulate that pipework should be wrapped in impermeable tape. This may well isolate pipework from potential chemical reactions with a surrounding screed which may be aggressive towards the pipework – but will not protect the pipework from accidental damage or damage from structural movement. More thought is needed to extend the regulations to cover more eventualities.

Copper pipe can be obtained ready coated in plastic which should protect it from aggressive environments.

BRE (Berry, R. W.), *Remedial Treatment of Wood Rot and Insect Attack in Buildings*, BRE Report 256, Building Research Establishment, 1994

BRE Digest 245, *Rising damp in walls: diagnosis and treatment*, Building Research Establishment, 2007

BRE, *Treating Condensation in Houses*, Good Repair Guide 7, Building Research Establishment, 1997

BRE, *Wood-Boring Insect attack: Part 1 – Identifying and assessing damage, Part 2 – Treating Damage*, Construction Research Communications Ltd, 1988

BSI, BS 5930:1981 *Code of Practice for Site Investigations*, British Standards Institution, 1981 (updated 1999)

BSI, BS 8215:1991 *Code of Practice for the design and installation of damp-proof courses in masonry construction*, British Standards Institution, 1991

Building Construction (undated), The Reference Library of Bennett College

Building Research Association of New Zealand, *Restoring a House after Flood Damage*, Building Information Bulletin 240 CI/SfB (L36), Building Research Association of New Zealand, 1984

Burkinshaw, R., 'Moisture Monitoring – How do the various instruments measure up?', *Recovery* (BDMA journal) Vol 4, Issue 4, 2003

Burkinshaw, R., 'Investigating Damp: What you need to know for a home condition report: Explanation of "diagnosis"', SAVA *Home Inspector* Issue 05 Oct, 2004

Burkinshaw, R. (undated) 'What is the moisture meter trying to tell us?' (various tests on moisture meters described): www.emeraldinsight.com/ Insight/viewContentItem.do?contentType=Article &contentId=844783

Burkinshaw, R. (undated) 'Which instruments should surveyors use to monitor moisture condition?' Includes a useful test where a floor screed is cured, and its moisture condition monitored using a variety of surveying instruments: www.emerald insight.com/Insight/advancedSearch.do?hdAction =button_search&dummy=&searchOptions1=& searchTerm1=%22monitor+moisture+condition %22&searchFields1=All+fields

Burkinshaw, R., 'How far should a surveyor take dampness investigation in a building survey?' Stewart, H. Conference Paper, Building Surveys/ Appraisals, 2004

BWPDA, *Code of Practice: Remedial Timber Treatment*, British Wood Preserving and Damp-proofing Association, 1995

Carll, C. G. and Highley, T. L., *Decay of Wood and Wood-Based Products Above Ground in Buildings*, American Society for Testing and Materials, 1999

CDA, *Copper Tube in Domestic Water Services – Design and Installation*, Publication 33, Copper Development Association, 1999

Chilton-Young, F., *Every Man his own Mechanic*, Ward, Lock & Co, 1895

CIRIA, *Structural Renovation of Traditional Buildings*, CIRIA Report 111, Construction Industry Research and Information Association, 1986

Clarke, M., 'Maximising Space – The Use of Basements for Housing in Britain', *Science in Parliament*, Journal of Parliamentary and Scientific Committee, Summer 2000

CLG Planning Policy Statement 25: *Development and Flood Risk*, Department for Communities and Local Government (see www.communities.gov.uk)

Critchley, R., 'Slow Progress', *Environmental Health Journal*, June, 2001

CSM, 'Flooding: pool your information', *Chartered Surveyors Monthly*, Nov/Dec. 2001

EBS, *Moulds, Damp and Dry Rot*, English Heritage Lecture Theatre, Savile Row, London, EBS Conference 13/14 June 2005

EA, *Lessons Learned Autumn 2000 Floods*, Environment Agency, 2001

EA, *After a Flood – How to restore your Home*, Environment Agency (undated)

EA, *Damage Limitation – How to Make your home flood resistant*, Environment Agency (undated)

EA/CIRIA, *After a Flood: How to restore your home*, Environment Agency/CIRIA (undated)

EPA, *A Brief Guide to Mold, Moisture, and your Home*, US Environmental Protection Agency, (undated), www.epa.gov/mold/moldguide.html.

Evening Standard 7/1/92, 'The Spectre of our Drowning City'.

Federal Emergency Management Agency (USA):

- FEMA 15 – *Design guidelines for flood damage reduction*
- FEMA 102 – *Floodproofing non-residential structures*
- FEMA 234 – *Repairing your flooded home*

Foster, J. S., *Structure and Fabric* (5th edition), Part 1, Mitchell's Building Series, Longman Scientific & Technical, 1994

Guardian 3/11/89, 'Rising water threatens buildings'

Harrison, H. W. and Pye, P. W., *Floors and Flooring*, Building Research Establishment, 1997 (General useful advice on control of dampness and methods of insulation).

Hodgkinson, P. E. and Stewart, M., *Coping with Catastrophe: A Handbook of Disaster Management*, Routledge, 1991

Howell, J., 'On the Trail of the Timber Treaters', *Chartered Surveyors Monthly*, February 1996

Hughes, P., *Patching Old Floorboards*, SPAB Information Sheet 10, (undated)

Hydraulic Lime Mortar Best Practice Guide, Donhead Publishing

IEHO, *Environmental Health Professional Practice*, Chapter II 'Mould fungal spores, their effects on health, and the control, prevention and treatment of mould growth in dwellings', IEHO, 1985

Institute of Medicine, *Damp Indoor Spaces and Health*, The National Acadamies Press, 2004

Johnson, A., *Converting Old Buildings*, David & Charles, 1988

Lead Sheet Association, *Pocket Guide for Specifiers, Surveyors and Supervisors*, Lead Sheet Association, 1997

Lead Sheet Association, *Pocket Guide No 1 Flashings and weatherings*, Lead Sheet Association (undated)

Lead Sheet Association, *Pocket Guide No 2 Roofing and Cladding*, Lead Sheet Association (undated)

Lsitburek, J. and Carmody, J., *Moisture Control Handbook: Principles and practices for residential and small commercial buildings*, RICS, 1998

Marley Plumbing and Drainage, *Underground Drainage Systems Design and Installation Guide*, November 2004, Marley Plumbing and Drainage, 2004

Melville, I. and Gordon, I., *Structural Surveys of Dwelling Houses* (3rd edition), Estates Gazette Ltd, 1992

Microclean, *The Micro-Clean Method, A Chemical-free Process for Total Mould Control*, Microclean Ltd, Denmark, 2004

Molloy, Gould and Drury, *Builder's and Decorator's Reference Book* (2nd edition), George Newnes Ltd, 1957

National Press Office, 'Boscastle Flood study – Key Findings', National Press Office, 2005

National Research Council of Canada 'Flood-proofing of buildings', *Canadian Building Digest*, National Research Council of Canada (undated)

Netherton, C., 'Taking the fear out of flooding' *Cleaning and Maintenance Journal*, The National Flood School, 2002

Oliver, A., *Woodworm, Dry Rot and Rising Damp* (3rd edition), Sovereign Chemical Industries Ltd, 1990

Oxley, R., *Survey and Repair of Traditional Buildings: A conservation and sustainable approach*, Dunhead Publishing, 2003

Oxley, T. and Gobert, E., *Dampness in Buildings* (2nd edition), Blackwell Science, 1983

Property Care Association Codes of Practice (all published in 2008):

- *Code of Practice for Remedial Timber Treatment*
- *Code of Practice for Remedial Waterproofing of Structures Below Ground*
- *Code of Practice for the Installation of Remedial Damp Proof Courses in Masonry Walls*

Proverbs, N. and Holt, *Surveying flood damage to domestic dwellings: The present state of knowledge*, RICS Research Foundation, November, Vol. 3, 2000

Proverbs, N. and Soetanto, R., *Flood Damaged Property*, Blackwell Publishing Ltd, 2004

Research Matters 'Partnership in Health Research', Issue 26, Autumn 2006

Richardson, B., *Remedial Treatment of Buildings* (2nd edition), Butterworth-Heinemann, 1995

Richardson, M. D. and Johnson, E. M., *The Pocket Guide to Fungal Infection* (2nd edition), Blackwell Publishing, 2006

Richardson, M. D. and Warnock, D. W., *Fungal Infection: Diagnosis and Management* (3rd edition), Blackwell Publishing, 2003

Rivington's Building Construction, reprint of 1904 edition, Donhead Publishing Ltd (ref on slag, Vol III, p.216), 2004

Rudge, J. and Nicol, F. (eds), *Cutting the Cost of Cold*, E & FN Spon, 1991

Rushton, T., *Investigating Hazardous and Deleterious Building Materials*, RICS Books, 2006

Safeguard Chemicals Ltd, 'Rising damp and its Control', *Safeguard*, Safeguard Chemicals Ltd, 2000

Scottish Office, *Design Guidance on Flood Damage to Dwellings*, HMSO, 1996

Singh, J., Email from J. Singh of Environmental Building Solutions Web: www. ebssurvey.co.uk, 2006

Sunday Times 28/10/01, 'Here comes the rain again'

Taylor, J. B., *Plastering* (4th edition), Longman Scientific & Technical, 1985

Thomas, A. R., *Treatment of Damp in Old Buildings*, SPAB Technical Pamphlet 8, Society for the Protection of Ancient Buildings, 1986

Thompson, P., 'Toxic Mould Remediation and Testing – experiences from Scandinavia' Conference Paper, 2005

Times 10/1/05, 'Five Dead as storms leave trail of flooded devastation'

Times 17/8/04, 'Rescuers fight to save villagers hit by floods'

Times 23/12/04, 'Household Chemicals in Direct Link to Asthma Rise' (Nigel Hawkes, Health Editor)

Times 27/6/05, 'Hay fever sufferers enduring worst June on record'

Times 8/7/04, 'Insurers balk at risk from sewage floods'

Watts Group plc, *Watts Pocket Handbook*, RICS Books, 2008

White, Singh, et al., *Searching for Answers at the Roof of the World*, Building and Facilities Management for the Public Sector, 1995

Zureik, C., Neukirch, B., et al., 'Sensitisation to airborne moulds and severity of asthma: cross sectional study from European Community respiratory health survey', BMJ, 325:411 (24 August), 2002

VIDEOS AND BROADCASTS

BBC2 (2004) Documentary: *A Seaside Parish* (Boscastle flooding of 2004)

Dri-Eaz Products Inc (1993) *Psychrometry Made Simple*

Dri-Eaz Products Inc (1994) *The Residential Inspection*

USEFUL WEBSITES

Equipment manufacturers

Borescope manufacturers and flexible endoscopes – Litetec Ltd: www.lite-tec.co.uk

Data loggers – Gemini Data Loggers (UK) Ltd: www. Geminidataloggers.com

Leak detection and pipe testing devices: www.vernon morris.co.uk

Metal detection and laser levelling equipment: www. bosch.co.uk

Remote monitoring – HygroTrac system: www. gesensing. com and www.yorksurvey.co.uk

Thermometers, humidity sensors and pressure gauges – for consumer and industry: www.brannan.co.uk

Damp meters: www.gesensing.com/protimeter and www.tramex.co.uk

Useful organisations

Basement Information Centre: www.basements.org.uk

BDMA: www.bdma.org.uk

Building Science Corporation: www.buildingscience. com

Defra: www.defra.gov.uk/environ/fcd/default.htm

Environment Agency: www.environment-agency.gov. uk (flood advice booklet: www.highpeak.gov.uk/ environment/flood/EAbooklet_flood_product_gu ide.pdf and the advice sheets)

Environmental Health Officers' website: www.enviro health.co.uk

HHSRS: www.communities.gov.uk/hhsrs

Property Care Association: www.property-care.org

Scottish Environment Protection Agency: www.sepa. org.uk

Damp proofing/waterproofing

British Wood Preserving and Damp-proofing Associ-ation: www.bwpda.co.uk

John Newton and Company: www.newton-membranes. co.uk

Moisture Control handbook: www.epa.gov/iaq/school design/moisturecontrol.html

Timber treatment and damp-proofing chemicals and systems: www.safeguardeurope.com, www. sovereignchemicals.com, www.ruberoid.co.uk and dampcoursing ltd: www.dampcoursing.com

Mould remediation

European Community Respiratory Health Survey: www.bmj.com/cgi/reprint/325/7361/411

Mould cleaning and protection, and wood treatment products: ACS Limited: see www.wood-protection. co.uk and www.facadeprotection.co.uk

Mould measurement (biomass): www.mycometer.com or info@mycometer.dk

Mould remediation in Canada: www.bioremediate. com/vancouvermold.htm (This shows services available across the Atlantic and how the service links to the key mould cleaning areas, e.g. the 10 square feet watershed.)

Mould steam cleaning method: www.microclean.dk or www.microcleanltd.co.uk

Ventilation systems

Kair Ventilation Ltd: www.kair.co.uk

The Nuaire Group: www.nuaire.co.uk

Vent Axia Ltd: www.vent-axia.com

Sample/material testing

Chemical test tablets: www.palintest.com

Laboratory tests water/material samples: www.eclipse scientific.co.uk

Eurofins (for testing water samples): www.eurofins.co. uk

Mobiair Diagnositics Ltd, Laivakatu 5, 00150, Helsinki, Finland: www.mobiair.info (Laboratory that mould samples can be sent to for analysis, contact Malcolm Richardson +358 44 5040888.)

Flood remediation/training

Case histories of Carlisle flood victims: www.bbc.co.uk/ insideout/northeast/series7/floods.shtml

CIRIA flooding advice sheets: www.ciria.org/flooding/ advice_sheets.html

Computer data recovery/forensic services: disklabs: www.disklabs.com

Corroventa: www.corroventa.com/Eng/torkteknik.htm (This shows a good example of a modified psychro-metric chart. The standard chart shown has achieved a 'triple toe loop'. Move up or down the chart as temperature changes, and sideways as moisture is added or removed from the subject air. You may or may not find this easier to use than the standard version, in which dry bulb temperature is on the X axis, and moisture in air on the Y axis. Once you know air temperature (dry bulb) and relative humidity, plot the position on the chart and move directly upwards to check grams per kilogram of moisture in the air (i.e. specific humidity), and then move down and to the right to read off dew point.)

Damage management contractors/drying equipment hire: www.restoration-express.co.uk

Dri-Eaz Ltd: www.dri-eaz.com; www.dri-eaz.com/ PRODUCTS/Dehumidifiers.html (This shows a selection of modern drying machines, such as LGR 2000 a 'low grain' dehumidifier.)

Fast technical drying: www.actiondry.co.uk

Floodskirt website: www.floodskirt.com

National Flood School: www.nationalfloodschool.co.uk

General

The Lime Centre: www.thelimecentre.co.uk

Dust Mite cleaning: www.silentmites.co.uk

Showers and bathrooms: Matki Ltd: www.matki.co.uk

Sika Ltd: www.Sika.co.uk

Index